The African Middle Ages

1400–1800

The African Middle Ages
1400–1800

ROLAND OLIVER
ANTHONY ATMORE

CAMBRIDGE UNIVERSITY PRESS

CAMBRIDGE
LONDON   NEW YORK   NEW ROCHELLE
MELBOURNE   SYDNEY

Published by the Press Syndicate of the University of Cambridge
The Pitt Building, Trumpington Street, Cambridge CB2 IRP
32 East 57th Street, New York, NY 10022, USA
296 Beaconsfield Parade, Middle Park, Melbourne 3206, Australia

First published 1981

Printed in the United States of America

Phototypeset in V.I.P. Plantin by
Western Printing Services Ltd, Bristol, England
Printed and bound by Vail-Ballou Press, Inc.,
Binghamton, New York

British Library Cataloguing in Publication Data
Oliver, Roland
The African middle ages, 1400–1800.
1. Africa – History – To 1884
I. Title II. Atmore, Anthony
960'.2 DT20 80–40308

ISBN 0 521 23301 1 hard covers
ISBN 0 521 29894 6 paperback

Contents

Maps

Acknowledgements

The authors wish to record their gratitude to Professor Richard Gray and Dr Andrew Roberts, who read the manuscript in draft and made very many useful suggestions for its improvement.

Introduction

The first volume in this series, *Africa in the Iron Age* by Roland Oliver and Brian Fagan, deals with the period from about 500 B.C. till A.D. 1400. This is a period for which, although there are some important literary sources, the evidence comes mainly from archaeology. What we here call the African Middle Ages is, in contrast, one for which, although archaeology continues to contribute, the dominant sources are literary and traditional. For a part of the continent at least, we now have chronicles, by which we mean historical information collected and written down, more or less within the lifetime of living witnesses of the events, by learned men concerned to establish facts accurately and in detail and to arrange them in chronological order. For our period there is continuous evidence of this kind for Egypt and the Maghrib countries, Ethiopia and the western Sudan, and in some measure also for the central and Nilotic Sudan and a portion of the East African coast.

At one end of the spectrum, chronicle material shades off into recorded tradition, by which we mean information about the past remembered by non-literate witnesses of events, and handed on by word of mouth from one generation to another until eventually it was told to a literate person who recorded it in writing. Most of the evidence about most of Africa between 1400 and 1800 is of this kind, and obviously it is less reliable than evidence recorded directly from eye-witnesses. People tend to forget the things which are not in some way relevant to their daily lives, and non-literate people lack the means to place past events within an accurate chronological framework. So long as it remains in an oral state, tradition is liable to be distorted in order to serve the ideological and propaganda needs of succeeding generations. Much therefore depends on how soon and how carefully oral traditions came to be recorded.

In most of Africa this process had to wait until some members of the societies concerned began to adopt literacy in the late nineteenth or early twentieth centuries. However, in that part of Africa which was in some kind of touch with the civilisation of Islam – and this included a wide zone stretching for 800 to 1,000 kilometres to the south of the Sahara – some traditional history was recorded much earlier. Ibn

Khaldun, the great Maghribi historian who died at the very beginning of our period, incorporated much traditional material from the Sahara and the western Sudan in his 'History of the Berbers'. The mid-seventeenth-century chronicles of Songhay and Timbuktu by al-Sa'di and Ibn al-Mukhtar incorporate traditions of the earlier empires of Ghana and Mali. The fragmentary chronicles of Hausaland, Aïr and Bornu, though known only in nineteenth-century versions, clearly contain material that had existed in written form long before.

Finally, there is the most valuable kind of historical evidence, which is the record written by the eye-witness himself. This may take the form of the narrative of a journey or the report of a mission or the accounts of a trading venture or the correspondence generated by any ongoing enterprise by literate people, whether commercial, religious, diplomatic, military or colonial. Here, although the world of Islam has the first word, it is the European world that comes, by the end of our period, to occupy the dominant role. In 1400 there was no European foothold on African soil, and no European had made any significant journey into the African interior. Yet already from the previous century we have Ibn Battuta's lively accounts of his journeys across North Africa from Morocco to Egypt, from the Persian Gulf down the East African coast to Mogadishu, Mombasa and Kilwa, and from Morocco across the Sahara to the western and central Sudan. From the early sixteenth century we have the no less vivid reminiscences of the Granadan Moor al-Hassan ibn Muhammad al-Wazzani, later converted to Christianity as Leo Africanus, who travelled extensively in Morocco and Songhay and perhaps as far afield as Hausaland, Bornu and Kanem.

However, following the conquest of Ceuta in 1415, the Portuguese began their systematic exploration of the ocean coastlines of Africa, reaching Cape Verde in 1446, the Bight of Benin in 1475, the Congo estuary in 1483, and the Cape of Good Hope, Sofala, Kilwa, Mombasa and Malindi, all in 1497–8. Spurred on by the spread of the printing-press and the expansion of secular education, the Christians of western Europe made a much wider use of literacy than their Muslim contemporaries. From the fifteenth century onwards royal and ecclesiastical archives began to bulge with instructions, reports, accounts and itineraries, and from the sixteenth century there issued from the printing-press a swelling stream of voyages, handbooks, histories and geographies, all of which constitute precious sources for the history of the coastal regions. Fortunately perhaps for Africa, but unfortunately for the study of its history, it is only here and there that these European records shed their light at any distance into the interior. Taking the continent as a whole, between A.D. 1400 and 1800 it is to the sources of traditional history, with all their difficulties, that the historian must mainly turn.

Another reason for calling the period from 1400 to 1800 the African Middle Ages is because certain features of it correspond with the period of European history known as the Middle Ages, or medieval times. The Middle Ages of European history comprise an earlier period than the African Middle Ages – from about 800 to 1500. One similarity of the Middle Ages of both continents was the emergence and growth of states. In Europe there was an early time of loose-knit empires, such as the Holy Roman Empire instituted by Charlemagne and the large kingdom of the Angevins which straddled the English Channel. In some respects these were not unlike the African empires of the western and the central Sudan, such as Mali and Kanem–Bornu, in which only limited power was exercised from the centre and in which the territorial extent of the empire depended not upon the ethnic or cultural unity of the subjects but upon the military predominance and the dynastic alliances of a small ruling group. Later in medieval western Europe, states began to evolve which were based on the concept of nationality; the examples of France, England and Spain come to mind. In these, power was becoming centralised and institutionalised, and the state institutions reflected, at least to some extent, particular linguistic, cultural, religious or ethnic characteristics. The parallels in Africa were states such as Asante, Oyo, Benin, Kongo and Rwanda, although there were of course many differences. The steady growth of state systems, however different they might be, is one of the dominant features of both European and African medieval history.

A more particular common aspect was the history of the city states, in parts of Italy and Germany on the one hand, and in Hausaland, Yorubaland and the coastal cities of eastern Africa on the other. Finally – and connected with the growth of states and cities – there was the increasing importance of trade, commerce and financial matters, of economic changes generally, in the Middle Ages of both continents. Again, there were many differences, but these are less outstanding than the differences between medieval and modern economies, which are essentially those of scale and conceptualisation. In this respect, medieval Africa and medieval Europe are more similar to one another than they are in their modern counterparts. What sets Africa apart was that this modernising process *began* in Europe long before it did in Africa. Europe had started on the long, hard road of modern, capitalistic economic change while Africa remained in its

3

Middle Ages, and this difference more than any other accounts for the difficulties and violence that were to mark many of the contacts between Africa and Europe. Despite the extent and violence of the Atlantic slave-trade, however, these contacts remained limited during the period up to 1800. They were to dominate African history only as the nineteenth century wore on.

1   The African dimension of Islam

To an impartial observer living in the year 1400 Africa would have seemed inevitably destined to join the world of Islam. By 1400 Islam had been established in Egypt and the Maghrib for more than seven centuries. In origin the religion and culture of the Arab conquerors, it had been strengthened by the westward migration of farmers and nomads (bedouin) from the Arab lands, and it had been adopted by a steadily growing proportion of the indigenous populations. In Egypt Muslims by now outnumbered the Christian Copts, and Arabic, which had long supplanted Coptic as the literary language, was displacing spoken Coptic even in the countryside. In the Maghrib Latin Christianity had ceased to exist. The mixed populations of the towns and the coastal plains were solidly Muslim and Arabic-speaking, as were the pastoral nomads of the Atlas foothills and the desert fringes. Only the Berber farmers of the high mountains preserved their ancient speech and practised a more syncretistic kind of Islam, of which the characteristic leader was the 'holy man' (*marabout*) rather than the teacher, the preacher and the jurist who animated the religious life of the cities and the plains.

Politically, Egypt and the Maghrib had long ceased to observe any common authority. Egypt, together with Palestine and Syria, had been ruled since 1250 by the military despotism of the Mamluk sultans, enforced by a constantly renewed foreign army recruited from Turkish slaves (see Chapter 3). Mamluk authority extended westwards to include Cyrenaica. Tripolitania, on the other hand, formed part of Ifriqiya, a state somewhat larger than modern Tunisia, ruled since the early thirteenth century by the Hafsids, a dynasty originally placed there as provincial governors by the Almohad caliphs of Morocco. Beyond Bougie, in the centre and west of modern Algeria, lay the state of Tlemcen, ruled by another successor dynasty of the Almohads, called the 'Abd al-Wadids or Zayanids. Finally, in lowland Morocco the Almohads had been succeeded since 1248 by the Marinids, Zanata Berbers from the Saharan fringes south of the Atlas, who had moved north as conquerors and had made their capital   5 at Fez. In all three kingdoms Berber dynasties had consolidated themselves by making close alliances with groups of Arab bedouin immigrants who provided military contingents in exchange for the right to gather taxes from specific areas. The Marinid kingdom, especially, had enjoyed periods of considerable military power, when it had conquered and imposed tribute on Tlemcen and Ifriqiya and had even intervened in Spain. However, by the fifteenth century this dynasty had more than once failed to resolve its succession problems, power was becoming decentralised to the provinces, and what remained at the centre was passing into the hands of the hereditary vizirate of the Wattasids. Such was the situation in which, in 1415, the Portuguese were able to establish a bridgehead at Ceuta on the southern shores of the Strait of Gibraltar.

Despite the rough and ready nature of political power, however, and despite much internecine warfare between state and state, and among the mountain peoples, the nomads and the plainsmen, there remained in the Maghrib enough basic security and good order to permit a great deal of regular, long-distance movement by civilians in the service of trade, religion and education. Trade routes at this time ran mainly north and south, linking the Maghrib with southern Europe on the one hand and with the western and central Sudan on the other. Merchant shipping was almost entirely in European hands, and communities of European traders lived in factory enclaves (*funduq*) in all the large ports such as Oran and Bougie and, above all, Tunis. Maghribi shipping was largely concerned with piracy, preying upon the European trade, and deeply involved in the capture of Christian slaves, who were an important element in all Maghribi armies and navies. Land transport on both sides of the Mediterranean was by pack-animals and not by wheeled vehicles. In the Maghrib donkeys, mules and horses were used in large numbers for short hauls, but the main long-distance baggage animal was the camel. Though usually associated with the desert, it was a familiar sight in every port and market-town from the Mediterranean coast to the Senegal and the Niger.

In contrast to the movements of trade, however, those occasioned by religion and education went mainly east and west. Islam revered knowledge and stressed the virtue of pilgrimage. Knowledge acquired abroad was preferred to the home product, and the ambitious scholar would migrate from one famous law school (*madrasa*) to another, keeping open regular links between Fez and Meknes, Tlemcen and Bougie, Tunis and Kairouan, Cairo and places further to the east.

6   Pilgrimage attracted ever larger numbers. Young men and old, rich

and poor, some riding but many on foot, swelled the caravans moving to and fro across the Maghrib, from Morocco and Tlemcen across the wastes of southern Tunisia and Tripolitania and on across the Libyan desert to the Siwa oasis and Cairo, and so up the Nile to the Wadi Hamamat, the port of 'Aydhab and the Red Sea crossing to Jidda and Mecca. Often two or three years would be spent on the journey. A large part of Islamic alms-giving and public works was devoted to the provision of hostels and caravanserais for scholars and pilgrims. All this wide world of North African Islam was thus in a real sense intercommunicating. Few Muslim communities can have existed from Morocco to the Nile which did not count some members who had made the journey to the Holy Places. Every town and village along the pilgrimage routes was likewise familiar with a wide cross-section of the population of the Islamic West, from the desert foothills of the Atlas to southern Spain.

ISLAM SOUTH OF THE SAHARA

By 1400 this intercommunicating world of western Islam was by no means confined to the Maghrib. For the desert, too, was regularly crossed by great caravans during several months of every year. The grand trunk routes passed through the Fezzan to Kanem, Bornu and the other states of the central Sudan, and through Sijilmasa and Taghaza to Timbuktu and the empire of Mali. Ibn Battuta, who travelled by the western route in 1352, described a twenty-five days' march from Sijilmasa in the Atlas foothills to Taghaza, the great salt-pan almost halfway across the desert. There followed another twenty-five days, with only a single watering-place, between Taghaza and Walata, still in the desert, but only a few days' march from its southern edge. It took Ibn Battuta twenty-four more days to travel by land from Walata to Niani, the capital of Mali, situated on the Sankarani tributary of the upper Niger, in the forest fringes of modern Guinea. By the beginning of the fifteenth century, most caravans were by-passing Walata and travelling straight from Taghaza to the growing city of Timbuktu, with its river-port close by on the Niger, where the great loads of Saharan salt and other merchandise could be transferred directly from the backs of camels to the bottoms of large canoes for transport up and down the Niger waterways. From Gao, on the north-eastern curve of the Niger bend, another great desert highway led away eastwards through the highlands of Adrar and Aïr to the Fezzan and Egypt.

Though much less thoroughly Islamised than the Maghrib, the   7 western Sudan was thus by 1400 in full contact with the rest of the Muslim world. The empire of Mali, embracing within its suzerainty all the lands between the eastern arm of the Niger bend and the Atlantic coast from Senegal to the Gambia, was ruled by a Muslim dynasty, several of whose kings had themselves made the pilgrimage to Mecca. These men, and many of their leading subjects, had met the rulers of Egypt and Syria, had visited al-Azhar, the university mosque of Cairo, had mingled at Mecca with fellow pilgrims from Baghdad and Basra, from Zeila and Zanzibar. At their courts in the Sudan were Turkish slaves and Andalusian architects, Maghribi merchants and scholars and green-turbaned Sharifs claiming descent from the Prophet's own family. Already at Timbuktu the Sankore mosque was providing education in Arabic for indigenous Sudanese preachers and jurists, many of whom would pass on to the *madrasas* of the Maghrib and Egypt before returning to practise their skills to the south of the desert. Foreigners were welcomed and their goods protected. On the trade routes from Timbuktu northwards there operated Maghribi trading firms like that of the five Maqqari brothers, of whom the senior brother lived in Sijilmasa, with two of his juniors in Tlemcen and two more in Walata. South of the desert the merchants were local Mande, of the occupational caste called Dyula, or Wangara. Muslims to a man, they operated the donkey caravans and the files of human porters which at about this time were beginning to trade salt and manufactured goods for the gold and kola-nuts of the Guinea and Akan forest, and to penetrate eastwards into the central Sudan as far as Katsina and Kano. Though the written word was still expected to serve the needs of religion before all else, here were societies in touch with the outside world, whose affairs were known and understood from Fez to Cairo, from Marrakech to Mecca and Mombasa.

In the central Sudan there was, around 1400, only one area where Islam was well established, and this was Kanem, the country to the north and east of Lake Chad, which had been in regular trading contact with the Fezzan, Ifriqiya and Egypt for more than five hundred years. At Bilma, in the desert between Kanem and the Fezzan, was a salt-mine as inexhaustible as that of Taghaza, which constituted the main resource of the southward trade. Its northward element consisted almost entirely of slaves, captured by the military forces of Kanem in annual campaigns around its extensive frontiers. The rulers of Kanem were essentially nomads, and their capital at Njimi had never grown into a great town like those of the western Sudan. Nevertheless, Kanem had long possessed a class of literate Muslim clerics. Its kings, like those of Mali, had often made the

8

pilgrimage, lingering on the way to see the wonders of Cairo, and to establish there hostels for students and pilgrims from their own country. For Muslims living on a religious frontier, as in Kanem, there was no perceived contradiction between the profession of intense piety at home and the levying of perpetual war against the surrounding nations of unbelievers. Indeed, on the eve of our period, dynastic rivalries in Kanem had caused the main ruling house to retreat westwards into Bornu, to the west and south of Lake Chad, there to establish another great expanding frontier between the Kanuri invaders and the former Chadic-speaking inhabitants of the land, remembered in Bornu traditions as the Sao.

While Islam was being carried into Bornu by migration and conquest, in nearby Hausaland it was being introduced peacefully by Dyula traders from Mali. According to the traditions preserved in the chronicle of Kano, there were initially only about forty of these strangers. They so impressed the king that he appointed one of them his preacher and another his muezzin, while a third cut the throats of

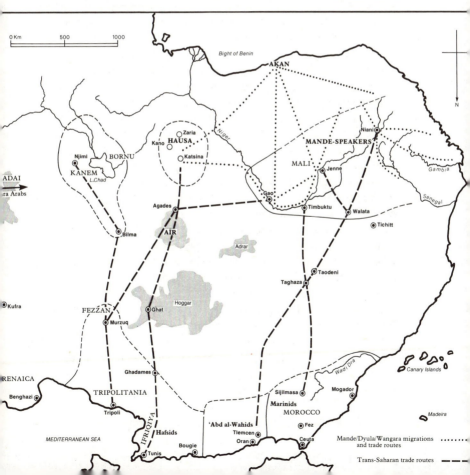

whatever flesh was eaten, and a fourth was appointed *qadi* or judge of the Islamic law. And the king commanded every town in the land of Kano to observe the times of prayer. Though by no means the beginning of Hausa history, the coming of Islam seems to have been quickly followed by the development of cavalry forces and the establishment of a regular slave-raiding frontier against the still pagan lands to the south. Kano raided the Jukun, Zaria raided the Nupe, and the captives from this perennial warfare were settled in slave villages around the Hausa towns and put to work in agriculture and industry. The new situation soon led on to the arrival of camel caravans and to the opening of a new trade route running northwards through Aïr to Ifriqiya and Egypt. Another section of the Sudanic Belt had been added to the Muslim world.

ISLAM AND CHRISTIANITY IN NORTH-EAST AFRICA

In the Nile valley south of Egypt Christianity, not Islam, had remained the dominant religion until the fourteenth century, and even by the fifteenth century the transformation to Islam was far from complete. Although the Mamluk sultans of Egypt had at the critical moment helped to overthrow the defences of the northern Nubian kingdom of Maqurra, the real momentum of the Islamic advance into this sector had come from Arab nomads pressing southwards from the deserts of Upper Egypt towards the wider pasture-lands to the east and west of the upper Nile. There was nothing systematic or co-ordinated in these migrations. The newly Islamised dynasty of Maqurra certainly did not control them, and they soon swept far on towards the south, occupying the lands on either side of the southern kingdom of Christian Nubia, called 'Alwa. The earliest and most far-reaching movements occurred to the west of the Nile, where Arab bedouin known as Kababish (from Arabic *kabab*, ram), herding camels and sheep, occupied the grazing lands between Dongola and Darfur, while others known as Baqqara (from Arabic *baqara*, cow) spread out across an even larger territory stretching from Kordofan through southern Darfur and beyond. In Kanem the impact of the nomads was reported in a letter from the King of Bornu to the Sultan of Egypt in 1391. It was in fact one of the causes of the retreat of the Magumi dynasty from Kanem to Bornu.

East of the Nile the bedouin, here known as Juhayna, moved south down the line of the Red Sea hills, reaching the Butana plain between the Atbara and the Blue Nile by the end of the fourteenth century, and the Gezira country between the Blue and White Niles only a century

2 Christian and Muslim north-east Africa, *c.* 1400

later. The kingdom of 'Alwa was thus encircled and cut off both from its former trading partners in Egypt and Arabia and from the metropolitan bishop of its church in Alexandria. A long-drawn-out process of disintegration was eventually followed by conquest, but the scene

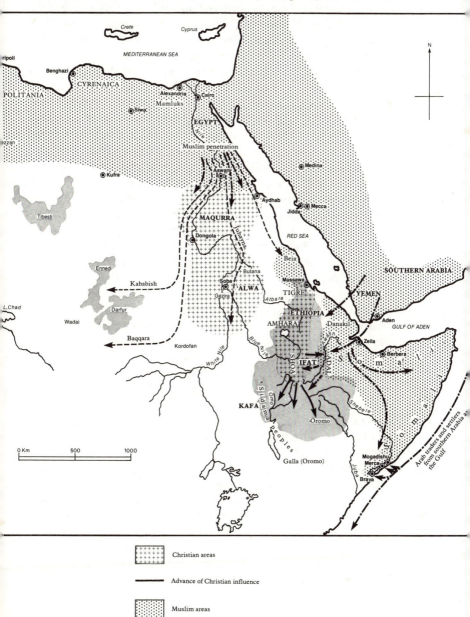

Christian areas

Advance of Christian influence

Muslim areas

Advance of Muslim influence

Movements of Arab (or Beja) pastoralists and settlers

at the beginning of our period was essentially one of chaos, in which an old order was crumbling but had not yet been replaced by a new one.

In the Horn of Africa, Christianity and Islam had existed side by side for many centuries – Christianity in the central highland plateaux, Islam in the lowlands to the north and the east. At the beginning of the fifteenth century the spheres of both were expanding rapidly. By a combination of migration, conquest and cultural assimilation, the centre of the Christian population had moved steadily southwards through the highland region from Eritrea and Tigre through Lasta to Shoa. The Christian kingdom was now consolidating its supremacy in the Rift Valley region to the south of the upper Awash. Islam had long been embraced by the Beja, the Saho and the Danakil living in the arid plains between the highland escarpment and the Red Sea coast: these peoples were, after all, separated only by a short voyage from the heartlands of the faith. Further east, the Somali living on the southern shores of the Gulf of Aden had begun to be converted in the tenth and eleventh centuries by shaykhs from southern Arabia, and the movement had rolled slowly southwards from there, reaching the line of the Shebele River by the thirteenth or fourteenth century.

In general, Christianity and Islam in the Horn of Africa had expanded in parallel, the first a religion of highland farmers, the second of pastoral nomads inhabiting a different kind of country. There was friction at the edges, however, and in origin this was conflict over trade and trade routes. Till the thirteenth century the Christians had used trade routes leading northwards to the Bay of Massawa in the Red Sea, while the Muslims had developed the routes leading inland from Zeila and Berbera on the Gulf of Aden. From Adal, behind Zeila, they had ascended the Awash valley, and opened a rich trade in slaves and ivory, gold and civet with the Sidama peoples living in the Rift Valley and beyond. As the Christians advanced southwards into Shoa, they competed for this trade and sought control of the trade route, and at the turn of the fifteenth century they clearly enjoyed the ascendancy. They had driven the Muslims from their footholds in the highlands, and their raids were soon to reach Zeila itself. In the longer term, however, the environmental factors were to reassert themselves. A noteworthy feature of Christian Ethiopia was that, like the Muslim lands by which it was surrounded, it had its place of pilgrimage. Ethiopian Christians kept open their links with Jerusalem, and there they made contact with the Christians of the West. In their mutual struggle Christians as well as Muslims were conscious of belonging to a wider world.

3 Muslim trading in the Indian Ocean, *c*. 1400

THE ISLAM OF THE INDIAN OCEAN COAST

Thanks to the regular alternation of the monsoon winds, navigation in the Indian Ocean was much simpler and safer than in the Atlantic, and it is no wonder that on this side of Africa the world of Islam extended its influence far to the south of the Equator, indeed almost to the southern tropic. By the beginning of the fifteenth century there was certainly a colony of Muslim traders established at Sofala, to the south of the Zambezi mouth, while others were soon to be active far up the river itself, at Sena and even at Tete. These were the outposts of an interlinked and intercommunicating system embracing settlements on Madagascar and the Comoros, Kilwa and Mafia, Zanzibar and Pemba, Mombasa and Malindi, Manda and Pate, Brava and Mogadishu, and various trading ports on the southern coast of Arabia, the Persian Gulf and western India. The main African product exported through these settlements was ivory, which found its way in large quantities to India and China. Other exports included gold, copper, timber, foodstuffs, tortoise-shell and slaves.

By the beginning of the fifteenth century the maritime trade of the western Indian Ocean was approaching the peak of its activity in

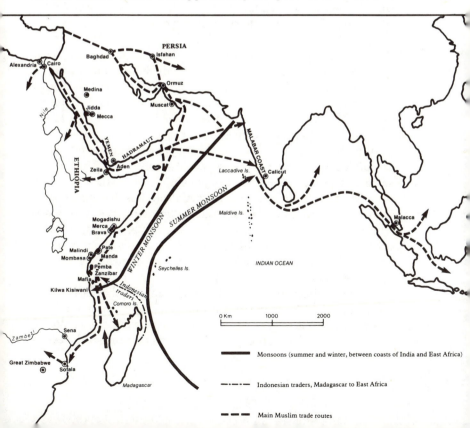

mainly Arab hands, and it could be that the annual procession of dhows sailing between the Persian Gulf and East Africa carried a weight of merchandise nearly equal to that which was crossing the Sahara by the great camel caravans. The coastal cities of eastern Africa may in a very real sense be likened to the cities at the southern termini of the desert crossings. In East Africa as in the western Sudan, these were entrepôt cities, where merchandise changed from one kind of transport to another. They were cities full of foreigners in varying stages of assimilation to the local environment. They were supported by slave populations who performed most of the agricultural and other manual work. In both regions slavery was accompanied by concubinage, so that after a few generations the descendants of immigrants were physically indistinguishable from the local peoples, and all of them spoke the local languages. In both regions those in contact with the entrepôt cities were gradually assimilated into the Muslim faith of the immigrants.

At the same time, the Islamic civilisation of the East African coast had a character very much more exotic than that of the western Sudan. Perhaps because they arrived by sea rather than by land, the Muslim immigrants to eastern Africa maintained a separateness from the local societies which was well symbolised by the fact that, wherever possible, they made their settlements on offshore islands. They were in daily touch with individual Africans as slaves and concubines. No doubt there were market-places where the inhabitants of the settlements met as trading partners with individuals and groups from the local societies and from the interior. But with the local societies as such, contacts seem to have been always minimal and frequently hostile. The richest settlement was certainly that at Kilwa Island, which exercised a near monopoly over the gold- and ivory-trade of the lands to the south. Here Ibn Battuta in 1332 was received by a sultan of South Arabian ancestry who was a deeply pious Muslim. His subjects were mostly very black with tribal marks on their faces. But his relations with the people of the mainland, less than a mile away, was one of perpetual warfare and raiding, no doubt mainly for slaves. This seems to have been a normal pattern. At all events, it is clear enough that the Muslim settlements of the East African coast were in no sense African societies which had been penetrated by Islam, but foreign settlements into which African elements had been incorporated. The difference was highly significant. In the East African settlements the leaders in religion and politics were from immigrant communities. There was no deep contact between the immigrant societies and the indigenous ones. There was no basis for the expansion of Islam into the interior – unless perhaps from the settlements up the Zambezi river, where alone do we know of Muslims travelling inland. But the Zambezi settlements developed late, and were soon to be taken over by Portuguese successors. Elsewhere in the East African interior the spread of Islam dates only from the nineteenth century.

The East Coast settlements excepted, Islam had by 1400 established a front line, from one side of the continent to the other, which tended to move steadily southwards. The Muslims of the southern frontier were already for the most part black people drawn from the urban populations of the sub-Saharan states. Some of them were soldiers, especially cavalry knights, whose contribution to Islamic proselytism consisted in the capture of slaves who would be acculturated to the Muslim faith in their new homes whether to the north or the south of the Sahara. Others, however, were merchants, for whom membership of a universal faith was an almost indispensable passport for long-distance travel beyond the borders of tribe and language. It was usually merchants rather than soldiers who planted new communities of Muslims to the south of those already existing. For wherever they settled they married. And wherever their children were born, there they sought to establish a Koranic school with a Muslim cleric as teacher. The cleric, once recruited, would not limit his impact to the merchant community, but would soon be found writing letters and charms for the local chief and advising him on his foreign relations, his physical health, and his spiritual welfare. Religious conversion might be a long time in coming, but the atmosphere for it was soon created. Nakedness was covered with decent cotton clothing. Magic was alphabeticised. Administration and justice were slowly permeated by Islamic ideas and ideals. The northern, intercommunicating part of Africa grew at the expense of the more isolated regions to the south.

We have seen that, around 1400, the parts of Africa which were in regular touch with the outside world formed a broad belt across the northern third of the continent, which also extended in a narrow thread down much of the Indian Ocean coast. For the most part, it was on land routes that long-distance communication depended. There was no maritime traffic anywhere between southern Morocco and the Limpopo, and for those living between these points the ocean marked the end of the world. The coastal regions had their resources in salt and fish and sea-shells, but in general the peoples of Guinea, and of western-central and southern Africa lived with their backs to the sea. Some of the larger ethnic and linguistic groupings touched the seacoast – notably the Wolof kingdoms between the Senegal and the Gambia, the Akan peoples of Ghana, a few of the southern Yoruba, the Kongo and Mbundu peoples of Zaïre and Angola, and on the eastern coast of South Africa representatives of the great Nguni family

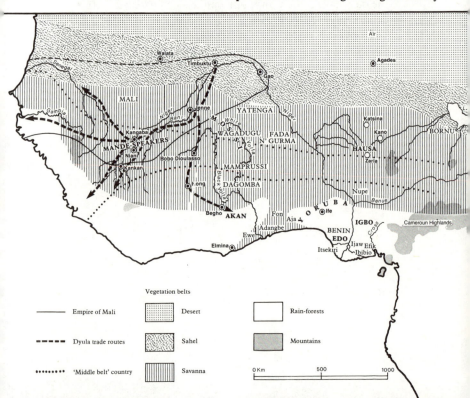

Vegetation belts

—————— Empire of Mali   Desert   Rain-forests

- - - - - Dyula trade routes   Sahel   Mountains

•••••••• 'Middle belt' country Savanna   0 Km   500   1000

of Bantu peoples. In no single case, however, were the capitals or other major centres of these peoples situated by the sea. The Nguni, though dwelling in coastal plains, were notorious for their dislike of boats and their taboo against eating fish. In most other cases the fishermen of the ocean coast were peripheral members of their societies, leading an isolated and specialised existence rather like that of the specialised hunters of the forest.

More than half of the coastline between Senegal and the Limpopo was, in fact, occupied by small ethnic groups, culturally and linguistically distinct from those of the neighbouring interior. In western West Africa, the great Mande-speaking family of people was separated from the coast by a whole series of very small linguistic areas, known collectively as West Atlantic, which covered most of the territory of modern Guinea, Sierra Leone, Liberia and Ivory Coast. In eastern Ghana, Togo and Bénin (Dahomey) the large groupings of Ewe and Fon were bordered to the south by a thin belt of coastal Adangbe, who fished the lagoons between the Volta mouth and the Ogun. In the western Niger Delta the Itsekiri intervened between Benin and the sea. In the mangrove forest south of the Igbo lived the Ijaw, the Ibibio and the Efik – all specialised fishermen and salt-refiners, who were destined, after the opening of the Atlantic trade, to become the 'middleman tribes' of the intercontinental trade in slaves and palm-oil, but who until then occupied a much lowlier position. In Cameroun the Duala, and in Gabon the Mpongwe, fulfilled the same role. Along the immense desert coastline of southern Angola, Namibia and the Cape Province it was Khoi *strandlopers* who exploited the fruits of a sea still unfurrowed by the keel of any sailing ship.

UPPER AND LOWER GUINEA

The region of 'back country' nearest to the Islamic orbit around the beginning of the fifteenth century was that lying between the western Sudan and the Atlantic seaboard, where Upper Guinea may be taken as meaning the area west and south of the Mali empire, while Lower Guinea includes the area from the Volta to the Cameroun highlands. The Wolof were still at the beginning of our period united under a supreme ruler, the *burba*, who had his capital some 300 kilometres inland from the mouth of the Senegal. The *burbas* had been tributaries of the Mali empire for a brief period during the fourteenth century, and the ruling class had been touched by Islam. Most of the Wolof territory was open savanna, and so was easily dominated by an aristocracy of horse-owning warriors, who took slaves for export and also 17 used them extensively for their own farms and households. When the Portuguese reached their shores in the mid-fifteenth century, they became the first suppliers of Negro slaves to Christian Europe.

South of the Gambia, the terrain was more heavily wooded, turning into thick forest on either side of the mountain watershed dividing the tributaries of the upper Niger from the rivers flowing directly to the Atlantic coast. As far south as the forest margin most of the population was Mande-speaking, though most of it was beyond the political control of Mali. Within the forest lived stateless peoples of the West Atlantic group. The main source of wealth here was the kola-nut, and it seems to have been around the beginning of our period that traders from Mali began to penetrate the region. These Dyula were operating far beyond the frontiers of Islam. To succeed, they had to move their caravans through 300 to 500 kilometres of 'middle belt' country, lacking in exportable commodities and inhabited by pagan Mande organised in very small states, or *kafus*, strung out along the valleys of the upper Niger and its tributaries. The caravans were protected by bands of mercenary soldiers, and in the areas of kola production Dyula families would settle on a long-term basis, intermarrying with the local West Atlantic-speaking societies and slowly winning their confidence and commercial co-operation. At places like Kankan in the interior of modern Guinea, and Bobo Dioulasso and Kong in northern Ivory Coast, there grew up large Dyula communities, whose military escorts and garrisons were a factor to be reckoned with in local politics. Sometimes these forces would turn from protection to slave-raiding and so to conquest, and thus a host of little states ruled by Mande warriors gradually emerged in West Atlantic-speaking country. When the Europeans reached the river estuaries of Guinea and Sierra Leone, it was among the Mande warlords that they found their trading partners.

To the south of the Niger bend, the commercially unproductive 'middle belt' country continued eastwards, separating the great states of the savanna from the equatorial forest region. Here, however, the 'middle belt' peoples were no longer Mande but a succession of stateless groups such as the Senufo and Dogon, the Tallensi and Konkomba, in whose midst flourished five separate islands of military, slave-raiding feudality, the so-called 'Gur states', consisting of the two Mossi states of Wagadugu and Yatenga in modern Upper Volta, the Mamprussi and Dagomba states in the north of modern Ghana, and the Fada N'Gurma state in the west of modern Niger. In the forests of eastern Ivory Coast and the southern part of modern Ghana lived the Akan, who, around 1400, were probably organised in scores of very small states, rather like the *kafus* of the southern Mande. Unlike the West Atlantic peoples living in the same latitude, whose staple food was rice, the Akan cultivated mainly yams. Like the West Atlantic peoples, however, they had kola trees growing in their forests. They also had some of the richest gold reefs of the world beneath their soil. No doubt they had long been familiar with the metal and had panned it in the rivers and worked it for their own use since the first introduction of metallurgy. However, the beginning of outside interest in their wealth, leading to its more intensive exploitation by mining, seems to have occurred only around the late four-teenth century, with the advent of Dyula traders from Jenne, the Mande merchant city on the Bani tributary of the Niger, which was separated from the upper Volta only by a narrow watershed. A large Dyula settlement developed at Begho on the north-western border of Akan territory, and from there the traders entered into contact with the rulers of the various gold-bearing localities of the forest region. By the second half of the fifteenth century Dyula traders were well known on the Atlantic coast around Elmina. When the Portuguese in 1482 negotiated the lease of a site for a fort, they did so with a chief called Karamansa, whose title was certainly of Mande origin.

Between the Volta and the Cross River, the Ewe, Aja, Yoruba, Edo and Igbo peoples succeeded each other in the yam-producing belt comprised by the forest and its northern woodland margin. The Ewe to the west of the region and the Igbo to the east, though both very numerous, were mainly stateless. Between them, the Aja, the Yoruba and Edo were mostly organised, from well before the beginning of our period, into powerful and economically developed city states. One of these, the Edo city of Benin, had already started upon a career of systematic conquest, coupled with the elaboration of centralised poli-tical institutions, which was to make it by the end of the fifteenth century an empire of almost Sudanic dimensions. As developed characteristically among the Yoruba, however, the city state consisted of a single walled town, inhabited by perhaps half of the total popula-tion, while the other half was scattered around it in a circle of smaller but still densely occupied settlements. While agriculture was carried on both from the city and its dependent settlements, the pride of the city and much of its social and political organisation were based on specialised industries – smithing and other metalwork, weaving and dyeing, carpentry and wood-carving, glass-making, leatherwork, pot-ting and basketry. At the apex of the craft system, a very few very highly skilled artists and brass-founders in the service of the most powerful rulers were already producing some of the finest sculpture in 19 the history of the world. Along with the craft specialisation went a high degree of monetarisation, probably based on some kinds of sea-shells, so that, for example, much of the food grown on the farms was sold in the town markets and even small services were paid for in cash. The city state, however, was not just an expression of its citizens' preference for an urban life. The main reason for its existence was undoubtedly military. Year in, year out, state warred against state. Prisoners were taken for enslavement. Crops and booty were carried off. North of the forest, knights in armour raided on horse-back. Within the forest, where horses were useless in battle, they were nevertheless kept by rulers as symbols of authority, thus indicating that the tradition of military rulership had originated in the savanna region.

It is impossible as yet to discern how and when the pattern of city states common to so much of northern and south-western Nigeria spread among so many diverse peoples. It is noticeable, however, that in western Nigeria and Bénin (Dahomey) there occurs a break in the east–west line of 'middle belt', stateless peoples. The city states of the Hausa border on those of Nupe, which in turn border on those of the Yoruba. Certainly, however, it would be a mistake to regard the state systems of the south as a response to the slaving warfare of Muslim Hausaland which we mentioned in the last chapter. Some at least of the Yoruba cities are as old as those of the Hausa, and if they have a common origin, it must long antedate the introduction of Islam in the north. For our present purposes, they may be regarded as separate systems.

AROUND THE CONGO FOREST

We have seen that from the West Atlantic coast to the Cameroun highlands it was typical for the 'middle belt' – the woodland region south of the savanna and north of the equatorial forest – to be inhabited by strongly agricultural and self-sufficient peoples organised either in very small states or else having no kind of states at all. This was also true of the region between the Cameroun highlands and the White Nile. Here, to the south of the Nilo-Saharan and Arabic-speaking peoples of the savanna, lived Central Sudanic-speakers such as the Sara and the Madi, and Eastern Negritic-speakers such as the Banda, Baya and Wute. All of these people were probably, at the beginning of our period, stateless. Their northernmost representatives were perpetually harried by the horse-borne slave-raiders of the savanna states – Bagirmi, Kanem, Wadai and Darfur. For this

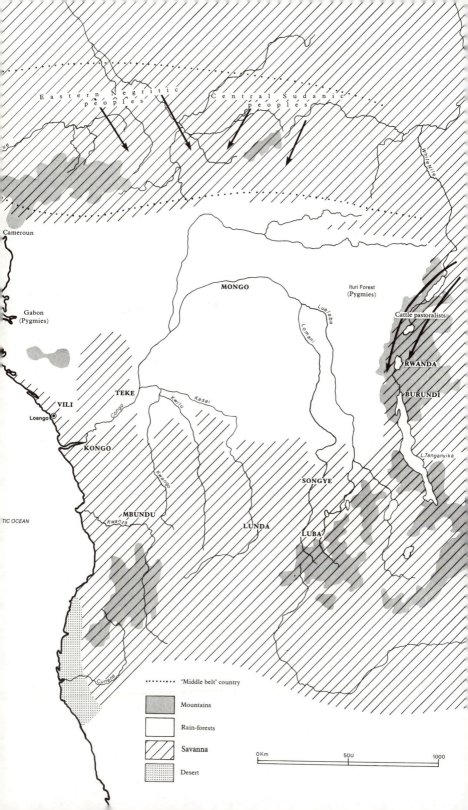

Eastern Negritic peoples

Central Sudanic peoples

Cameroun

Gabon (Pygmies)

MONGO

Ituri Forest (Pygmies)

Cattle pastoralists

Lualaba

Lomani

VILI
Loango

TEKE

Kwilu   Kasai

RWANDA

Congo

BURUNDI

KONGO

Kwango

L.Tanganyika

SONGYE

TIC OCEAN

MBUNDU

Kwanza

LUNDA

LUBA

Cunene

·········   'Middle belt' country

▨   Mountains

☐   Rain-forests

▨   Savanna

▨   Desert

0 Km   500   1000

reason, and perhaps also because of climatic change, there was a slow drift of population from north to south, which is clearly reflected in the traditions of most of these peoples. It is probable that over the centuries many of their southernmost representatives drifted southwards into the equatorial forest, adopting Bantu speech and becoming culturally absorbed by such Bantu-speaking groups as the Mongo, living within the great bend of the Congo river. Later on a few of them, such as the Mangbetu from the Central Sudanic group, and the Nzakara and Azande from the Eastern Negritic-speakers, were to become involved in processes of active conquest and state-formation.

In general, however, the region to the north of the Congo forest was one of small communities, and, unlike the West African 'middle belt', it was crossed by no long-distance trade routes corresponding to those of the Mande and the Hausa. The Congo forest had neither gold nor kola. It was inhabited only very sparsely, with food-producers more or less confined to the river lines, and pygmy hunter–gatherers elsewhere. Not only was the Ituri forest, to the east of the Congo bend, then as now a pygmy domain, but so also was the vast forested area forming the watershed between the Congo drainage system and the rivers flowing directly to the Atlantic such as the Ogowe and the Sanaga. It may be that even within the great bend of the Congo large areas were still at the beginning of our period inhabited mainly by pygmies, whose physical traces are still visible in many of the modern food-producers of that region. Pygmy hunting bands tend to number thirty to forty individuals. The riverside settlements of the forest cultivators, though much denser, were no doubt then as now subject to very frequent changes of site, due to the rapid deterioration of forest soils. While the Congo waterways may have provided a considerable stimulus to medium-distance trade, involving the exchange of produce between forest and savanna, there is no tradition of large-scale political organisation within the forest region.

It was to the east and south of the forest that, already by the beginning of our period, areas of comparatively dense population were beginning to be organised in states at least as large as those of the southern Mande and Akan, and in some cases large enough to require a hierarchy of ruling chiefs. The most important factors in this situation were no doubt ecological and demographic. To the east of the forest, along the frontiers of northern Zaïre, Uganda, Rwanda and Burundi, the Nile–Congo watershed with its volcanic soils offers some of the richest farming lands in the whole continent. To the south of the forest, the great tributary rivers of the Congo drainage system rise far out in the southern savanna and flow northwards through several hundred kilometres of forest/savanna mosaic, which likewise offers a favourable environment for farming combined with fishing and hunting. In this respect the southern margins of the forest are more favourable to human settlement than the northern ones, where the Congo tributaries rise close to, or even within, the forest.

In addition to these local environmental factors, however, there were others of wider geographical scope. The savanna to the east of the forest was much more open than the forest itself to migration from the north, and especially to the migration of pastoralists, who were by occupation much more mobile than cultivators. Whatever the origins of this process, which may go back to the end of the first millennium, it is certain that by about 1400 communities of fairly specialised pastoralists were living in among the agricultural populations on both sides of the Western Rift Valley. In the grasslands of western Uganda a dynasty of pastoralists was already powerful enough to be surrounding its main cattle-camps with extensive earthwork defences. Pastoralists had already penetrated the grasslands of eastern Rwanda and Burundi: soon they would be moving into the islands of mountain pasture astride the Nile–Congo watershed, where the agricultural population was densest. Though we have less information from eastern Zaïre, it is clear that a basically similar situation prevailed right down the grassland corridor between the forest and the Western Rift. Wherever pastoralists lived in close contact with cultivators, a symbiosis developed which tended to become institutionalised in state organisations. The grassland of the western Rift may thus have been a corridor not only for migrants but, even more, for political ideas, which gradually spread by contact and borrowing through the comparatively dense communities to the south of the forest.

At all events we may be sure that, by the beginning of our period, Songye, Luba, Lunda, Mbundu, Kongo, Vili and Teke, to name only the most important of the ethnic groups to the south of the forest, had all entered upon the process of state-formation. In particular, the kingdom of Kongo, with its centre in the plateau country of northern Angola, was on the way to establishing a hegemony comparable to that of Benin in southern Nigeria, stretching over a territory of perhaps 10,000 square kilometres to the south of the lower Congo, and incorporating as tributary provinces three or four pre-existing states, themselves of not negligible size. In the plateau country to the north of the lower Congo, the Teke or Tio were organised in another large kingdom, which was perhaps already supplying slaves to Kongo and would soon be doing the same for the Atlantic trade of the Portuguese. Between the Teke and the Gabon coast were the three Vili kingdoms

23

of Loango, while on the Kwanza river to the south of the Kongo kingdom a considerable state was being built up among the Mbundu people by a dynasty with the title *ngola a kiluanje*, which was to give its name to the Portuguese colony of Angola. It is clear that throughout all this region there can have been no really long-distance trade prior to the coming of the Portuguese. On the other hand, the fact that all these kingdoms used a common currency, consisting of the sea-shells called *nzimbu* fished from the shallow waters around Luanda island, argues that local trade, involving the exchange of products between the forest, the savanna and the sea coast, was probably quite intensive. On the political and ritual side, kingship was everywhere associated with smithing and metalwork, political allegiance was symbolised by the distribution of brands from the royal fire, and many other taboos and observances concerning the sacredness of the king's person were in force. It is these features, or some of them, which may have reached the lower Congo region from the east.

In a work of seminal importance, which will be discussed in more detail in Chapter 13, Joseph Miller has studied and reinterpreted the westward spread of rulership titles from Luba to Lunda, and so on to eastern Angola. His essential thesis is that political ideas and institutions can spread from one population to another with only minimal migrational movement by individuals, as ethnic groups reorganise themselves in response to the reorganisations of their neighbours. In the savanna/forest mosaic of southern Zaïre the crucial communicators of ideas were the guilds of specialised hunters who operated in the forest margins and in the no-man's-land between one settled community and another. These men were skilled smiths. They had the best weapons and the strongest magic. When new forms of leadership were required, it was to them that the agricultural populations would turn. A group of village settlements would combine to form a state ruled by a hunter chief and his coterie. Such reorganisations could happen over and over again, with fewer and larger units emerging on each occasion. At the beginning of our period, the part of the region where political organisation had developed furthest was probably among the Luba, in whose country the favourable environment of forest/savanna mosaic was enhanced by rich deposits of copper- and iron-ore, easily accessible in surface outcrops. On the high plateau of Shaba these deposits had been actively exploited since the late first millennium, and the existence not much later at Sanga, nearly 200 kilometres further north, of a currency consisting of H-shaped copper crosses (which also occurred, though later, in Zambia and Zimbabwe) argues the existence of an active system of local

24

trade. In Shaba, it would seem, was the industrial centre of Bantu Africa. According to Luba traditions, the rulers came from the north, from Songye and ultimately perhaps from the grasslands of the Western Rift. It is no less clear, however, that Lubaland was itself the scene of much technical and social innovation, which radiated influence to large parts of Africa lying to the south as well as to the west.

THE EASTERN AND SOUTHERN INTERIOR

Despite the existence of an active East Coast sea route connected to all the main lines of Indian Ocean trade, most of the interior of eastern Africa remained until late in our period a world apart. Behind the coastal plain of Somalia, Kenya and Tanzania lay a thorny wilderness, sparsely inhabited and difficult to cross. Behind that again were grasslands occupied by more or less specialised pastoralists of Cushitic or Nilotic speech. Here, Bantu cultivators were largely confined to the valleys and foothills of the high mountains – Mt Kenya and the Nyandarua range, Kilimanjaro, the Pares, the Usambaras. It was only beyond the grassland belt, in the region north and south of Lake Victoria, that ecological conditions favoured the cultivator or the mixed farmer keeping cattle as an adjunct to cereals or bananas. To the north, this region began around the southern periphery of the Nile marshes (Sudd). From here through the southern Sudan and northern Uganda stretched a land of orchard bush – in West African terms, typical 'middle belt' country, and occupied at the beginning of our period by agricultural and stateless peoples like the Central Sudanic-speaking Madi and Nilotic-speaking Bari and Lango. To the south of them lived the Interlacustrine Bantu, growing bananas in preference to cereals and reaching a considerable population density around the northern and western shores of Lake Victoria, which enjoyed a high and well-distributed rainfall. Here at the beginning of our period there were already small states existing in scores if not in hundreds, but so far as we know, the only large one was that of the pastoralists in the grasslands between the lake and the Western Rift, which we have noted above (p. 23). South of the lake, population was probably by comparison much thinner, with kinship-based settlements slowly proliferating amid sparsely cleared bush.

As yet there is no shred of evidence that this interlacustrine province of Bantu Africa was connected by trade to the Indian Ocean world. In so far as it was affected at all by outside influences, these came from the north in the shape of Nilotic migrants. Before 1400 the main Nilotic thrust had been that of the Eastern Nilotic peoples led by the Kalenjin, who had conquered and settled the western highlands of Kenya, absorbing the earlier Southern Cushitic-speaking population of this area. Further west, in northern and southern Uganda, the main thrust of Western Nilotic, Lwo-speaking peoples was yet to come. The identity of the specialised pastoralists who had already occupied the grasslands of the Western Rift is still uncertain. Most probably, they were Eastern Nilotes from the same stock as the Kalenjin and their northern neighbours. Otherwise, they can only have come from the Cushitic-speaking region still further to the east. The main conclusion to be drawn for the interlacustrine region, which was to continue through our period, is that political change was usually a response to the reception of northern immigrants whether as conquerors or as peaceful settlers.

South of the Great Lakes the picture changes. While northern influences were still important, particularly those reaching the region from the eastern Congo basin, there was an independent stimulus to political and economic development arising from the Indian Ocean trade in gold and ivory. Although the earliest agricultural settlement by Bantu-speaking peoples dates to the early centuries of the first millennium A.D., it would seem that the overall ethnic character of the region underwent considerable changes as a result of the immigration of later Iron Age groups between the eleventh century and the fourteenth. Most of these movements probably stemmed from southern Zaïre, where, as we have seen, the mining and working of copper and iron had already reached a high degree of development before the end of the first millennium. Certainly it is with the advent of the first waves of later Iron Age peoples that the evidence of gold-mining and of Indian Ocean trade goods begins to appear in the archaeological record of western and central Zimbabwe. Archaeological evidence from Mozambique is still very scanty, but from the tenth century onwards Arab geographers testify to the existence of an important trade in ivory, and perhaps also in gold, with a country called Sofala, which evidently formed part of modern Mozambique and probably included the area south of the Zambezi delta, where the Arab trading settlement called Sofala later developed.

We do not know whether it was the hunting and transport of ivory or the mining and monopolisation of gold resources that provided the main impetus to political centralisation among the ancestors of the Shona peoples, but the architectural history of Great Zimbabwe provides ample evidence of the steady growth of at least one major centre of power. The earliest stone buildings on the Acropolis Hill date from the late eleventh century. By the early thirteenth century a

26

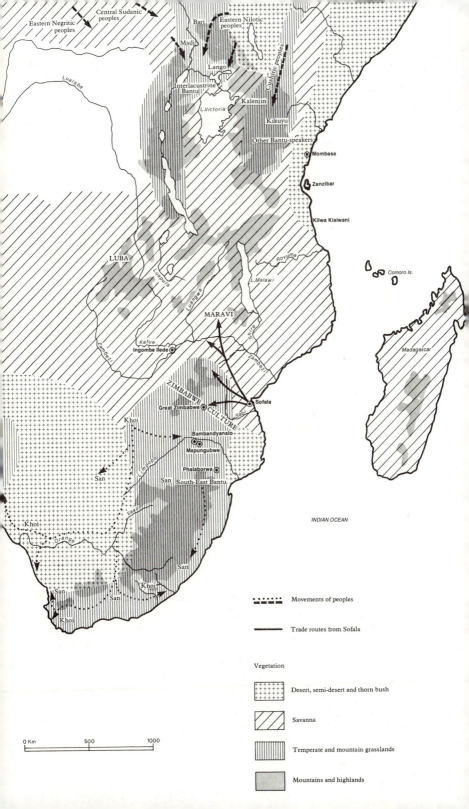

Eastern Negritic
peoples

Central Sudanic
peoples

Bari

Eastern Nilotic
peoples

Madi

Lango

Interlacustrine
Bantu

L.Victoria

Kalenjin

Cushitic peoples

Kikuyu

Other Bantu-speakers

Mombasa

Zanzibar

Kilwa Kisiwani

Lualaba

LUBA

Luapula

Luangwa

Rovuma

L.Malawi

MARAVI

Kafue

Shire

Zambezi

Ingombe Ilede

Zambezi

ZIMBABWE CULTURE

Great Zimbabwe

Sabi

Sofala

Khoi

Bambandyanalo

Mapungubwe

Limpopo

Phalaborwa

San

San

South-East Bantu

Vaal

Khoi

Orange

San

San

Khoi

San

San

Khoi

Comoro Is.

Madagascar

INDIAN OCEAN

Movements of peoples

Trade routes from Sofala

Vegetation

Desert, semi-desert and thorn bush

Savanna

Temperate and mountain grasslands

Mountains and highlands

0 Km   500   1000

new stage of prosperity had been reached, characterised by larger houses, built on stone platforms and surrounded by walled enclosures of massive proportions. By the late fourteenth or early fifteenth century the Zimbabwe masons were capable of the dressed stone and regular coursing of the great girdle wall surrounding the Elliptical Building of the Valley Ruins, while the finds associated with this period include valuable items of glazed Chinese porcelain along with multitudinous imported glass beads, rich jewellery in gold and copper, large copper ingots evidently used for currency, and a wealth of advanced ironwork. It is abundantly clear that, while the export trade was a major stimulus to activity, the architectural conceptions, and no doubt also the political and religious institutions they embodied, were wholly African in their inspiration.

By about 1400, then, Great Zimbabwe was approaching the peak of its prosperity, and certainly it represented a concentration of power unique in the region as a whole. It did not, however, enjoy a monopoly either of political centralisation or of long-distance trade. Besides the routes leading directly inland from Sofala, there was the immense system of navigable waterways provided by the Zambezi and its tributaries. To the north of the main stream, in the wide territory between the Shire and Luangwa tributaries, there flourished at this period the Maravi empire, uniting Chewa and Nyanja, Manganja and Nsenga, under the rule of chiefs of the Phiri clan, remembered in tradition as conquerors from the Luba country in southern Zaïre. Much of the ivory-trade of the region around Lake Malawi probably passed through Maravi hands. Further inland, beyond the Kafue confluence, a rich trading centre at Ingombe Ilede probably served as the collecting-point for ivory from the Gwembe (middle Zambezi) valley and for copper and gold from south of the river. Here, as also among the Maravi, cotton was grown, spun and woven, probably as a result of Muslim influence from the coast.

Again, to the south of Zimbabwe, the Limpopo valley formed the midrib of another series of long-distance trade routes leading from the Indian Ocean coast to the mineral resources of the interior. These led past the copper of the Messina district towards the gold workings of south-western Zimbabwe; and at Mapungubwe, just above Messina, there occurs just the kind of rich, chiefly capital and burial site that one would associate with the control of a long-distance trade route which was functioning around the beginning of our period. Southward from the Limpopo ran the tributary valley of the Olifants River, with its iron and copper mines at Phalaborwa in active use from about the ninth century onwards.

While the Early Iron Age occupation of South Africa dates to the middle of the first millennium A.D., the area affected by it seems to have been confined to the Transvaal, Swaziland and the eastern half of Natal. As in other parts of Bantu Africa, the main means of subsistence was by cereal agriculture combined with hunting: cattle were present only in small numbers. In South Africa, as in Zimbabwe and Zambia and much of eastern Africa, it was only within the present millennium that cattle-keeping became the most prestigious element in food-production and capital-accumulation, with a consequent pressure to occupy every available area of actual or potential grassland. The earliest stages of this revolution are still shrouded in mystery. There is a good deal of linguistic evidence to suggest that the introducers of specialised pastoralism were Khoi or Central Bushmen, who migrated with their herds from southern Angola, western Zambia and northern Botswana by a route which seems to have passed to the east rather than the west of the Kalahari Desert. At this rate, the fusion of the pastoral with the agricultural way of life in this region might have occurred somewhere in the western Transvaal and some time around the twelfth or thirteenth century A.D. It is likely that by the fourteenth century the grasslands of the Vaal were becoming overcrowded, and that a part of their already Bantuised populations were seeking new homes across the Drakensberg, in Natal and the Transkei. We know that by the sixteenth century the coastal plains to the east of the Kei were occupied by Nguni-speaking peoples whose lives centred on their herds of sleek, well-fed cattle, in whose interests they were still clearing and burning the bush, so that the Portuguese described their country as 'the land of fires'. The genealogical evidence collected from the Nguni clans suggests that they may have come from the interior about a century earlier.

All in all, it would appear that by about A.D. 1400 much even of the back country of Africa was in a state of active development. Stateless societies there were, exhibiting a quality of passivity and relative changelessness, but these were rare. Throughout much of the southern two-thirds of Africa it would seem that populations were growing and that societies and economies were alike becoming more complex. In many, if not in a majority of, cases, the increase in scale and in complexity of economies was achieved only with the use of forced labour. In particular, the growth of agricultural production generally involved slaves and other forms of servile labour. All over the continent there was raiding or trading for slaves, using violence of some kind, to obtain labour which was not forthcoming freely from the peoples who lived at the place of such production. We have to 29 remember that African societies operated in economic situations quite unlike the systems of mercantilism and capitalism which were to emerge in western Europe.

As we have seen, there had long been an external trade in human beings across the Sahara and across the Red Sea into the heartlands of Islam (and further afield). Almost the first activities of the Portuguese on the Lower Guinea coast were to act as transporters of slaves from Benin to the Akan country – a comparatively small step which was to lead to further steps in the sea-borne trade, to Portugal itself, to the Portuguese Atlantic Islands, to São Tomé and Principe, and finally to Brazil and other parts of the New World. This was an extension of the usual manner of obtaining a supply of labour in Africa. Slaves transported across the Sahara and across the Atlantic could not, of course, be put to long-term economic use in Africa, and there were many African communities which suffered enormous human losses, both to the internal and external trade. But other African societies thrived, not just on the use of slave-labour in the productive processes, but in the trade to foreigners of such slaves.

Where there was a connection between regions of Africa and the outside world, however tenuous, that usually made the difference to the pace of change. But there were regions, notably in southern Nigeria and around the lower Congo, which were developing rapidly without any such connections, and where indeed the opening of long-distance communications following the appearance of the Portuguese in the Atlantic was to prove more of a setback than a stimulus. Nevertheless, the general rule would appear to be that human societies in Africa which could take advantage of the new opportunities grew larger and richer in proportion to the spread of their outside connections. The greatest handicap which these parts of Africa had to suffer was their geographical remoteness.

3   Egypt and the Nilotic Sudan

Although the lands now comprised within Egypt (the United Arab Republic) and the Republic of Sudan are geographically contiguous, and although the Saharan barrier to communication is here mitigated by the Nile valley on one hand and the Red Sea on the other, the histories of the two parts of the region have at many periods run surprisingly different courses. During the six centuries following the Arab conquests, the contrast was at its sharpest. Egypt was at first an Arab colony and later the centre of a Muslim state extending eastwards and northwards into Palestine and Syria. The Sudan was oriented around two strong and prosperous Christian kingdoms, comprising all of the riverain population and stretching out their cultural influence far to the west, across Kordofan, Darfur and Wadai. From about 1250 onwards, however, Egypt and the Sudan began to draw together again, with a great expansion of pastoral bedouin Arabs as the main connecting link. Between about 1300 and about 1500 the Sudan was overrun by Arabic-speaking Muslim tribes, so that a single literary language and a single great religion held sway both north and south of the desert. At the end of our period, in 1821, Egypt conquered the Sudan, and there followed almost a century of strong Egyptian influence in the south. Although the two countries were to draw apart again during the colonial period, it is clear that the Sudan, more than any other sub-Saharan country, is part of the Arab world, and that the reasons for this go back to the expansion of Arab people during the late medieval period.

EGYPT: THE MAMLUK SULTANATE

For more than four thousand years before the start of our period, from the first emergence of the Pharaohs' kingdom, Egypt had carried the most densely packed and the most easily accessible agricultural population of any part of Africa. This population was concentrated entirely in the delta and beside the flood plain of the main Nile, where the fertility of the soil was maintained by silt carried down by the river and deposited over the farmlands by the annual flood. The water which carried the precious silt carried also the boats of the corn-merchant and the tax-gatherer. Every cultivated holding was within sight of the river or the canal bank. Every peasant smallholder (Arabic *fellah*, pl. *fellahin*) could be made to produce a taxable surplus: if he failed, there would be many another to take his place. Thus, although the *fellahin* might live very near the subsistence level, suffering severely in the seasons following a poor flood, their combined taxes could support a rich and powerful superstructure of centralised government and military might. It made little difference to the system if the ruling elite were a foreign one, and in fact since early in the first millennium B.C. it had always been so. The Persians were followed by the Greeks, the Greeks by the Romans, the Romans by the Byzantines, and the Byzantines by the Arabs. From 1250 until 1517 the ruling elite was composed of Turks from the steppes of southern Russia and Circassians from the mountains of Georgia. Its members were known as Mamluks, a term used for slaves from the regions to the north of the Arab heartlands.

First introduced into Egypt by the famous Salah al-Din (Saladin) and his Ayyubid successors as an answer to the threat of the Crusaders, the Mamluks were all of them in origin slaves. They were taken from the most warlike of the Turkish tribes of the South Russian steppes, peoples long specialised to fighting on horseback, whose main military skill was as mounted archers. Captured as young boys and shipped to Egypt through the Black Sea and the eastern Mediterranean, they were trained deliberately to be members of a *corps d'élite*. When fully qualified as cavalry knights, they were manumitted and given an income corresponding to their rank, which normally consisted of the revenues from a specified area of land (*iqta*). Each Mamluk, according to the size of his *iqta*, had the obligation to mount and arm anything between five and five hundred men, and in the case of the highest ranks, the *amirs* or commanders, revenues were substantial enough for the purchase and training of fresh Mamluks for their units. An *iqta*, however, was essentially a grant in usufruct, ending with the life of the owner. Moreover, although Mamluks could marry, their children could never become Mamluks: thus, the foreign elite had constantly to be replenished by fresh recruits from abroad, educated in the discipline of a military camp or 'household', dependent for their manumission and their subsequent promotion upon their professional patrons and superiors. It is thought that, at their peak, there may have been about ten thousand Mamluks, ruling over an Egyptian population of three to six million.

In 1250, following their decisive victory over the crusading army of King Louis IX of France at Mansura in the delta, a group of Mamluk officers staged a coup d'état against Turan Shah, the last of the

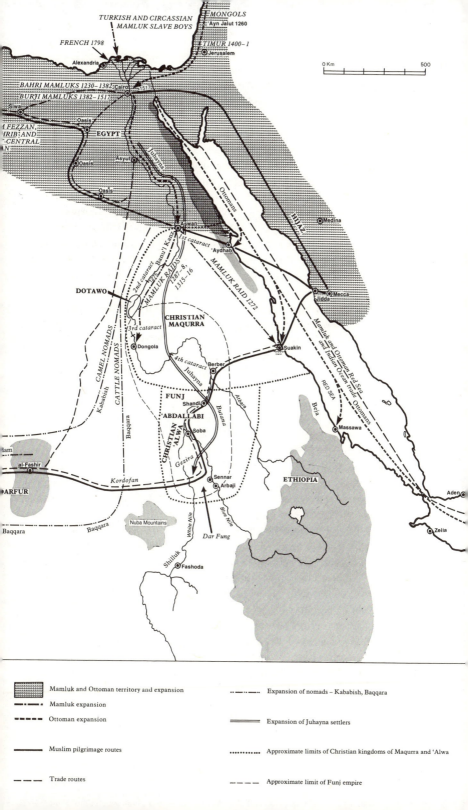

TURKISH AND CIRCASSIAN
MAMLUK SLAVE BOYS

MONGOLS
'Ayn Jalut 1260

FRENCH 1798

TIMUR 1400–1

Jerusalem

Alexandria

0 Km   500

BAHRI MAMLUKS 1230–1382 Cairo 1517

BURJI MAMLUKS 1382–1517

Siwa

A FEZZAN
RIB AND
-CENTRAL
N

Oasis

EGYPT

Asyut

Juhayna

Oasis

Oasis

Aswan   1st cataract

Aydhab

Medina

HIJAZ

Ottomans

Banu'l Kanz
1275

2nd cataract

DOTAWO

MAMLUK RAIDS
1287–8,
1315–16

MAMLUK RAID 1272

3rd cataract

CHRISTIAN
MAQURRA

Suakin

Jidda

Mecca

Dongola

4th cataract

Berber

Mamluk and Ottoman Red Sea
and Indian Ocean trade Ottomans

CAMEL NOMADS

CATTLE NOMADS

Kababish

Juhayna

Shandi

FUNJ

RED SEA

Baqqara

ABDALLABI

Soba

Butana

Atbara

Beja

Massawa

CHRISTIAN
ALWA

Gezira

Kordofan

Sennar

Arbaji

ETHIOPIA

lam

al-Fashir

ARFUR

Baqqara

Nuba Mountains

White Nile

Dar Fung

Blue Nile

Aden

Baqqara

Shilluk

Fashoda

Zeila

▨ Mamluk and Ottoman territory and expansion	–··–··– Expansion of nomads – Kababish, Baqqara
–·–·– Mamluk expansion	
– – – – Ottoman expansion	═══ Expansion of Juhayna settlers
——— Muslim pilgrimage routes	·········· Approximate limits of Christian kingdoms of Maqurra and 'Alwa
– – – Trade routes	– –– – –– Approximate limit of Funj empire

Ayyubid sultans. Henceforward, for 267 years, the sultanate was invariably held by a Mamluk. In theory, though not always in practice, the *iqta* system applied equally to the ruler, who was merely the largest *iqta*-holder, receiving one-quarter of all the revenues levied in this way. At the death of a sultan, a designated son or nephew carried on the office for a few days or weeks, while the leading *amirs* fought among themselves over the succession. When the new sultan was elected, the natural heir withdrew into an honourable retirement. The Bahri (River) Mamluks, who ruled from 1250 until 1382, were not therefore a dynasty, despite the fact that a number of sultans were in practice succeeded by their children or relatives. The designation merely referred to the island headquarters of the regiment or 'household' from which they came. The Burji (Citadel) Mamluks, who succeeded them from 1382 until 1517, had scarcely any cases of hereditary succession. These sultans were drawn from the mainly Circassian regiments which guarded the Cairo citadel, and their ascendancy marked a change in the balance of power between Turkish and Circassian elements in the military elite.

The Mamluks seized power in Egypt at a period which was critical for the whole of the Islamic world. For the fading menace of the European Crusaders there was now substituted the far more terrifying threat of the Mongol hordes advancing from central Asia, and rolling up year by year the map of the old 'Abbasid caliphate. Baghdad fell to the Mongols in 1258. Early in 1260 they and their Armenian allies had occupied all Syria. As Bernard Lewis has written, 'Throughout the early, formative period of the Mamluk sultanate, the dominating fact of life was the presence of a hostile heathen power in central and south-west Asia, which had conquered half the world of Islam, and seemed poised to conquer the other half.'[1] On the Muslim side the heroic figure was Baybars, the commander of the Bahri regiment, who had been the victor against the Crusaders at Mansura and the leader in the overthrow of Turan Shah, and who now marched north to Galilee and, at 'Ayn Jalut on 3 September 1260, fought a decisive battle against the Mongols. It was the first time that a Mongol army had suffered defeat, and a few weeks later Baybars crowned his victory by forcefully supplanting the Mamluk sultan, Qutuz.

Baybars (1260–77), Qalawun (1279–90), al-Nasir Muhammad (1293–1340, with two intervals) – these were the great Mamluk sultans of the Bahri line, who reorganised and defended the western half of the Islamic world during the vital half century of the Mongol threat.

[1] *Cambridge History of Islam*, vol. 1 (Cambridge, 1970), p. 215.

Their first contribution was military. They modernised their armies, even engaging Mongol bands to teach the latest methods of cavalry warfare. Their battles were fought far beyond the frontiers of Egypt, above all in Palestine and Syria, where they finally dislodged the Crusaders, annexed the remaining Ayyubid principalities, drove back the border peoples of the north, and established a firmly held northern province based on Damascus. The new imperial communications through Palestine were so good that Baybars boasted that he could play polo in Cairo and Damascus in the same week, while an even more rapid carrier-pigeon post was maintained between the two cities. Refugees from Iraq and Persia poured into the Mamluk domains. One of the earliest was an 'Abbasid prince from Baghdad, who was installed as caliph in Cairo in 1261. Although quite powerless, the reinstatement of the caliphate in Egypt brought the allegiance of the rulers of the Holy Places in the Hijaz and greatly enhanced the importance of Cairo as a staging-post on the pilgrimage routes. Other refugees included teachers, preachers and scholars from Baghdad and other eastern cities, who helped to make Cairo the undoubted centre of orthodox, Sunni Islam and also of Arabic scholarship. Finally, Mamluk Egypt gained greatly by the Mongol disruption of the more northerly trade routes connecting Europe and Asia. The Mamluk sultans sent embassies to the Indian Ocean lands to advertise the merits of the Red Sea route, and, even while they were chasing the Crusaders from their last outposts in the eastern Mediterranean, they were carefully encouraging the settlement of European merchants in specially protected enclaves (*funduqs*) in Alexandria. The so-called Karimi merchants and bankers of Egypt were far more than the middlemen who bought at the Red Sea ports and sold at those of the Mediterranean. They operated great fleets of ships on the Red Sea and the Indian Ocean. They had agencies in Ethiopia and Nubia, in Arabia and the Persian Gulf, in India and Ceylon, in Indonesia and southern China. At home in Egypt, they vied with the sultans as patrons of religion and the arts.

For the first century and a half of Mamluk rule Egypt prospered exceedingly. But during the reign of Barquq (1382–99), the first of the Burji sultans, a further wave of Mongol invaders from central Asia under the leadership of the great conqueror Timur (Tamarlane) broke upon the northern frontiers of the Mamluk empire. In 1400–1 Syria was invaded and completely devastated. Damascus and many other cities were put to the sack, and their inhabitants deported to the east. Egypt was saved by Timur's abrupt departure to deal with a crisis at the eastern end of his dominions, and the situation in Syria was 35 gradually restored. Nevertheless, the military expenditure of the Burji sultans started the Egyptian economy on a slow but steady decline. Overtaxation, state monopolies and depreciation of the currency were short-term remedies which produced long-term damage. The initiative of the Karimi merchants in the eastern trade was declining when the Portuguese at the end of the fifteenth century sailed into the Indian Ocean and began to divert maritime trade routes around the Cape of Good Hope. By this time even the military machine of the Mamluks was becoming outdated, as heavy-armed cavalry knights were overtaken by fire-arms, especially in the neighbouring and rapidly expanding armies of the Ottoman Turks.

Nevertheless, until the final and sudden collapse under Ottoman fire-power in 1516–17, the decline of the Mamluks was less visible in Egypt than in the northern dominions, and less visible in Cairo than in the rest of Egypt. The Burji sultans were great builders and restorers of mosques, schools, hostels, baths and other public works, and the reign of Qa'it Bey (1468–96) saw the finest development of Mamluk art and architecture. Roads, bridges, markets and caravanserais were well maintained throughout the Burji period, and so were the splendours of the 'palace city' within the Cairo citadel, where incense burned and wine flowed, where musicians played and poets recited to a court society clad in silk and sprinkled with rose-water, its beards well perfumed with the musk of civet. This was the Cairo visited by the great men of the western Sudan on their way to pilgrimage. This, even more importantly, was the Cairo where West African scholars went to study the authentic doctrines of Islam, in a bookish atmosphere very different from the popular enthusiasms of the Maghrib or the Nilotic Sudan. Though ruled by Turks, Mamluk Egypt preserved the older Arabic civilisation of Islam, which was being replaced to the east and the north by the new Islamic cultures of recent converts whose main languages were Persian and Turkish, and whose influence upon Africa was to be much slighter.

THE ARABISATION OF NUBIA

There was one region of Africa where the proximity of the great Mamluk state in Egypt exercised an influence of a very different and a very much more direct kind. Primarily this influence was that of the nomadic bedouin Arabs, who from early Islamic times had pastured their camels and goats in the deserts to the east and the west of the Nile valley. In the eastern desert of Egypt these were known collectively as the Juhayna. Further south, the inhospitable region between the first and second cataracts, though politically a part of the Christian king-dom of Maqurra, was early occupied by bedouin Arabs called the Banu'l Kanz, who formed an unruly border community which was constantly raiding the settled riverain populations to the north and the south and interfering with the pilgrim traffic passing between Aswan on the Nile and 'Aydhab on the Red Sea. There was thus a situation in which punitive action against the nomads, whether from Egypt or Maqurra, could have serious repercussions upon the other country. The Fatimids, perhaps because of their dependence on the black slave recruits from Nubia for their armies, never sought to exploit this situation. Ibn Selim of Aswan, who travelled through Nubia in the late tenth century, noted that, except for the cataract region, the only Muslims permitted to enter Maqurra or the southern Christian state of 'Alwa were merchants. Under the Ayyubids the recruitment of black slave soldiers ceased abruptly. The Mamluks, while developing trade contacts with Nubia from the Red Sea ports, were quite pre-pared to treat Maqurra as a ready-made solution to the bedouin problem. Whenever the Juhayna raided the settled districts of Upper Egypt, they were attacked and driven south, thus adding to the overcrowding of the cataract region. And when in 1272 a Maqurran raid against the Banu'l Kanz reached 'Aydhab, Sultan Baybars responded by capturing the Maqurran port of Suakin and by despatching three expeditions up the Nile. Baybars did not succeed in dethroning the Nubian king, David, but his armies plundered as far as Dongola and did great damage, and the story was repeated under Qalawun in 1287 and 1289. Qalawun allowed himself to be bought off with an increased tribute, but not before Maqurra had been devas-tated and made incapable of further resistance. As a result, when the operation was again repeated by al-Nasir Muhammad in 1315 and 1316, the Christian king was captured without difficulty and replaced by a Muslim pretender. In the following year, as we know from an inscription on its walls, the Christian cathedral of Dongola was con-verted to a mosque. Only in the inhospitable region around the second cataract, now largely by-passed by caravan routes running straight across the desert from Aswan to Dongola, did a small Christian kingdom, that of Dotawo, survive until the late fifteenth century, paying tribute to the Muslim rulers of Maqurra.

The real result of the Mamluk intervention, however, was not so much to extend Egyptian influence as, by destroying Maqurra's power of resistance, to let loose the pent-up flood of bedouin Arabs from upper Egypt into the Sudan. These soon disposed of the puppet ruler installed by al-Nasir Muhammad, and replaced him by the Arab   37 chief of the Banu'l Kanz. Immigrants poured in – first the semi-sedentary Banu'l Kanz from the cataracts, then the Juhayna from upper Egypt. Many of them settled in the Dongola reach of the Nile valley, dispossessing and enslaving the former Nubian owners. Meanwhile, other more purely pastoral groups, such as the Kababish, spread through the deserts to the west of the Nile and out across the dry grazing lands of northern Kordofan and Darfur, one group of them, the Judham, reaching as far west as Kanem by the end of the fourteenth century. Later waves of Arab nomads had to push still further south, into the lightly wooded savanna of southern Kordofan, southern Darfur and Wadai. These moister grasslands were unsuited to camels and sheep, so the Arabs took over the cattle culture of the Nilotic- and Central Sudanic-speaking peoples of the area. There was much intermarriage, and gradually there emerged a racially mixed but Arabic-speaking population called the Baqqara, which lived in widely dispersed groups across the whole region.

By the end of the thirteenth century the southern Christian kingdom, 'Alwa, appears to have been much fragmented. The capital was reported to have moved from Soba on the Blue Nile to another site, known as Waylula, which cannot now be identified. A Mamluk emissary, one 'Alm al-Din Sanjar, who travelled through the region in the late thirteenth century, described his contacts with nine apparently independent rulers. Probably these represented the ancient provincial centres, based on a series of riverside towns from the Atbara confluence southwards to the Gezira. These 'Alwa chiefdoms continued in existence for at least two more centuries, until just before the emergence of the Funj sultanate. At the end of the fifteenth century the chronicler John of Syria reported that the Nubians had no kings, but were ruled by 'captains' who lived in castles along the Nile. Soon after this visit, however, large parts of 'Alwa, including the old capital of Soba, were united under the hegemony of an Arab chief, 'Abdallah Jamaa, who established his headquarters at Arbaji on the lower Blue Nile. Though a somewhat shadowy figure, it is likely that 'Abdallah Jamaa was initially the leader of Juhayna Arab migrants, who moved southwards from upper Egypt down the line of the Red Sea hills, reaching the Butana country between the Atbara and the Blue Nile during the fourteenth century, and the Gezira country between the Blue and White Niles about a century later. What is not clear is whether the preceding period of political fragmentation in 'Alwa was a consequence of the penetration of the Arabs, or whether it was in origin an internal process that was already under way before the Arabs arrived.

THE FUNJ SULTANATE

The origin of the Funj sultans, who ruled over the central part of the modern Sudan Republic from the early sixteenth until the early nineteenth century, is still a subject of debate. The explorer James Bruce, who recorded traditions of the kingdom in 1772, believed that the Funj were Shilluk, that is to say that they belonged to the northernmost of the Nilotic-speaking peoples, who in the seventeenth century built up a considerable kingdom astride the White Nile around Fashoda. Other sources, however, indicate that the home of the dynasty lay to the south of the Blue Nile, around the area still known as Dar Fung. The two areas are in fact not so far apart, and if we bear in mind that Shilluk traditions tell of a long period when their ancestors were engaged in driving out the previous inhabitants of their country called ap-Funy, the most likely conclusion would seem to be that the Funj came from the southern Gezira, and that they were Negroes and not Arabs. Quite possibly, they stemmed from one of the southern provinces of the old kingdom of 'Alwa, and their endeavour was to reconstitute that kingdom around a more southerly base. At all events, their first appearance in history, around the turn of the fifteenth and sixteenth centuries, was as pastoralists and horsemen, under the leadership of one 'Amara Dunkas, who invaded the Gezira from the south and defeated the Juhayna of 'Abdallah Jamaa in a great battle near Arbaji. The Funj henceforward occupied the grazing lands of the Gezira, but contented themselves with a loose suzerainty over the 'Abdallabs, who continued as the overlords of the Butana and of the Nile valley below the confluence. David Reubeni, a Jewish traveller who claimed to have travelled through the region with a merchant caravan in 1523, reported that the Funj dominions began to the north of Dongola: they thus encompassed not only 'Alwa but most of the old kingdom of Maqurra. Sennar, traditionally founded in 1504, was the commercial capital, but 'Amara Dunkas lived further to the south, perhaps in a peripatetic, tented capital like the Solomonid kings of Ethiopia. By the middle of the sixteenth century the dynasty had converted to Islam. By the early seventeenth century it had settled permanently at Sennar, with the dependent 'Abdallabi dynasty at Qarri, just below the confluence.

The power of the Funj sultans, as also that of their 'Abdallabi vassals, depended on the ability of their mounted soldiers to levy fairly regular taxes from the settled, riverain cultivators, and to exercise at least some periodic control over the cattle nomads of the Gezira and the Butana. Most of the pastoralists had to move their herds from 39 summer to winter grazing grounds, and so could be waylaid while on the move and forced to hand over some of their stock as tax or tribute. Again, the revenues of both Funj and 'Abdallabi rulers depended greatly on customs dues levied on trade. Essentially, they controlled a set of long-distance caravan routes leading to Egypt and the Red Sea ports, along which there passed commodities of considerable value, such as the gold and civet-musk of southern Ethiopia, the ivory and ebony of the White Nile, and the slaves drawn from all the weaker communities of the southern frontier. From the mid-sixteenth century onwards, the main direction of Funj expansion was westwards into Kordofan and the Nuba mountains, whence came most of the slave soldiers recruited into the sultans' armies. But Funj rule in these western regions was never very effective, and by the middle of the eighteenth century they had passed into the control of Darfur, the rapidly expanding Muslim state to the west of the Funj domains. To the east, the Beja people of the Red Sea hills, though converting gradually to Islam, remained politically almost independent; and, beyond them, the Ottomans ruled the Red Sea coast for most of the period. To the south, the Nilotic-speaking peoples in and around the area of the Nile marshes were quite unaffected by the Funj hegemony. The heartland of the sultanate was always the Gezira with, to the north of it, the long stretch of the Nile ruled by the 'Abdallabi, where the Funj were only the overlords.

During the sixteenth and seventeenth centuries, the Funj sultanate appears to have provided its subjects with long periods of relative peace and prosperity, during which the new Arab element in the population mixed and fused with the descendants of the Christian Nubians to form a new nation with a distinctive sense of patriotism. Very largely, this was a process which followed as more and more people, whose ancestors had entered the Sudan as nomads, became sedentary farmers in the more favourable parts of the Nile valley. It was particularly marked in the region around Dongola, where the term Ja'aliyyun came to denote the sedentary Muslims, who thought of themselves as Arabs but were in fact mostly of mixed race. Further south, the Arab element was certainly weaker and the Negro element stronger. All observers described the Funj rulers as black. Here, the sense of arabisation depended more upon the adoption of Islam, though religious conversion often involved the invention of fictitious Arab pedigrees. Strangely enough, the religious leaders who spread Islam so widely among the populations of the Funj sultanate during the sixteenth and seventeenth centuries came not so much from Egypt and the Hijaz as from the Maghrib. The Islamic law, the *shari'a*, was taught in the Maliki form prevalent in the Maghrib, not in the Shafi'i form of Egypt. And the pattern of 'holy men' and their descendants, each with his circle of enthusiastic disciples practising strict observance of the law and popular Sufi devotions, was likewise a feature of Maghribi Islam. In the Sudan the 'holy men', known as *faqi*, came to wield immense power. They became closely involved with the Funj and 'Abdallabi rulers, advising, criticising and supplying moral support for political actions. Frequently they were rewarded with large grants of land, so that many in time became important proprietors and political authorities in their own right. Other *faqis* practised as merchants and penetrated the trading community. Even the nomads had their *faqis*, who moved around with them performing magical and religious services.

By the second half of the eighteenth century the Funj sultanate was disintegrating, racked by internal conflicts, many of them caused by more intense competition for dwindling resources. From the 1760s till the 1780s revolts and power struggles were particularly severe, and both the main cities of the Gezira, Sennar and Arbaji, were badly damaged. In 1772 Bruce was so impressed by the atmosphere of instability and decline that he described the Funj as 'this horrid people, whom Heaven has separated by almost impassable deserts from the rest of mankind'.[2] When the Egyptian forces of Muhammad 'Ali invaded the sultanate in 1821, they met with scant resistance, and found to their dismay that Sennar, which had once enjoyed a legendary reputation for wealth and splendour, was little more than a heap of ruins. Nevertheless, the sense of a Sudanese nationhood, Muslim and Arabic-speaking, extending from the cataract region in the north to the Gezira in the south, had been born and was to survive.

EGYPT: THE OTTOMAN PROVINCE

While the Nilotic Sudan was developing its Muslim identity under the Funj, Egypt was by comparison languishing under a not very purposeful or well-organised kind of colonial rule. There was indeed a rather striking contrast between the discipline and stability of the Ottoman empire in its central provinces while its power was still growing, and the situation at the last conquered extremities of that empire as it turned towards decline. The Ottoman state had emerged in the fourteenth century as one of many Turkish principalities practising the holy war against the retreating frontier of the Byzantine

---

[2] James Bruce, *Travels to Discover the Source of the Nile* (1790), vol. IV, p. 476.

empire in Asia Minor (Anatolia). Within a century it grew into a world power by conquering the Byzantine provinces in south-eastern Europe (Rumelia), and establishing itself in the Byzantine capital of Constantinople (henceforward Istanbul) in 1453. Thus far, its military achievements had been mainly those of free Turkish soldiers seeking booty in this life and salvation in the next. But as the children of the conquerors settled to the enjoyment of their possessions, the military muscle of the empire, as well as much of its highly centralised bureaucracy, passed into the hands of slaves taken as a regular levy from the Christian populations of the Balkan provinces. The best known of the slave troops were the crack infantry corps called the Janissaries (Turkish *yeni cheri*, new troops), who were the first soldiers in the Muslim world to be regularly trained in the use of fire-arms. The Janissaries were formidable in warfare. They were also the hard core of the Ottoman provincial garrisons. Forbidden to marry while on active service, forbidden to introduce their children into the corps, well rewarded on retirement, they remained through the fifteenth and sixteenth centuries the most loyal element in the Ottoman power structure. By the seventeenth and eighteenth centuries, however, the system was breaking up. The bureaucracy resented the privileges and the social exclusiveness of the Janissaries, and the Janissaries were only too ready to be assimilated into the urban elite of the Ottoman provinces, marrying the local women, joining in the faction fights of local politics. So far as Egypt was concerned, Ottoman rule meant first of all an external metropolis to be satisfied with tribute, and secondly yet another military elite living on the fat of the land.

There was no compelling reason why the Ottomans should have attacked the Mamluks. Obviously, as the frontiers of the two empires approached each other in the borderlands of eastern Anatolia and northern Syria, there would be local friction, and from 1485 until 1491 there was some long-drawn-out fighting between the two powers over which of them should control the buffer state of Albistan. However, when the Portuguese burst into the Indian Ocean and began to threaten the Red Sea route, the Mamluks asked for, and received, much help from the Ottomans both in building up their Red Sea fleet and in belatedly converting some of their infantry to the use of fire-arms. It was really the rapid expansion of a third large Muslim state, that of the Safavid Shah Isma'il from Azarbayjan into western Persia and Iraq, which led, as a by-product, to the Ottoman conquest of Egypt. In 1514 the Ottoman sultan, Selim, began a war against Shah Isma'il, who called for the help of the Mamluk sultan, Qansawh al-Ghawri. Unwisely, in 1516 Qansawh led an army to northern Syria to threaten the flank of the Ottoman advance. Sultan Selim responded by switching his campaign from the Shah to the Mamluk, decisively defeating Qansawh near Aleppo in August, taking Damascus in September and Cairo in January 1517. The Mamluk empire was promptly broken up. Egypt, deprived of its Syrian territories, became a separate province under a system of government by which the Mamluk establishment continued to perform most of its old functions under the supervision of an Ottoman viceroy and a Janissary garrison.

Although Selim's conquest of the Mamluk empire had been undertaken on impulse, Egypt proved to be the most profitable of all the Ottoman provinces, at least during the sixteenth century. The wealth of the country was in its agriculture, and with the Ottoman conquest most of the land allocated in *iqta* holdings reverted to the state, which made a considerable profit by farming the taxes. Egypt continued to profit as the assembly-point for the pilgrimage caravans from the Maghrib and West Africa; and the trade of the trans-Saharan routes, particularly those from Darfur and Sennar, was far from negligible. Moreover, despite the activities of the Portuguese in the Indian Ocean, Egypt's share of the Eastern trade remained very considerable throughout the sixteenth and most of the seventeenth century. The Ottomans also inherited and developed the Mamluk interests in Arabia and on the African shores of the Red Sea. In 1538 the Ottoman viceroy of Egypt, Sulayman Pasha, led an unsuccessful expedition to oust the Portuguese from the Indian port of Diu, but on his return took control of Aden. A few years later, Ozdemir Pasha, a Circassian general in the service of the Ottoman sultan, led an expedition through Upper Egypt into northern Nubia (known to the Turks as Berberistan), where he captured and garrisoned Aswan, Say and Ibrim, all important caravan towns in the Nile valley. Ozdemir then led his forces across the desert to the Red Sea ports of Suakin, Massawa and Zeila. The Ottomans set up a new province, which they called Habesh (Abyssinia), with its capital at Massawa, in a largely successful attempt to exclude the Portuguese from the Red Sea and from access to Christian Ethiopia.

Throughout the reigns of Suleyman the Magnificent (1520–66) and Selim II (1566–74), Ottoman rule in Egypt delivered peace and good order within the province. Thereafter, with the decline of the central institutions of the empire, fewer Ottoman officials and fewer garrison troops were sent from Istanbul, and power slipped steadily back into the hands of the Mamluks. Though still organised in 'households', they were now increasingly a hereditary caste, including not only

43

soldiers but officials and tax-farmers, and it has been reckoned that by the eighteenth century something like two-thirds of the revenues of Egypt remained in their hands. The leaders of the Mamluk households, formerly called *amirs* but now *beys*, conducted increasingly violent faction fights in the capital for the control of revenue-bearing offices, and from time to time a boss figure would emerge with such a concentration of wealth and power that the transitory Ottoman viceroys were quite overshadowed. Such were Ridwan Bey al-Faqarri, who dominated Egypt in the mid-seventeenth century, and 'Ali Bey, who was a commanding figure from about 1760 until his death in 1773. Indeed, 'Ali Bey became a national and not merely a Mamluk leader, and may be regarded as a precursor of Muhammad 'Ali Pasha, who in the first half of the nineteenth century succeeded in establishing effective autonomy for Egypt under a hereditary local dynasty. 'Ali Bey, however, failed to transmit his ascendancy to his children, and the end of the century saw an unstable triumvirate of *beys*, only nominally under Ottoman control, until the French invasion of 1798.

4 The north-eastern triangle

In north-eastern Africa two great cultures, one Christian and the other Muslim, had long been expanding their influence over the Semitic- and Cushitic-speaking populations of the region. The Christian element, planted in the fourth century, had its base in the central highland area extending from Tigre in the north through Wag and Lasta to the Shoan plateau in the south. The Islamic element, dating from the ninth and tenth centuries, was based upon the coastlands to the west of the Red Sea and to the south of the Gulf of Aden, whence it had spread southwards through the Somali country and westwards up the Awash valley to encompass the Semitic-speakers of southern Shoa and the Chercher highlands and the fringe of the Sidama (Omotic or Western Cushitic-speaking) peoples living in the Rift Valley and beyond it. For three or four centuries the two systems had expanded side by side, and peaceably enough, at the expense of pagan systems existing to their south. By the fourteenth century, however, Christians and Muslims were no longer merely in contact along a common border, but were beginning to compete actively for commercial and political dominance over the Sidama peoples of the south-west. By the fifteenth century warfare between Christians and Muslims had become endemic. By the sixteenth it had reached proportions that were really destructive. Perhaps sensing the self-inflicted weakness of their Christian and Muslim neighbours, the pastoral and pagan Galla (Oromo) living to the south of Somali migrated northwards and in the course of the sixteenth and seventeenth centuries occupied the grass-lands of the Rift Valley and the upper Awash, as well as the eastern foothills of the central plateau. To a large extent these grasslands coincided with the border areas between the Christian and Muslim spheres, and one effect of the Galla migrations was to isolate the protagonists from each other. As if to underline this role, the majority of the invading Galla were to be nominally incorporated under a greatly weakened Christian rule, while becoming mainly Muslim in religion. Thus, the fierce religious nationalism of the fifteenth and sixteenth centuries gradually gave way to a pragmatic pluralism in the seventeenth and eighteenth. It was to be revived only by the late-nineteenth-century kings of Ethiopia, and by the emergence of Somali

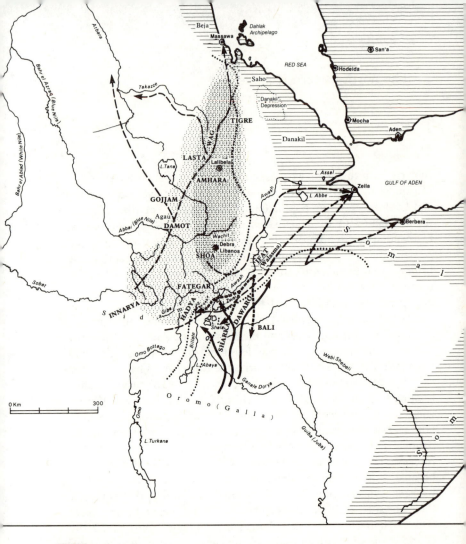

nationalism under the leadership of Muhammad 'Abdallah Hassan in the early twentieth.

THE SOLOMONID ASCENDANCY

The advent of the Solomonid dynasty in 1270 inaugurated a period of 250 years when Christian Ethiopia dominated the whole surrounding region and reached its pinnacle of prestige and power. The Solomonids abandoned the fixed capitals of their Zagwe predecessors and lived as military leaders in vast, tented camps pitched for a part of each year near the scene of the season's campaign. Themselves Amharic-speakers from the southern marches of the old kingdom, their first concern was to consolidate and extend this southerly base. Their early aims were thus primarily territorial, to make room for further settlement of Christian Amhara on the delectable lands of the Shoan plateau and in the highlands of Gojjam situated within the great bend of the Blue Nile. Their first conquests, therefore, were directed westwards, among the Agau-speaking (Northern Cushitic) peoples who had previously been incorporated in the great pagan kingdom of Damot. The conquered Agau were to a great extent assimilated into Amharic Christian culture by a combination of large-scale deportations, resettlement by Amhara colonists and evangelisation by Amhara clergy trained at the monastic schools of Debra Hayq and Debra Libanos.

With armies strengthened by contingents from the new provinces, the great conquering king Amda Siyon (1314–44) shifted the main direction of expansion towards the south and the east. Henceforward, the emphasis was less on settlement and assimilation and more on economic and political control. In pre-Solomonid times, when the kingdom was centred in Tigre, Wag and Lasta, the main caravan routes to the outside world had been the northern ones leading down the Eritrean escarpment to the Bay of Massawa and down the Atbara valley to Nubia. Once the centre of power had shifted southwards to Shoa, the vital route to the sea, and to the salt of the Danakil desert, was that which descended the valley of the Awash, following more or less the same line as the modern Addis Ababa–Djibouti railway, and reaching the seacoast at Zeila. The key section of this route was the Awash gorge, where the river makes its tortuous descent through 1,800 metres of altitude between the Shoan plateau to the north and the Chercher plateau to the south. The population hereabouts spoke a number of Southern Ethio-Semitic languages only remotely related to Amharic, and politically they were much divided. Where the valley

47

8 The north-eastern triangle (1): Solomonid expansion, 14th–16th centuries

route descended to the foothills, however, there had emerged the state of Ifat, ruled by a Muslim dynasty called the Walasma, which effectively controlled the main line of access to and from the kingdom of the Solomonids. Furthermore, the merchants of Ifat had long been active to the south of the Christian kingdom among the Sidama peoples of the Rift Valley and the south-western highlands, where lay the sources of a valuable trade in slaves and ivory, gold, civet and musk. In half a dozen small Sidama states like Dawaro and Hadya, Fategar, Bali and Sharka, Ifati Muslims had preached Islam and had intermarried with the local dynasties whose war-bands supplied them with their slaves and whose hunters went in search of elephants and civet. It was inevitable that a Christian kingdom growing in strength on the Shoan plateau should attempt to lay hands on this trade.

At the very beginning of his reign Amda Siyon passed on from destroying the last remnants of Damot to the conquest of Hadya, the northernmost of the Sidama states and that most famed for the slave-trade. Soon he was picking quarrels with Ifat for interfering with his coastbound caravans. Finally, in a great campaign in 1332, his armies invaded Ifat, and swept through Dawaro, Bali and Sharka, laying them all under tribute. Basically, these conquests were to endure for two centuries. Hadya, like the Agau provinces, was fully annexed and was to become a major centre of Christian evangelisation. But the other Sidama states continued to be ruled by their own dynasties, paying tribute which had to be enforced by periodic military expeditions. The most sustained resistance, however, came from Ifat, where Islamisation had gone furthest, and where, because of its strategic situation, Solomonid interference was greatest. Throughout the fourteenth century the Solomonid kings employed the classic tactics of the powerful neighbour, by inviting Walasma princes to their court and supporting in the periodic succession struggles those who promised loyalty and conversion to Christianity. The result was to split the dynasty, one branch ruling a puppet state in Ifat, the other retreating south-eastwards with the hardcore of the Muslim community to the Chercher plateau and developing a system of alliances with the warlike Somali nomads of the Haud plains. Aided by Somali war-bands, the Muslim Walasma conducted fierce raids upon the tributary provinces of the Rift Valley, in Dawaro and Bali, and only for one brief period was the Christian kingdom able to excise this thorn in its eastern flank. This was when King Dawit in 1403 led a series of military expeditions into the heart of the Chercher plateau and pursued the Walasma ruler right down to the seacoast at Zeila, where he was at last captured and killed. Thereupon the Walasma princes retreated to the Yemen, it is said for twenty years, before returning to rebuild their fortunes in the same mountain fastness, from which a century later they were to break out and overrun the Christian kingdom.

Meanwhile, during the whole course of the fifteenth century, the empire of the Solomonids enjoyed a period of stable government, of economic prosperity, of religious and cultural activity unparalleled in any part of Africa south of the Sahara. Dawit was succeeded by three kings of exceptional ability – Yishaq (1413–30), Zara Yaqob (1434–68) and Baida Maryam (1468–78). During these reigns the system of garrison armies stationed permanently in each of the frontier provinces reached its full development. There followed three more reigns – those of Iskander (1478–94), Na'od (1494–1508) and Lebna Dengel (1508–40) – during most of which the established equilibrium was maintained. Especially towards the end of this period, Christian Ethiopia was visited and described by some European Christians, notably by the Portuguese embassy of 1520–6. As a result, in addition to the royal chronicles with their inevitable concentration on military and dynastic affairs, we begin to have some picture of the economic and social life of the country as a whole. To these men from western Christendom medieval Ethiopia seemed strikingly lacking in the close-built towns of Europe and the Middle East. Only Aksum, the ancient capital in the far north, still used by the Solomonid kings for their coronation rituals, was a town in this sense. On the other hand, the Ethiopian countryside, extending for some 1,000 kilometres from north to south along the line of the central highland massif, struck them as unusually populous and well husbanded. The rich volcanic lands were tilled with oxen and ploughs to yield harvests of wheat and barley as well as millet. Large herds of cattle and sheep grazed the mountain pastures. Horses, donkeys and mules carried produce to the weekly markets, where cotton and coffee, beeswax and honey were exchanged for the salt carried up on camel-back from the Danakil desert.

Even to Portuguese visitors, whose own society was barely emerging from feudalism, it was obvious that Christian Ethiopia was a land where every man had a master. Francisco Alvarez, the chaplain to the embassy of 1520, commented that there would have been 'much more fruit and tillage if the great men did not ill-treat the people'.[1] In fact, most peasant farmers were near to serfs, bound to the land and compelled to yield at least one-third of their crops and many other

---

[1] C. F. Beckingham and G. W. B. Huntingford (eds.), *The Prester John of the Indies*, Hakluyt Soc. (Cambridge, 1961), vol. II, p. 515.

customary services to the feu-holder, who might be the king or a chief or a parish or a monastery or a regiment or an individual knight or soldier. More still of the peasant's production was taken for the tribute which flowed in from every province to the royal court. From Shoa and the southern provinces much of the tribute was delivered in kind – in food and drink, cattle and mules, honey and wax. Some provinces had access to gold and ivory, which could be accumulated in the royal treasure houses. But much of the external trade of the northern provinces must have arisen from the need to convert country produce into portable wealth for delivery to the capital as tribute. Much of the agricultural surplus of the highlands was probably carried down the escarpment to the coast and sold as provisions for the Red Sea shipping and food for the pilgrims of Mecca. Thus the lords of Eritrea and Tigre were able to pay their tribute in Arabian horses and Indian silks and cottons, swords and coats of mail from Syria and Turkey, and in gold, some of which may ultimately have come from West Africa.

Treasure and luxuries apart, the royal encampment, with its officials and ecclesiastics, its nobles and their retinues, its military commanders and their troops, its artisans and armourers, its cooks and grooms and herdsmen, represented a huge agglomeration of people, which drained the resources of a vast stretch of country. At its centre were pitched five or six thousand tents for the king and the nobility, and the attendant population probably numbered ten times as many. The Ethiopians told Alvarez that they were unable to understand that Europeans lived in permanent cities, seeing that their own capital had to move every three or four months in order to solve the problems of supply, and that an area once occupied could not be revisited for at least ten years. The same pattern was repeated on a smaller scale at the courts of provincial governors and local grandees. When the royal court moved from one site to another, Alvarez described the scene thus:

The tenth part of them may be well-dressed people, and the nine parts common people, both men and women, young people and poor, some of them clothed in skins, others in poor stuffs, and all of these common people carry with them their property, which consists of pots for making wine and porringers for drinking. If they move short distances these poor people carry with them their poor dwellings, made and thatched as they had them; and if they go further they carry the wood with them, which are some poles. The rich bring very good tents. I do not speak of the great lords and gentlemen, because each of these moves a city or a good town of tents, and loads, and muleteers, a matter without number or reckoning . . . The court cannot move with less than fifty thousand mules, and from that upwards, the number may reach a hundred thousand.[2]

At the centre of all this activity, his great white tents shielded from the public gaze by a double enclosure of high curtains, there lived and worked the Christian king. He was surrounded by many of the trappings and ceremonial customs of other African monarchs. The greatest in the land appeared before him bared to the waist, and he interviewed them from behind a gauze curtain, communicating through intermediaries. Individuals were promoted and destituted with a nod. Even the most religious kings kept at least three official queens, and the complex network of royal kinship was a vital factor in the affairs of state. Yet there were important ways in which the long-established Christian culture of the country gave the Ethiopian state a very different world-view from those of its more sophisticated Muslim and half-Muslim neighbours. The world of Islam was all around, and national security no less than trade demanded a wide knowledge of its strengths and weaknesses, its doctrinal divisions and its political rivalries. The Christian archbishop was always an Egyptian Copt, and this fact in itself demanded a working relationship with the Muslim rulers of Egypt. But the king's subjects also went on pilgrimage to Jerusalem. Many of them stayed there, and from there dispersed in the company of other Christian pilgrims over the northern Mediterranean lands. In time some of them returned, carrying letters from European courts, or even with European ecclesiastics or artificers in their train. When the Portuguese embassy arrived in 1520, they found a Florentine painter, Brancaleone, who was on friendly terms with the king, and there was no difficulty in finding a Latin interpreter so that Alvarez could be subjected to minute investigation on matters of doctrine and liturgy by King Lebna Dengel himself.

All this, of course, reflected the very intense hold of Monophysite Christianity upon the core populations of the kingdom. No more than their rulers did most Ethiopians find it easy to observe Christian marriage law, with the result that communicant membership was largely confined to the very young, the very old and the very sick. Nevertheless, there was a steadily growing recruitment to the monastic life, accompanied in the fourteenth and fifteenth centuries by a notable revival of biblical studies and by the emergence of a religious literature expressed in the Amharic language. In this revival the Old Testament found especial favour and helped to give religious educa-

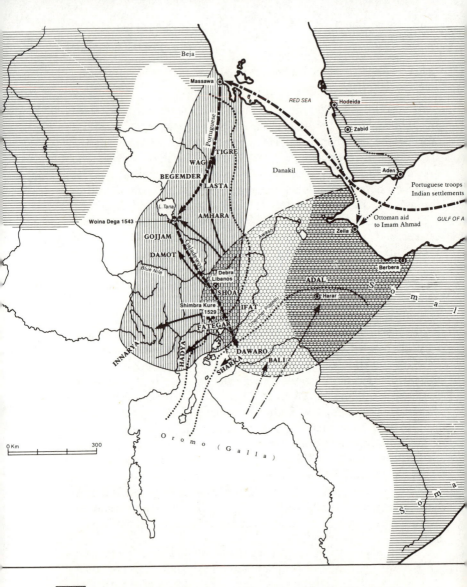

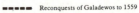

tion a nationalistic slant. The children of the royal house and those of the great nobles shared in this education, and at least one of the great kings of the fifteenth century, Zara Yaqob, lent the whole weight of his office to the reorganisation and consolidation of the national Church. Divergent monastic traditions were reconciled. The monasteries were given tribute-bearing lands for their support and territorial spheres in which to exercise their influence. The king's soldiers accompanied the abbots on their visitations, and all Christians were enjoined to carry signs of their faith on their persons, their dress and even on their ploughs. Churches were built within the reach of all Christian communities, and attendance at Saturday and Sunday observances made compulsory. While it may be that Zara Yaqob in his zeal was far in advance of the mass of his subjects, it will be clear to any reader of Alvarez that he and his Portuguese companions felt themselves to be travelling in a deeply Christian country.

ADAL, THE SOMALI AND THE GALLA

The fall of Christian Ethiopia from the position of strength and security which it had built up over 250 years at the heart of the north-east African region was extraordinarily sudden and swift. No doubt with the eye of history it is possible to see that the collapse was in part the result of a process of decline which had set in with the death of Zara Yaqob sixty years before, with the growth of factions at the royal court, with the persistent election of kings who were minors, with the mounting power of the provincial nobility over against the royal officials. In practice, however, the system had not been severely tested, and therefore it had endured. Following a number of local defeats on the Adali frontier during the reigns of Iskander and Na'od, Lebna Dengel had in 1516 won a major victory over the Adali general Mahfuz. Hence, from 1520 till 1526, he dallied with the Portuguese embassy like a man who had no need at all of a new ally from the Christian West. Yet in 1529, at the battle of Shimbra Kure in southern Shoa, he suffered a crushing defeat at the hands of a young Adali general, Ahmad ibn Ibrahim, who was to spend the next fourteen years laying waste his kingdom from Bali in the south to Tigre in the north, from Damot in the west to the Awash gorges in the east.

Ahmad, nicknamed 'Gragn', the left-handed, was one of those rare individuals who combined at an early age the talents of a soldier and a statesman. Born in one of the minor emirates bordering on Ifat and Adal, he came to the fore as a cavalry knight on the Christian frontier and in the faction fighting between the various allies of the Walasma

53

9 The north-eastern triangle (2): the 16th century

dynasty which made up the internal politics of Adal. While still in his teens he assumed the leadership of a group which overpowered the ruling sultan and reduced him to the position of a figurehead in Harar, while the real rule passed to Ahmad, who took the religious title of *imam* and built up an effective alliance of Danakil and Somali clan sections from the region between Harar and Zeila, with the jihad against Christian Ethiopia as the uniting theme. The nomads were interested in booty, above all in cattle and slaves, and in his opening campaigns Ahmad led them to the lush pastures of Dawaro at the head of the Rift Valley, and on westwards to Fategar in the broad valley of the upper Awash. A counter-expedition by Lebna Dengel's governor in Bali was crushed and all its members enslaved. At Shimbra Kure in 1529 Ahmad faced the assembled might of the Christian heartlands, with armies summoned even from the far northern provinces to confront him, and he won a decisive victory. All the southern provinces of the Christian empire were now in his hands, and he devoted a year to dismantling their defences, mopping up their garrisons and replacing their Christian rulers with Muslims.

For any previous sovereign of Adal this would have been more than enough. But Ahmad was intent upon the complete destruction of the Christian state. In 1531 he was back in Shoa, with plans to take over and administer every province in the kingdom. When Lebna Dengel retreated westwards into Damot, Ahmad followed him as far as the Blue Nile gorges, burning the great monastery of Debra Libanos, where his biographer described the monks hurling themselves into the flames like moths into a lamp. Then, turning north-eastwards, he circumvented the high redoubts of the central watershed by passing through the coastal lowlands into Tigre and so westwards again to Begemder, Lake Tana and northern Gojjam. Thus, by 1535 Ahmad had encircled the northern heartlands of the Christian kingdom. All along his path Christian governors had been replaced by Muslims; churches had been looted of their treasures, their books burnt, their clergy slain. Even in the central mountains of Wag and Lasta no place was free from his raiders, and effective Christian government was paralysed.

Nevertheless, from this time onwards not everything went well for the *imam*. With the flow of booty diminishing, his nomad followers drifted away back to their warm plains, leaving him to govern his conquests with the aid of renegade Christians of dubious loyalty. In the highlands the end of open opposition marked the beginnings of covert resistance. The emperor remained at large and refused Ahmad's overtures for a peaceful settlement. When Lebna Dengel died in 1540, he was succeeded by an able warrior prince in Galadewos (1540–59), who was free from the stigma of his predecessor's defeats. In 1541 the Portuguese from India responded to Christian appeals by landing a small force of matchlockmen at Massawa, whose fire-arms put courage into the Christians of Tigre. The Turkish governor of Zabid in southern Arabia countered by sending a parallel force of troops equipped with fire-arms and light cannon. The Portuguese suffered heavy losses, but when in 1543 they were at last able to join forces with Galadewos, they met the Muslim armies in battle at Woina Dega near Lake Tana and Imam Ahmad was killed in the fighting. It was the end of the Adali occupation of the highlands, but it left a Christian state demoralised and in ruins, which could never until the later nineteenth century recover either its medieval territory or its political and cultural ascendancy.

The long-term result of the Adali occupation was that it fatally undermined the whole system of frontier defences against the nomadic, pastoral peoples by whom the Christian kingdom was almost surrounded. These defences consisted of a kind of standing militia, of which each unit depended upon the dues and services arising from a particular area of land. Most of the regimental lands were situated near the frontiers, and the majority of them near the eastern escarpment, where lowland pastoralists constantly attempted to raid the crops and cattle of the highland peasantry, and where in the absence of military resistance raiding was always liable to develop into conquest and settlement. In the far north the pastoral neighbours were Beja and Arab. In the Red Sea plains from Massawa to Zeila they were the Danakil. To the east of the Rift Valley provinces they were the Somali. To the south of the Rift Valley provinces they were the Galla. Had Imam Ahmad's conquest been consolidated, it would certainly have led to a large colonisation of the highlands by the Somali. In the event it was mainly the Galla who broke in. They did so in the southernmost province of Bali, and they did it around 1531–2, at the precise moment when the imperial garrisons had been wiped out by Imam Ahmad, and when Ahmad himself had moved on to the conquest of Shoa. There was therefore nothing marvellous about the beginnings of the Galla expansion. They saw a vacuum on their northern frontier, and they filled it by driving their cattle a hundred kilometres further up the Rift Valley than they had ventured before. And they moved slowly. It was an encroachment rather than an invasion, for the Galla lacked any central political organisation. It was the members of the warrior age-group who pushed the cattle camps a little further north year by year, operating in bands of a few thousand

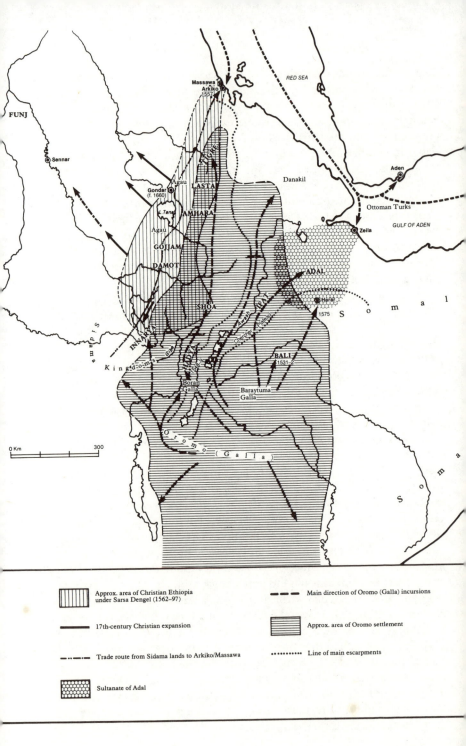

FUNJ

RED SEA

Massawa
Arkiko
1557

Sennar

Aden

Agau
Danakil

Gondar
(f. 1660)

Ottoman Turks

L. Tana

GULF OF ADEN

AMHARA

Zeila

Agau

GOJJAM

ADAL

DAMOT

Harar
1575

S   o   m   a   l

SHOA

Awash

Chercher Plateau

INNARYA

BALI
1531-2

Gibe

Kingdom

Baraytuma
Galla

Boran
Galla

0 Km   300

Oromo   (Galla)

S   o   m   a

| | Approx. area of Christian Ethiopia under Sarsa Dengel (1562–97) | | | Main direction of Oromo (Galla) incursions |

— 17th-century Christian expansion

Approx. area of Oromo settlement

Trade route from Sidama lands to Arkiko/Massawa

Line of main escarpments

Sultanate of Adal

at most. They were armed only with spears, and at this stage they had no horses. By the time of Imam Ahmad's death they had by no means completed the occupation of Bali. Even a vestigial relic of the former imperial garrison could have stopped them in their tracks. But such was the state of insecurity around the frontier as a whole that the Galla were able to drive in their wedge.

The emperor Galadewos was still very much preoccupied with Adal and its Somali allies, who, although they had evacuated the central highlands, had not abandoned their attempt to occupy Dawaro, the province at the head of the Rift Valley, immediately to the north of Bali. This area was the scene of very severe fighting between Christians and Muslims during the period from 1543 until Galadewos's death there in 1559. It was at this time that the Galla completed their occupation of Bali, unopposed. And it was their subsequent expansion into the Chercher highlands, the heartland of Adal, which from about 1575 onwards relieved the Christian kingdom from Muslim pressure. Meanwhile the Baraytuma Galla, who had led the advance, had been followed by other Galla tribes, notably by the Boran, who moved up the western side of the Rift Valley, reaching the province of Hadya by 1548 or 1549. From this time onwards they were too numerous and too scattered to be stopped. Put in the simplest way, what the Galla did during the century which followed was to occupy the land between 1,200 and 1,800 metres above sea level. In terms of rainfall and vegetation these were the intermediate lands, too dry to be reliable for settled agriculture, but admirable for transhumant pastoralism combined with a little wet-season cereal-farming. Geographically, these areas were disposed in the shape of a cross dividing the three main mountain massifs of the region, with the Red Sea and the Gulf of Aden forming the fourth quadrant. The main axis was formed by the Rift Valley in the south and the foothills of the great eastern escarpment in the north. The crosspiece consisted of the Chercher highlands to the east, and the broad plain of the Awash–Gibe watershed in the west. Many of these areas were only lightly populated before the Galla came, and the most lethal fighting by the Galla was probably against fellow pastoralists such as the Somali and the Danakil and the many small groups of Semitic-speaking pastoralists around the borders of Ifat and Adal. Elsewhere, the arrival of the Galla often contributed a new and complementary feature to the economy. It was an infiltration comparable to that of the pastoral Fulbe among the sedentary farmers of the western Sudan, with the same liability to sudden bursts of violence, especially from the most recently arrived.

10 The north-eastern triangle (3): the Oromo settlements

Still, if the Galla were not as terrible as they have been painted, there is no underrating the problem which they posed to the rulers of the Christian kingdom, whose southern provinces were now lost beyond recovery, and whose whole eastern frontier from Tigre south to Shoa was soon to be thrown into a state of the utmost chaos. Sarsa Dengel (1562–97) was the last emperor who had any chance of restoring stability within greatly reduced frontiers, and his policies have given rise to great controversy among historians. Certainly he devoted much effort to rebuilding a central army to counter-balance the increasingly local loyalties of the feudal militia. But the direction in which he employed his forces was not that most directly threatened by the Galla. Instead, writing off the Zeila trade route so fundamental to an empire based in Shoa, he concentrated upon reopening the older routes to the rich Sidama lands from the north. His great campaigns were in the Agau regions around Lake Tana, and further south in Gojjam, Damot and Innarya. These gave him a full treasury, not least from a regular trade in Sidama slaves, of whom some ten thousand were sold each year to the Turks, based since 1557 at Arkiko, and soon to seize Massawa and Zeila. But he left his south-eastern frontier unguarded, and his successors were prevented by the westward expansion of the Galla into Innarya from exploiting even the contacts opened with the south-west. In the withering judgment of Merid Aregay, 'Sarsa Dengel contributed to the dismantling of the system of defences by using the soldiers to ravage peaceful provinces, thereby clearing the way for the Galla.'[3] The kings of the seventeenth and eighteenth centuries had narrower options, and Susenyos (1607–32) set a new pattern by incorporating Galla groups from the eastern escarpment frontier as units of the imperial militia (*chewa*), enjoying the traditional rights to tribute and services from the local Tigre and Amhara peasantry. In one sense this amounted to legitimising the occupation of lands which the Galla had already seized. In another sense, however, it gave the longer-settled Galla an interest in resisting further incursions by newcomers. It was an age-old expedient of failing empires facing barbarian attack. It meant that some of the Galla became to some extent 'amharicised', but at the cost of no one any longer knowing quite what he was supposed to be defending.

Faced with the alienation of large territories on the east and south, and with perennial disturbances even in the heartlands of the old empire, in Shoa, Lasta, Angot and Tigre, it was natural that the seventeenth-century kings should concentrate their attention increas-

[3] 'Southern Ethiopia and the Christian Kingdom 1508–1708', unpublished Ph.D. thesis, University of London, 1971, p. 230.

ingly upon the west and the north. This was not historically Christian territory. Its people were not Semitic Amhara, but Cushitic Agau. Before the sixteenth century the Christian empire had largely passed them by, with only an occasional nibble at their eastern fringes. These were the areas regularly raided by Sarsa Dengel, where first Susenyos and later Fasiladas (1632–67) established their capitals at Dunqaz, Enfraz and finally Gondar. Here the Christian kings became increasingly divorced even from their old Amharic nobility and clergy, their households served by Agau slaves and protected by Galla mercenaries. It was in these circumstances that Susenyos began to cultivate the friendship of the Portuguese Jesuit missionaries who had been present in the country since 1557, and who probably led the king to believe that he could best re-establish his authority with the help of the Christian West. Susenyos announced his own conversion in 1612 and that of his country in 1622. By 1632 he had abdicated in favour of Fasiladas and the national Monophysite Church had been re-established.

The Galla, by this time, were sated in their territorial ambitions, and the momentum of their expansion had run down. They were still seen at their most characteristic in the cruciform area best suited to the pastoral life. Within that area their culture was dominant. Beyond it, the Galla were militarily in control of wide regions, where they imposed themselves as overlords but where their culture rapidly succumbed to that of their subjects. The Christian kingdom was now almost confined to the north-western quadrant, and here, as we have seen, the Galla occupied a privileged position as feudal soldiery at the price of some cultural assimilation. In the north-eastern quadrant the Galla had acquired a similar position in relation to the Muslim population of Adal, though they had not descended into the Somali-occupied lowlands north and east of the Chercher plateau. In the south-eastern quadrant it was essentially a pattern of Galla in the hills and Somali and Bantu in the coastal plains. In the south-western quadrant Galla ruled in most of the former Sidama provinces of Christian Ethiopia, taking over the political systems of the Sidama inhabitants, trading through Harar to Zeila and in the eighteenth century becoming increasingly Muslim in religion. Throughout this period the Christian kingdom was becoming more and more a shadow of its former self, confined within a shorter and shorter radius of Gondar. The Christian Church, however, retained a wider ambit, maintaining its hold over the old provinces of the central highlands, which had long ceased to pay more than a nominal allegiance to the dynasty at Gondar. It was around the local Christian nobility of Tigre and Shoa that the modern Ethiopian empire was finally to be constituted.

5 The states of Barbary

The eastern and central Maghrib, from the Egyptian frontier in the east to that of Morocco in the west, underwent great changes during our period, which can almost be compared with those in West Africa described in the following chapter. The changes in West Africa arose from the opening of the Atlantic seaboard to the maritime trade of the Portuguese, the Dutch, the British, the Danes and the French. The changes in North Africa arose from the great conflict between the Spanish empire in the western Mediterranean and the Ottoman empire in the east. In this conflict neither side was primarily concerned to gain a North African empire, but only to deny strategic control to the other. Externally, the result was to leave North Africa marginally within the Ottoman camp. Internally, however, the basis of power in North Africa was radically shifted from the elements, mainly Berber and Arab, which had dominated the land, to the much more cosmopolitan elements – Turkish, Andalusian, Maltese, Greek and Jewish – which made their living mainly from the sea. The transition was most vividly symbolised in the growth of Algiers from an unknown fishing village into the premier city of the region. Algiers had no importance for any of the great land routes of the Maghrib, either for those linking Egypt with Morocco or for those crossing the Sahara to the Sudan. It was a purely Mediterranean city, just as Elmina on the Gold Coast, or St Louis at the mouth of the Senegal, were purely Atlantic cities. As in West Africa, however, the old interior lines of communication showed a persisting vitality throughout the period. Though the main centres of power had changed, pilgrims and scholars still travelled to the Holy Places of Islam. Gold and slaves still crossed the Sahara by the desert caravans. Fundamental changes in the economic field were to come only with the advent of the steamship, the railway, the motor lorry and the aeroplane, and with the discovery of oil below the surface of the desert.

THE EASTERN AND CENTRAL MAGHRIB IN THE FIFTEENTH CENTURY

60 During most of the fifteenth century the forces which were to trans-

form the political geography of North Africa were barely perceptible. In Spain the Christian kingdoms were still engaged in the reconquest of the Moorish south. Aragon and Castile were to be united by the marriage of Ferdinand and Isabella only in 1484. Granada, the last of the Moorish emirates, was to fall only in 1492. In Asia Minor, the Ottoman Turks were at the beginning of the century still assaulting the eastern flanks of the Byzantine empire. Constantinople was to fall in 1453, mainland Greece in 1460 and the Aegean islands much later. In Egypt the Mamluk sultans continued to rule throughout the century, including Cyrenaica (the north-eastern third of modern Libya) within their dominion. To the west of Egypt, the great power of the eastern Maghrib was the Hafsid kingdom of Ifriqiya, with its capital at Tunis, its agricultural base in the fertile Tunisian plain and its rule extending from Tripoli in the east to Bougie in the west. Under the strong and long-lived sultans Abu Faris (1394–1435) and Abu 'Amir 'Uthman (1435–83) Ifriqiya reached the very peak of its economic prosperity and international influence.

The abiding strength of Ifriqiya lay in its rich agricultural lands, laid out in a patchwork of vegetable gardens, wheatfields and olive groves, which covered the whole northern half of the Tunisian plain. From Carthaginian and Roman times onwards, these had enabled it to absorb and acculturate wave upon wave of immigrants, and to feed a great metropolitan city with its outlying seaports. Tunis, dominating the narrow seas between the eastern and the western Mediterranean, had been among the earliest of the North African cities to welcome the Christian merchants of southern Europe – from Pisa, Genoa and Marseilles to the west of the Italian peninsula, and from Venice to the east. Under Hafsid rule, moreover, Ifriqiya had grown into a maritime power in its own right, importing timber for shipbuilding from as far afield as Norway, and manning its shipyards and its galleys with Christian captives taken in privateering raids around the coasts of Malta, Sicily and southern Italy. Though Tunis was comparatively distant from the desert, its control of the central Mediterranean enabled it to command a goodly share of the profits from the Saharan trade. A major caravan route went south from Tunis to Ghadames and thence to Timbuktu. On the southern shore of the Gulf of Sirte, Tripoli stood almost in the desert, at the head of the great central routes to the Fezzan, Kawar, Bornu and Hausaland. The Hafsids of Ifriqiya, no less than the Marinids of Morocco, minted the gold of Mali and Songhay. In addition, they received the slaves and ivory of the central Sudan. In this direction they were in regular touch with the rulers of Bornu, with whose emissaries they discussed arrangements 61

11*a*   The states of Barbary: eastern half
11*b*   The states of Barbary: western half

BAGIRMI

WADAI

DARFUR

KANEM

FUNJ

Shari

B

White Nile

Bilma
KAW

Tubu

TIBESTI

peopl

HIJAZ

Mecca

Nile

Aswan

Kufra

Mur
FEZZAN

EGYPT

OTTOMANS

Pilgrims
to Mecca

Siwa

Awjila

Pilgrims to Mecca from the Maghrib

OTT
TR

MAMLUK SULTANATE

Cairo

Alexandria

CYRENAICA

OTTOMAN
CONQUEST 1517

Benghazi

OTTOMANS

TRIPOLIT

SYRIA

CONQUERED FROM
CYPRUS VENICE 1571

CONQUERED FROM
VENICE 1669

CRETE

DRAGUT

KHAIR AL-DIN

Malta
(Knights Hospitallers)

OTTOMANS

SICILY

Reggio

Palermo

ANATOLIA

Lepanto

OTTOMAN CONQUEST 1517

OTTOMAN

Istanbul (Constantinople)

EMPIRE

N

0 Km   500   1000

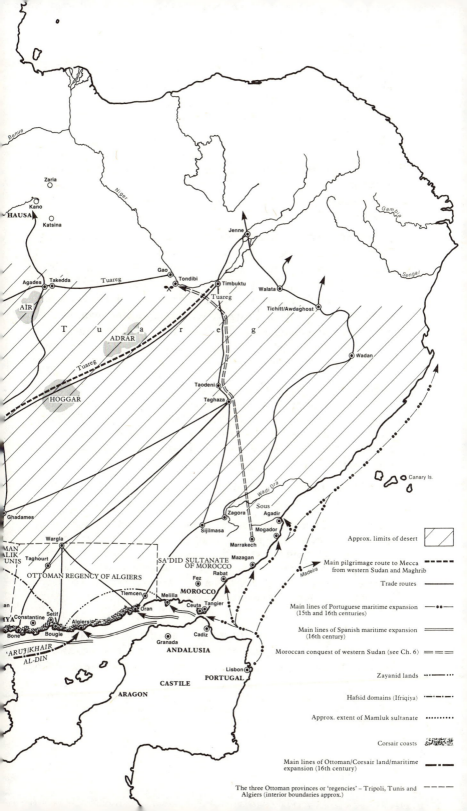

Benue

Zaria ○

Kano ○

HAUSA
Katsina ○

Niger

Gambia

Jenne ◉

Senga[l]

Agades ◉ Takedda ◉   Tuareg   Gao ◉ Tondibi ⚔ Timbuktu ◉

AIR

Walata ◉

Tuareg

Tichitt/Awdaghost ◉

T   u   *a*   r   e   g

ADRAR

Wadan ◉

Tuareg

Taodeni ◉

HOGGAR

Taghaza ◉

Canary Is.

○ Ghadames

Wadi Dra

Zagora ◉   Sous   Agadir ◉

Sijilmasa ◉   Mogador ◉

Marrakech ◉

Wargla □

Madeira

MAN
LIK
UNIS

Taghourt ○

OTTOMAN REGENCY OF ALGIERS

SA'DID SULTANATE
OF MOROCCO

Mazagan ◉

Rabat ◉

an

Tlemcen ◉   Melilla ◉

MOROCCO

Fez ◉

IYA

Constantine ◉ Setif ○   Oran ◉   Ceuta Tangier

Bone ○   Bougie ○   Algiers

'ARUJ/KHAIR
AL-DIN

Cadiz ◉

Granada ◉

ANDALUSIA

CASTILE

Lisbon ◉

PORTUGAL

ARAGON

Approx. limits of desert ╱╱╱

→ Main pilgrimage route to Mecca ▬ ▬ ▬
from western Sudan and Maghrib

Trade routes ───────

Main lines of Portuguese maritime expansion ──•••──
(15th and 16th centuries)

Main lines of Spanish maritime expansion ═══════
(16th century)

Moroccan conquest of western Sudan (see Ch. 6) ═ ═ ═

Zayanid lands ─··─··─

Hafsid domains (Ifriqiya) ─·─·─·─

Approx. extent of Mamluk sultanate ············

Corsair coasts ⦚⦚⦚⦚

Main lines of Ottoman/Corsair land/maritime ▬·▬·▬
expansion (16th century)

The three Ottoman provinces or 'regencies' – Tripoli, Tunis and ─ ─ ─
Algiers (interior boundaries approx.)

for the security of the caravan routes through the Fezzan and Kawar. Moulded by the pleasant environment of the Tunisian plain, the Hafsid sultans were cultivated and civilised men, who kept a sumptuous court.

The Hafsid sovereigns [writes Julien] marked their power by formality of etiquette in public audience, and above all in their processions. Surrounded by sheikhs and men at arms, and later by foreign guards, they paraded on horseback in great pomp, to the beating of kettle-drums and tambours, and the rustling of multi-coloured standards of embroidered silk, overshadowed by their own white ensigns.[1]

It was only in the region to the west of Ifriqiya that the portents of change and disintegration were already by the fifteenth century becoming clearly visible. Here, to begin with, was a very different geographical setting. The warm, semi-tropical countryside of Ifriqiya was bounded to the west by the Aures mountains, a series of densely wooded escarpments and ridges, building up to the high, dry cold plateaux of the Saharan Atlas. The vivid contrast between the lands on either side of this frontier has been described by the French historian Fernand Braudel in modern terms:

In the west, the storks, the ash and elm trees, the roofs of heavy brown tiles under a sky of mountain storms; in the east, the terraced roofs, the houses with their white domes declare the kinship between the cities of Tunisia and the cities of the East . . . Qayrawan is a single vast white cube . . . the antithesis of Constantine, the latter still in many ways a large tribal village with undistinguished rustic houses.

And the same author comments that the contrast would have been just as visible to observers at the beginning of our period.

The Constantine merchant who travelled down into Tunisia, found in this vision of white terraced houses and sun-baked cities a rich land, looking to the East . . . a land of ordered civilisation, where the Arabic tongue was predominant both in town and countryside . . . The central Maghrib, as far as Tlemcen, was amazingly uncivilised. Algiers was to grow up in a country as yet without a leavening of culture, a virgin land, peopled by camel-drovers, shepherds and goatherds.[2]

At the beginning of the fifteenth century the central Maghrib was still predominantly peopled by Berber-speaking tribesmen. Most led the hard life of transhumant pastoralists on the high plateaux falling

---

[1] C.-A. Julien, *History of North Africa*, tr. C. C. Stewart (London, 1970), p. 155.
[2] F. Braudel, *The Mediterranean and the Mediterranean World in the Age of Philip II*, tr. S. Reynolds, vol. II (London, 1973), p. 772.

from the Saharan Atlas. A fortunate few were settled farmers living in towns and villages in the narrow coastal plain. As far west as Bougie, taxes and tribute were paid to the irregular soldiery of the Hafsids. From Bougie to the Moroccan frontier lay the territory of the Zayanid dynasty of Tlemcen, with its graceful capital situated far to the west in the hills behind Oran. Tlemcen was the only city in the central Maghrib with a strong connection with the African interior, for it bestrode a caravan route leading southwards between the Saharan and the Great Atlas to Sijilmasa, the oasis terminal of the western desert crossings. It thus competed with Ifriqiya and Morocco for the gold and slaves of Mali and Songhay, and was the main intermediary for these commodities with Andalusia and the expanding Christian kingdom of Aragon. Jews from Barcelona were early active in organising the long-distance trade with Tlemcen, and the country also benefited from the flow of Spanish Muslims fleeing before the Christian reconquest, many of whom were skilled and educated men.

As a state, however, Tlemcen had long suffered both from the nomadic elements in its own population and from the proximity of more powerful neighbours in Morocco and Ifriqiya. The fifteenth century saw an aggravation of these problems. Externally, the Zayanids became tributary to the Hafsids. Internally, as the state became weaker, more and more of its agricultural lowlands were invaded by the nomads of the Saharan Atlas, reinforced by bedouin Arabs, descendants of the Hilalian migrants of the eleventh century, who were now spreading westwards from southern Ifriqiya and absorbing the Berber nomads into their own much stronger tribal groupings. The Zayanids, incapable of expelling the Arabs, had no option but to recognise them as feudatories, making over lands and revenues in exchange for tribute and protection. In the course of the fifteenth century the whole of eastern Tlemcen, which was to be the nucleus of the future state of Algiers, passed into the hands of semi-independent, Arabic-speaking tribes, who were ready to conduct their own negotiations with new migrants and invaders from across the sea.

THE STRUGGLE FOR POWER IN THE MEDITERRANEAN
1497–1581

For Spain in the Mediterranean, as for Portugal in the Atlantic, the idea of following through the wars of reconquest on to African soil was a natural one. In both countries the reconquest was seen as a crusade against an enemy whose ultimate bases lay in North Africa, whence, if allowed to regroup, the Moors might all too easily return across the narrow sea. Every Spaniard knew that during the later stages of the struggle many of the Moorish (Spanish *Morisco*) population had fled to North Africa, including, for example, the last emir of Granada who left with six thousand followers in 1493, while countless others remained to be a cause of anxiety to their Christian conquerors. These lived in dread of a Morisco insurrection inspired and aided by the refugees. North African 'corsairs' (privateers, pirates, from the Italian *corsare*, to chase), their ships often propelled by Christian galley-slaves chained to their oars, were known and feared in every coastal town and village of eastern Spain: sometimes they landed and carried off whole communities of isolated farmers and fishermen. Therefore it is hardly surprising that, in the very year of the conquest of Granada, the state secretary of Ferdinand and Isabella should have urged them to follow up their success, saying 'It looks as if God wishes to give Your Highnesses these African Kingdoms.'[3] Following careful naval reconnaissance, the port of Melilla, on the borders of Tlemcen and Morocco, was occupied by Spain in 1497.

What is perhaps surprising is the extreme prudence and hesitation shown by King Ferdinand (Isabella died in 1504) in following up this initiative. Braudel describes it as one of the great missed chances of history.[4] No further action was taken until 1505, when, following serious corsair raiding and a rising by the Moors of Granada, a systematic occupation of the main ports of the Maghrib was decided upon. Between 1505 and 1511 expeditionary forces were landed at and around Oran, Algiers, Bougie and Tripoli. Forts were built and military garrisons (Spanish, *presidios*) established, but no attempt was made to conquer the countryside surrounding these isolated bases, which were thus dependent even for their basic food on supplies shipped in from Spain. When these were delayed, foraging raids were undertaken, which alienated the local populations. Meanwhile, privateering against Spanish shipping continued from many small harbours in between the widely spaced *presidios*.

The largest gap in the Spanish system was the coast of central Ifriqiya, where from about 1504 onwards a nest of pirates developed under the leadership of two brothers, Greek Muslims from the Aegean island of Mytilene, called 'Aruj and Khair al-Din. At first they operated from Gouletta, the port of Tunis, under licence from the Hafsid sultan, Muhammad b. al-Hasan (1493–1526). When the Spaniards occupied Tripoli in 1511, 'Aruj set up a second base, on the

[3] Ibid., vol. 1 (London, 1972), p. 118.   [4] Ibid.

nearby island of Jerba, from which to harass the invaders. For a few more years 'Aruj worked hand in hand with the Hafsids, but increasingly it became clear that the pirate chief was growing more powerful than the sultan. On the death of Ferdinand in 1516, the people of Algiers invited 'Aruj to rid them of their Spanish garrison. From this time on 'Aruj acted as an independent ruler, using Turkish soldiers to establish his own authority at Algiers, and proceeding in the next year to attack the Zayanid capital at Tlemcen. The Zayanids at once made common cause with the Spaniards. Before long the Hafsids were to do the same. However indirectly, Spain and Turkey were henceforward engaged with one another on the North African scene, with the Spaniards as the 'protectors' of the traditional Islamic Berber dynasties, and the Turks as the aiders and abettors of the new men of the sea and the Arab war-lords of the hinterland.

'Aruj was driven out of Tlemcen and killed by a Spanish and Zayanid force in 1518. Thereafter, his brother Khair al-Din, nicknamed Barbarossa, 'the redbeard', by his European foes, became the leader of the North African war against the Spaniards, placing himself publicly under Ottoman protection and receiving the title of *pasha* and the military rank of *beylerbey* (commander-in-chief) in respect of the Turkish troops sent to his aid. Although initially forced to retreat from Algiers, he gradually built up a successful bridgehead further to the east, and in 1525 was able to return, capturing first the town and later the Spanish fortress on the offshore island called the Peñon. By building a causeway between the Peñon and the mainland he created a nearly impregnable harbour, which was to become the main Ottoman naval base in the western Mediterranean and the headquarters of an extensive and profitable corsairing enterprise. Territorially, the dominion of Khair al-Din now comprised the coastline of eastern Algeria and the island base of Jerba in the Gulf of Sirte. In between lay the crumbling state of the Hafsids with its harbours commanding the Strait of Bizerta. Prompted, no doubt, by his Ottoman overlords, Khair al-Din assaulted and briefly captured Tunis in 1534, but was dislodged by a Spanish counter-attack which restored the Hafsids to their capital for another forty years. Khair al-Din was soon afterwards recalled to Istanbul to become the admiral-in chief of the Ottoman fleets. It was left to his successors to defend Algiers against a mighty attack by the Spaniards in 1541, and then gradually to expand its territory westwards towards Tlemcen, where the last vestiges of Zayanid rule were eliminated by about 1550, though the Spaniards remained in Oran for more than two centuries longer.

Meanwhile, in the 1550s another centre of Ottoman and Spanish rivalry had developed in the Gulf of Sirte and on the seas to the north. Here Tripoli, occupied by Spain in 1510, had been handed over, along with Malta, to the Knights of St John, following their expulsion from Rhodes in 1522. Turkish corsairs had founded a base nearby at Tajura in 1531, but it was only twenty years later that Khair al-Din's successor as the Ottoman admiral-in-chief, Sinan Pasha, laid siege to Tripoli and drove out the Knights. A famous corsair captain named Dragut became governor of the town and developed it into an Ottoman province comparable to that of Algiers. Under Dragut's rule corsairs from Tripoli raided as far as Sicily and southern Italy, on one occasion removing into captivity most of the population of the town of Reggio, on the Italian side of the Strait of Messina. The Spaniards, as the rulers of Sicily and Naples, attempted a counter-attack, but were ignominiously defeated. There followed the famous siege of Malta in 1565, when a Turkish expeditionary force of 20,000, led by Dragut and the Ottoman admiral Uluj 'Ali, was successfully resisted by a handful of the Knights. Four years later, Uluj 'Ali, now pasha of Algiers, occupied Tunis, expelling the Hafsid sultan. In 1571 the Spaniards, with 208 ships, sank all but 30 of a Turkish fleet of 230 at the great battle of Lepanto in the Gulf of Corinth, killing 30,000 Turks and freeing 15,000 Christian galley-slaves. They thereupon retook Tunis and briefly restored the Hafsid sultan. Nevertheless, in 1574 Uluj 'Ali, with the help of Sinan Pasha, definitively conquered Tunis and put an end to Hafsid rule. Tunisia, like Tripoli and Algiers, became an Ottoman province, and in 1581 Spain and Turkey signed a truce which effectively ended their Mediterranean contest.

NORTH AFRICA UNDER OTTOMAN RULE

From the final capture of Tunis in 1574, all of the eastern and central Maghrib was in theory comprised within the three Ottoman provinces, known to Europeans as the Regencies. In practice, only the coastal districts were held, and each province had still to face the problems of internal conquest and consolidation inseparable from the establishment of any colonial regime. At the head of each province was a beylerbey, or pasha, nominated by the Sultan of Turkey, usually for quite short periods. Each beylerbey had to control and balance two rival sources of power. First, there was the sea-faring elite of the corsairs, known as the *taifa*, from whom the original impulse for Ottoman protection had come, and upon whose continuing activity the material prosperity of the provinces depended. With the exhaus-

68   tion of the Spanish and Turkish navies after their great struggle, the

Mediterranean was wide open to privateering, and profits were higher than ever before. A few of the corsairing leaders were Turks, but most were drawn from the miscellaneous elements of the North African coast – Berbers, Moors, Greeks, Jews and Christian renegades from Corsica, Sardinia, Malta, Sicily and Calabria. Secondly, there were the *ojak*, the soldiers, nearly all of them Turks, recruited from Anatolia under licence from the Ottoman Sultan. These, though free men, followed much the same system as the Mamluks of Egypt. Only first-generation recruits might be members of the military elite. Their descendants by local wives formed a favoured group, but were barred from military rank. When it came to the conquest and administration of the interior, the power of the *ojak* grew more rapidly than that of the *taifa*. Their numbers increased. They were tightly organised in 'rooms' and 'barracks', and the military commanders formed a *divan*, or council, which soon took over the real government of every province, leaving the beylerbey as a mere figurehead.

During the Ottoman period the preponderance of power and prosperity in North Africa swung decisively from Ifriqiya to the new state of Algiers. It was here that the movement towards Ottoman rule had started, here that the first *ojak* had developed and here that the most powerful navy had been built up. The most striking evidence of the gains from corsairing was seen in the rapid growth of the capital city, which soon overflowed the walls built by Khair al-Din and his immediate successors into a circle of luxurious suburbs spreading over the surrounding hills. This was the prosperous world of the *taifa*, based upon the harbour, the docks and the *bagnios*, the winter prisons of the galley-slaves, who were allowed to exercise their religion and to communicate with their relatives in the hope of ransom. Outside Algiers, it was the *ojak* who ruled. In the west of the country Tlemcen was early developed as an administrative centre, and garrisons were posted in the main towns. In the countryside the traditional shaykhs and leaders of the religious brotherhoods conserved much of their authority, but all those within reach of expeditions from the garrison towns were subject to taxation or tribute payments, and already in the sixteenth century the power of the *ojak* was felt along the caravan routes leading south from Tlemcen as far as Taghourt in the Atlas and Wargla on the desert margin. In its developed form, the government was organised in four provinces, each under a *bey*, and further into districts ruled by *qa'ids*, the central government sending troops three times a year to assist in the collection of taxes. At headquarters, the military government of Algeria was administered in a fairly modern bureaucratic style, with a chancellery controlled by four state secretaries, which kept efficient records of the booty brought in by the corsairs and the taxation paid within the country. One of the functions of the chancellery, which continued in name for more than 150 years, was to receive the written instructions sent from the Sultan of Istanbul and to present them at a weekly meeting of the *divan* held at the pasha's palace. Though lacking any means of enforcement, this practice ceased only in 1711, when a pasha sent from Istanbul was expelled by the *divan* and the office of pasha was amalgamated with that of the bey, the locally elected commander-in-chief of the *ojak*.

Tunisia, under Ottoman rule, comprised only the central part of the old sultanate of Ifriqiya. As such, it was not only more compact but stabler and more coherent. Here there was a large, fully settled, agricultural population, well accustomed to paying taxes. Only in the saline flats to the south of the Tunisian plain were there nomadic tribes requiring constant control by military expeditions. Above all, the whole country was fully Islamised and Arabic-speaking. In these circumstances the few thousand Turks who formed the *ojak* became much more assimilated to the local population than their counterparts in Algeria. They accepted non-Turkish elements into their ranks – Greeks, people of mixed race and even renegade Christians – and within a short time the Turkish language gave place to Arabic, even among the military elite. Even sooner than in Algeria, the local *ojak* took affairs into their own hands, placing the *divan* under the control of a commander-in-chief, or *dey*, elected by themselves. From 1594 until 1640 three strong deys ruled the province with conspicuous success, creating an admiral to command the corsair fleet and a general (bey) to command the land forces. Then, by a palace revolution, the bey took over the supreme position on a hereditary basis, though the offices of dey and beylerbey were still retained. Finally, in 1705 a change of dynasty occurred, and the new family of Husainid beys added to their own title that of beylerbey–pasha; their rule was to last into the middle of the twentieth century.

While Tunisia possessed a natural identity which quickly reasserted itself under Ottoman rule, and while Algeria achieved a kind of national integration under the strong rule of the *ojak*, the Ottoman initiative in Tripoli faced much thornier problems. In large measure these arose from the geographical environment. While Tripoli had an immense strategic importance at the terminus of the shortest trans-Saharan crossing and as an almost inevitable staging-post on the land route from Ifriqiya to Egypt, it lacked an agricultural base. The coastal plain enjoying a winter rainfall was nowhere more than 12 kilometres wide. Behind it there was only sparse grazing for a few pastoral nomads. The grain to feed the two or three coastal towns had to be carried 800 kilometres on camel-back from the oasis region of the Fezzan or else brought in by sea. Tripoli was a port and a caravanserai, but only with the utmost difficulty could it be made into a state. Thus, while the transition from rule by the Ottoman beylerbey to that of the dey of the local *ojak* followed much the same pattern as in Algeria and Tunisia, violent episodes were recurrent, and it was only in the middle of the seventeenth century that Tripoli emerged as a serious power in the eastern Mediterranean. Two strong deys of the Saqizli family, in origin Greek renegades from Chios, built up the corsairing fleet, which raided as far as Spain and Italy, and developed a force of swift cavalry to police the caravan routes to the Fezzan. When the caravan traffic was diverted eastwards to Cyrenaica to avoid the attentions of the corsairs, they seized Benghazi and began to impose tribute on the settled tribes of the Jebel al-Akhdar. Thus a viable superstructure was erected which reached its heyday under the Karamanli dynasty who held power as pashas of Tripoli from 1711 till 1823.

NORTH AFRICA, THE SAHARA AND THE SUDAN

The history of the Ottoman period in North Africa has often been written as though it had no connection with the African world to the south. In fact, the struggle for command of the southern shores of the Mediterranean had a profound significance for sub-Saharan West Africa. In the first place, it was a victory for Islam, which kept open the lines of communication not only in North Africa but across the desert. Had Spain during its greatest century not been diverted by the conquest of the New World and by dynastic ambitions in Italy and central Europe, the history of West Africa as well as North Africa might have been very different. As it was, Muslim teachers and Arabic books continued to cross the Sahara along with Barbary horses, Turkish guns and Venetian cloth and hardware. More important, African pilgrims continued to visit the heartlands of their faith, and African slaves contributed, probably on a greater scale than in the past, to the population of the Muslim lands around the Mediterranean. It has been remarked that whereas the Atlantic slave-trade removed a preponderance of young males to plantation slavery in the New World, the trans-Saharan caravans carried a majority of women and young children destined for service and concubinage in Muslim households. The penal conditions of the galleys and the mines were reserved for Christians.

The degree of interaction between North and West Africa   71 depended, of course, upon political conditions to the south of the desert as much as to the north. As we shall see in the next chapter, the political and commercial relations of the western Sudan were concentrated during our period very largely upon Morocco and the Atlantic coast. The north-eastward traffic was that of pilgrims, who crossed the desert from Timbuktu to Ghat and Ghadames and continued eastwards through the Fezzan and Awjila, keeping to the desert oases and avoiding the main centres of Ottoman government. The trade of the central Sudan, however, was much more closely linked with the eastern and central Maghrib. Here, throughout our period, the dominant state was Bornu, its external contacts and political dynamism based firmly on the slave-trade. The main instrument of slave-catching throughout the central Sudan was the horse, employed in annual dry-season expeditions against the smaller, less organised populations bordering the great Sudanic states. The Sudanic breed of horses, though long established, existed upon the very margin of horse-breeding country, and needed constant enrichment from the larger Barbary stock to the north of the desert. Cavalry forces also needed horse-trappings, armour and coats of mail. And increasingly during our period, guns became an element in Sudanese warfare. They were certainly in use in Bornu by the sixteenth century, and at the time of their introduction they were accompanied by 'Turks', that is to say, soldiers of fortune from Tripoli and Tunis, trained to fire and mend them and trained in the completely novel military tactics required for their use. All these were costly luxuries, and in a land without gold they could be paid for only with slaves. At the beginning of the period Bornu was in the course of shifting its centre from the north-east to the west of Lake Chad. Though usually presented as a retreat from the growing strength of a daughter dynasty, that of the Bulala, in Kanem, this event can also be seen as the opening of a new slaving frontier among the many small Chadic-speaking peoples to the west and south of the lake. At all events, Kanem continued to be a polity based upon slave-raiding under the Bulala, as it had been under the Magumi kings of Bornu, and slaving was likewise the motor of the new states which emerged during our period, both further to the east, as in Wadai and Darfur, and further to the south, as in Bagirmi.

From Bornu, Kanem and Bagirmi the slave caravans all went north through Kawar, where the great salt-mine of Bilma formed the centre of a wide circle of trade routes supplying all the population of the central Sahara and Sudan. From Kawar they marched a journey of three or four weeks to the Fezzan. Along this, the most difficult,

section of the route caravans depended upon the co-operation as escorts and guides of the Tubu (or Teda) people, whose homeland was the mountain massif of the Tibesti, where they bred great numbers of camels for use in the long-distance trade. On arrival in the Fezzan, the caravans paused to recuperate and regroup at one or other of the oasis towns, such as Zawila, Traghen or Murzuk, where the slaves were rehabilitated, clothed and sold to the North African merchants who operated along the northern desert routes leading to Egypt, Tunisia and, above all, Tripoli, whence cargoes were despatched to Istanbul and other markets in the Ottoman empire. During most of the period the rulers of the Fezzan were a dynasty of Moroccan origin, the Awlad Muhammad, who took tolls, guarded the routes and generally acted as intermediaries between the peoples of the north and the south. From time to time military expeditions arrived from Tripoli to assert a nominal suzerainty. For the most part, they were placated with gifts and honourably entertained until they departed. Nevertheless, the existence of relatively strong powers at either end of this trans-Saharan route did contribute to its security, and in some sense Tripoli and Bornu regarded each other as neighbours and partners in policing the Saharan tribes, just as Kanem and Ifriqiya had done in an earlier period. Embassies and gifts were exchanged, and the traffic in arms and slaves was recognised as a political as well as a commercial transaction.

To the west of the grand central route through Kawar there ran another, scarcely less important, which connected the cities of Hausa-land with Ghat in the northern foothills of the Hoggar massif and thence with Murzuk on the one hand and Ghadames on the other. The camel nomads on whom this system depended were the Tuareg, who from about the eleventh century onwards had shifted their grazing lands southwards from the Hoggar to the hilly regions of Aïr and Adrar of the Ifoghas. Their earliest contribution had been in developing the routes running north-eastwards from Mali and Songhay, and during the first half of our period these remained of great importance. The connection between Aïr and Hausaland seems to have emerged only in the fifteenth century, when the Tuareg began to export the copper of Takedda and to acquire a near-monopoly in the distribution of Bilma salt. This corresponded in period with the military expansion of Kano, Katsina and Zaria, when horses and armour began to be imported in quantity from the north, and when manufactures of cotton and leather goods began to be exported across the desert in exchange. With the fall of Songhay at the end of the sixteenth century, the route between Aïr and the Niger bend died out of use, but the Hausa trade continued to thrive. From the northern 73 entrepôts of Ghadames and Murzuk the cotton textiles of Hausaland were distributed throughout the countries of the Maghrib, and some were even re-exported southwards again to Timbuktu. What came to be known in Europe as 'Morocco leather' had often an origin in Hausaland. All in all, the Tuareg trade routes seem to have had a more purely commercial flavour than those of the Tubu to the east. The Tuareg themselves acted as transport agents, carrying goods for a commission and taking responsibility for safe delivery. There was no western counterpart to the special relationship between Tripoli and Bornu, and, perhaps for this reason, fire-arms did not appear in Hausaland until the eighteenth century. Nonetheless, Hausaland, even more than Bornu, belonged to the commercial hinterland of the Ottoman Maghrib.

In its long-term implications, the most significant development of the fifteenth century in Africa was the opening of its Atlantic coastline to European shipping. Starting with the Portuguese occupation of Ceuta in 1415, this was in origin a project to gain closer access to the trade in West African gold, first of all by approaching the Moroccan termini of the trans-Saharan routes, and then by circumventing the overland traffic itself. As governor of Ceuta, the Portuguese prince Henry, later called 'the Navigator', gained first-hand information about the desert caravans. He devoted the rest of his life to the improvement of Portuguese shipbuilding and cartography and to promoting the exploration of the African coastline. The earliest expeditions were directed to opening the ports of southern Morocco, a thousand kilometres closer than Ceuta to where the northbound caravans emerged from the western desert. Madeira, discovered in 1418, was regularly colonised in the 1420s; the Azores a decade later. Meanwhile, along the mainland coast the pioneers passed Cape Bojador in 1434 and Cape Blanco in 1441, south of which the little offshore island of Arguin offered a safe site for a trading settlement more than halfway down the desert coast. The place was already frequented by Moorish salt-traders, who were soon able to exchange Sudanese gold and Negro slaves for the commodities they were accustomed to buy more expensively in Morocco – horses, wheat, textiles, carpets and silver coin.

Beyond Arguin the Portuguese came in 1444 to the mouth of the Senegal, which was the effective boundary between the Sahara and the Sudan. To the north of it lived the nomadic Moors, to the south the sedentary Wolof, with their ruling dynasty and their equestrian nobility rich in slaves. The Portuguese chronicler Azurara described in moving language the arrival at Lagos in southern Portugal of one of the first consignments of these unfortunates, destined for work in the sugar plantations of the Algarve.

On the 8th of August 1444, early in the morning on account of the heat, the sailors landed the captives. When they were all mustered in the field outside the town, they presented a remarkable spectacle. Some among them were tolerably light in colour, handsome and well-proportioned; some slightly darker; others a degree lighter than mulattoes, while several were as black as   75 moles, and so hideous both of face and form as to suggest the idea that they were come from the lower regions. But what heart so hard as not to be touched with compassion at the sight of them! Some with downcast heads and faces bathed in tears as they looked at each other; others moaning sorrowfully, and fixing their eyes on heaven, uttered plaintive cries as if appealing for help to the Father of Nature. Others struck their faces with their hands and threw themselves flat upon the ground. Others uttered a wailing chant after the fashion of their country . . . But their anguish was at its height when the moment of distribution came, when of necessity children were separated from their parents, wives from their husbands, and brothers from brothers. Each was compelled to go wherever fate might send him. It was impossible to effect this separation without extreme pain . . .[1]

Up the broad, slow-moving waters of the Gambia, discovered in 1455, the Portuguese were able to sail their caravels for some 250

[1] Cited in R. H. Major, *The Life of Prince Henry the Navigator* (London, 1868), pp. 179–80.

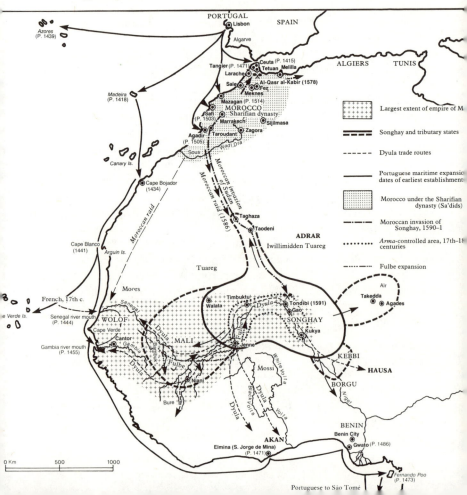

kilometres inland. This brought them into contact with a number of small states on the western periphery of the Mande-speaking world, and, more significantly, with the confraternity of Dyula traders, who responded quickly to the new commercial opportunities presented by the ocean route. At Cantor on the upper Gambia, the Portuguese were within about a fortnight's march of both the Bambuk and the Bure goldfields, which had supplied the needs of Europe and the Middle East for many centuries. Here, too, they were able to collect itineraries from merchants who had travelled as far afield as Timbuktu and even Kukya, the traditional capital of the Songhay kingdom on the eastern arm of the Niger bend. And here they were able to learn that south-eastwards from Jenne another network of trade routes led through even richer gold-producing countries to the shores of the great sea. This was the vital information which spurred the Portuguese to continue their explorations, despite the death of Prince Henry in 1460. In 1469 a Lisbon merchant, Fernão Gomes, was granted a temporary monopoly of the West African trade on the condition that he advanced the trading frontier by a hundred leagues a year. This brought him in 1471 to the shores of the Akan country – the Gold Coast, as it would later be called – where the creekside village soon to be named Elmina, 'the mine', was henceforward to be the heart of Portugal's West African trading empire. Here on a rocky promontory beside the village a royal 'castle' – in reality a fortified trading depot – was built in 1482. Elmina became the centre of a local trading network, collecting the produce which came down various trade paths from the interior. At the height of its prosperity in the late fifteenth and early sixteenth centuries, an average of 400 kilograms of gold a year passed through its vaults, and its warehouse was restocked at monthly intervals with copper, brass, textiles and cowry-shells – and slaves. The last, heavily in demand by the Akan for mining and porterage, were mostly brought from Benin, where a rapidly expanding military kingdom had many war captives to dispose of.

THE DECLINE OF MALI AND THE RISE OF SONGHAY

It has been estimated that by the end of the fifteenth century the maritime commerce of the Portuguese may have been attracting about a quarter of the total production of West African gold into its net.[2] In addition, by carrying something of the order of 2,000 West African

---

[2] V. Magalhães-Godinho, *L'économie portugaise aux XVe et XVIe siècles* (Paris, 1969), pp. 175–226.

12 Western West Africa (1): Portugal, Morocco and Songhay

slaves a year to the Cape Verde islands, the Azores and Madeira, as well as to its own homeland, Portugal had established a far-flung sugar industry of great significance for the further development of its world-wide trading system. All this was of revolutionary importance to a small European nation, but it had hardly scratched the surface of life in West Africa. There the first century of Portuguese contact had produced some coastward reorientation in the economic life of peoples living within 100 or 200 kilometres of the ocean, but over most of the region the commercial arteries remained firmly linked to the desert caravans and the Niger waterway. The economic determinant of this pattern, which prevailed until the coming of the railways, was undoubtedly the production and distribution of salt. There was no more economic way of getting this vital mineral into the scattered cooking-pots of the western Sudan than to mine it in mid-Sahara and carry it for a month on camel-back to the banks of the great river of West Africa at the northernmost point of its long course.

The fifteenth century did indeed see a change in the main, over-arching system of political control in the western Sudan, but this was in no sense a consequence of Portuguese outreach. Already from about 1360 onwards the Keita dynasty of Mali had been subject to severe internal dissensions based on the rivalry between the descendants of Mansa Musa and those of his brother Mansa Sulayman. Trouble at the centre of the system was soon reflected in disintegration at the periphery. Of the tributary states, Songhay in the east, and in the west the Wolof 'empire' south of the lower Senegal, were the first to break away. From the region south of the Niger bend Mossi horsemen made swift, devastating raids on the rich riverside towns from Jenne to Timbuktu. The Fulbe pastoralists from the upper Senegal moved in upon the areas of cereal production around the inland delta of the Niger. The Tuareg nomads advanced southwards upon the cities of the Niger bend, finally occupying Timbuktu in 1433. Thus, although the great king of the interior whose existence was reported by the Dyula traders to the Portuguese on the Gambia in 1455 was still the 'Bor-Melle' or 'Mande Mansa' of Mali, the range of his effective rule was already limited to the Mande-speaking centre of the former imperial system. Within twenty years more, it was to be reduced still further, to the southern half of that core region.

The state which expanded to fill the vacuum left by the break-up of Mali was Songhay. As a kingdom embracing much of the eastern arm of the Niger bend, it already had a long history. It had been the contemporary, and in some respects the counterpart, of ancient Ghana, commanding the caravan routes leading northwards and eastwards from the Niger in much the same way as Ghana controlled those leading to the north and west. With the expansion of Mali in the thirteenth century, Songhay had lost its northern province and its control of the desert routes. For much of the fourteenth century the remainder of the kingdom paid tribute to Mali. Yet the Songhay-speakers were still the predominant population of the river valley far beyond the political boundaries of the state. They were the fishermen, the boat-builders and the river traders right round the great bend of the Niger, forming the main ethnic stratum at Jenne and Timbuktu as well as at Gao and Kukya. Moreover, eastern Songhay, along with the neighbouring country of the Mossi, offered the best conditions for horse-breeding to be found anywhere to the south of the Sahara, and the mounted lancers of Songhay were swift and terrible, whether as slave-raiders on the eastern frontier or as the pillagers of Sahel towns. Thus, the potential existed for a Songhay revival, given only the leadership capable of directing it, and in 1464 this was found with the accession to the throne of Sonni Ali, who in a reign of twenty-eight years placed Songhay in the position formerly occupied by Mali.

Sonni Ali is remembered in the oral tradition of Songhay as a magician of unparalleled power, and in the chronicle of al-Sa'di of Timbuktu as an impious and unscrupulous tyrant. In fact, he was first and foremost a great military commander with a well-thought-out strategy of conquest, based on the Niger waterway. Whenever possible, he seems to have manoeuvred his forces within the arc of territory enclosed by the river, ferrying them to the north bank only to attack specific targets. In 1469 he took Timbuktu from the Tuareg, making his own headquarters at the river-port of Kabara, but sacking the rich city and driving out the Tuareg and Sanhaja clerics who had been the civic functionaries and the teachers and preachers at the famous Sankore mosque. A poignant passage of al-Sa'di's chronicle describes their donnish departure northwards to the desert city of Walata. 'On that day one saw bearded men of ripe age trembling with fright at the prospect of mounting a camel, and tumbling to the ground as soon as the animal got to its feet. The reason for this was that our virtuous ancestors used to keep their children at their apron-strings, with the result that they grew up helpless because they had never played games when they were young.'[3] Having established control of this vital junction between the land and water routes, Sonni Ali pursued his conquests upstream, reaching Jenne, which he besieged with four hundred boats in 1473. This gave him command of the gold and kola routes leading southwards to the Volta basin. It

[3] Al-Sa'di, *Tarikh es-Soudan*, tr. O. Houdas (Paris, 1900), p. 106.

remained to secure the important food-producing regions around Lake Debo and the inland delta of the Niger from raids by Mossi from the south and Fulbe from the west. It was only in fact towards the end of his reign that Sonni Ali's forces were in direct contact with those of the already much reduced kingdom of Mali, in the region to the west of the upper Niger. Here, broadly speaking, he was successful in the savanna, but not so in the forest, where his cavalry, impeded by the dense vegetation, was at the mercy of the Malian archers.

In methods of government, it seems that the new Songhay leadership mainly took over the old Malian system, and this tendency became clearer when, soon after the death of Sonni Ali, power was seized by one of his generals, the Askiya Muhammad Ture, whose name would strongly suggest that he was not of Songhay but of Soninke (i.e. northern Mande) origin and that his coup d'état represented a return to Mande leadership in what was predominantly a Mande-speaking empire. In another important respect Muhammad Ture's accession signified a return to the traditional Malian ethic. Before all else, he was an orthodox and pious Muslim, who was able to re-enlist the support of the literate class of the great cities of Gao, Timbuktu and Jenne. During his reign the scholars returned to Timbuktu, the princes were educated in the Sankore mosque and the princesses were married to the rich merchants who managed the trans-Saharan trade. Relations with the Tuareg and the Sanhaja were restored, and through them Songhay established virtual control over the salt-mines of Taghaza and the copper-mines of Takedda, which were the keys to the successful working of the long-distance trade. Again the Muslim clerics, once restored to favour, supplied the ideological support and the legal framework necessary for the efficient government of a large territory within which many people were constantly moving around outside their traditional ethnic areas.

At a more material level, the Songhay empire depended greatly on its colonies of royal slaves and on its privileged castes of craftsmen, which had probably been built up originally from the more skilled groups of war captives, such as smiths, weavers and leatherworkers. Here again, Songhay took over a system already developed by Mali, while adding greatly to the numbers of slaves by means of the regular annual raids carried out by the Songhay cavalry among the unprotected, stateless peoples living to the south of the Niger bend. Some of these captives went to the trans-Saharan markets, especially at this period those of southern Morocco with its developing sugar industry. Others were sold to the free citizenry of Songhay. Others again became the property of the ruler and were either recruited into the army or settled in colonies on the state farms. These were spread right across the empire, to supply the government and the garrisons, but the highest concentration was in the well-watered inland delta region upstream of Timbuktu, where the food was grown for the cities of the Sahel, the desert caravans and even for the workers in the far-off desert salt-mines. There is an interesting account in the seventeenth-century Sudanese chronicle of Ibn al-Mukhtar of how Sonni Ali, when he died, bequeathed to his successor twelve 'tribes' of slaves, some of which he had inherited from his own ancestors in pre-imperial Songhay, and three of which he had obtained, presumably by conquest, from the emperor of Mali. These three 'tribes' were composed of pagan Mande, or Bambara, from the regions to the south of the Mali empire, and when they belonged to Mali each man and wife had been obliged to cultivate forty measures of land for the king. But when they were taken over by Songhay, Sonni Ali divided them into groups of a hundred – fifty men and fifty women – and each group was allotted two hundred measures of land to cultivate in common and given a production quota, after supplying which they were allowed to keep any surplus. The children of slaves were slaves, and if a slave married a free woman, the king would pay a dowry of 40,000 cowries to the girl's family in order to establish his right of ownership over the children. The king would also take some of the children of slaves and sell them in order to buy horses for his cavalry.[4]

The Songhay empire, like that of Mali before it, thus involved a gigantic effort of state enterprise in production and trade as well as in military operations and civil government. Under Muhammad Ture (1493–1528) its territories were greatly extended, especially towards the west, until it encompassed the whole northern half of the old Mali empire. To the east of Songhay, Muhammad led at least two spectacular military expeditions, the first to Borgu, the second passing through the Hausa states of Zaria and Kano to the city of Agades in Aïr. But these were raids, not wars of conquest. As Muhammad himself explained, they were undertaken to distract the Songhay-speaking element in his armies from meddling in the Mande-speaking western part of his empire, where his own interests were strongest, and where he preferred to rule through slave armies recruited from his own war captives. Not under Muhammad only, but also under the succession of sons and grandsons who followed him as Askiyas until 1591, the real thrust of Songhay was towards the west and the north. It was an impetus based upon Timbuktu, both as the centre of Islamic

---

[4] Ibn al-Mukhtar, *Tarikh al-Fattash*, tr. O. Houdas (Paris, 1913), pp. 19–22.

learning in the western Sudan and as the meeting-point of river and desert communications. It was an impetus, largely successful, to reconstruct as much as possible of the old Mali empire around this northerly base. While it lasted it was certainly more significant in every way than the reconstruction of the coastal fringes of western West Africa under the impact of the European maritime advance.

THE RESURGENCE OF MOROCCO

As we saw in Chapter 1, Morocco by the fifteenth century had fallen into a state of great weakness and incipient fragmentation under the later Marinids and their hereditary Wattasid viziers, who finally seized the sultanate in 1472. The impotence of Morocco had indeed been one of the main factors leading Portugal into African adventures. Portuguese trade with southern Morocco developed steadily alongside the longer-distance maritime trade with West Africa, with the result that northern Morocco was virtually excluded from the profits of the trans-Saharan caravans. By the early sixteenth century the Portuguese were consolidating their initiative by occupying and fortifying the southern Moroccan ports of Agadir (1505) and Safi (1508), Asemmour (1513) and Mazagan (1514). The resurgence of Morocco originated in the opposition to Portuguese encroachments in this southern region. Its leaders were the marabouts (holy men) of the Islamic brotherhoods of the Saharan borderlands. They were headed by a Sharif, Abu 'Abdullah Muhammad, who gathered an army in the far southern district of the Sous and began to attack the Portuguese at Agadir. His successor, Ahmad al-A'raj, made his headquarters at the ancient capital of the Almoravids and Almohads at Marrakech, where he was recognised as sultan of the south by the Wattasid sultan of Fez. In 1541 Ahmad was deposed by his brother, Muhammad al-Mahdi, who finally chased the Portuguese out of Agadir in 1541 and in 1550 conquered the rest of Morocco from the Wattasids.

During the third quarter of the sixteenth century, Morocco, under its new 'Sharifian' dynasty, faced threats both from the Ottoman governors of nearby Algiers and from the Portuguese, who were still active on the northern coastline. One son of Muhammad al-Mahdi gained the throne for a brief period with Ottoman support. Another fled to Portugal, whence he returned with an expeditionary force led by the Portuguese king, Sebastian. All three protagonists perished at 'the battle of the three kings', fought near Al-Qasr al-Kabir in 1578. The battle was a resounding defeat for the Portuguese, however, and it was a third brother, Mawlay Ahmad, who now succeeded to the sultanate, adding to his name the title al-Mansur, 'the victorious', in token of his triumph over the Christians. Mawlay Ahmad, who reigned until 1603, turned Morocco into a great power. He thoroughly modernised the army, introducing fire-arms and employing Turkish and Spanish mercenaries familiar with their use. With his capital at Marrakech, it was natural that he should seek to improve his victory over the Portuguese by re-establishing Moroccan control over the desert trade. A preliminary expedition in 1584 is believed to have penetrated to the Senegal, imposing Moroccan authority on the nomads of the westernmost desert route leading to the Wolof kingdoms in Senegambia. The busier route, however, ran further to the east, via the salt-mining centre of Taghaza, which was within the sphere of Songhay. In 1586 Mawlay Ahmad sent musketmen to occupy Taghaza, but the miners fled with their Tuareg masters into the sandy wastes, and soon discovered a vast new salt-pan 200 kilometres to the south-east at Taodeni. Soon afterwards, Mawlay Ahmad determined to invade the heartland of Songhay itself.

To send an expedition across 3,000 kilometres of desert, there to fight the host that held in subjection the whole of the western Sudan, was a conception of breathtaking boldness, and it is recorded that many wise heads were shaken when Mawlay Ahmad presented the plan to his council. The sultan, however, insisted that such would be the superiority of fire-arms when matched against spears and bows that the force need be no larger than an ordinary commercial caravan. Events were to prove him right. In October 1590 four thousand picked men under the command of a Spanish renegade, Judar Pasha, with two thousand five hundred muskets and supplies and ammunition loaded on ten thousand camels, wound their way out of Marrakech. Half perished in the desert, but the survivors reached the Niger bend in February 1591 and began to march downstream towards the Songhay capital at Gao. News of their approach had already reached the Askiya Ishaq, who advanced to meet them with, at the very least, ten thousand cavalry and thirty thousand foot-soldiers. Battle was joined at the riverside village of Tondibi, and the Moroccans won a decisive victory. Ishaq made his submission to Judar and offered tribute to the sultan in gold and slaves. This, however, was refused, and another pasha was sent from Morocco to replace Judar and complete the conquest. Mawlay Ahmad celebrated his victory by claiming the supreme Islamic political title of Caliph.

During the remainder of Mawlay Ahmad's reign more than twenty thousand Moroccan troops crossed the desert to reinforce those already established on the Niger. The result was the creation of a 83 military colony, by no means co-extensive with the former Songhay empire, but dominating through its monopoly of fire-arms the main axis of desert and river communications running from Taghaza and Taodeni to Timbuktu, and thence up the Niger to Jenne and down-stream as far as Kukya. The pasha resided at Timbuktu in a citadel constructed by forced labour in the foreign merchants' quarter of the town. Subsidiary garrisons commanded by *qa'ids* occupied the salt-mines in the north and the main river-ports to the south. A puppet Askiya, living under the eye of the pasha at Timbuktu, administered traditional law and custom among the Songhay-speaking population of the river valley. The Moroccans concerned themselves with tribute and taxation, squeezing the merchant community and levying tolls on the river traffic. For a few years the profits appeared to be fabulous. 'Following the conquest of the kingdoms of the Sudan, Mawlay Ahmad received so much gold dust that envious men were all troubled and observers absolutely stupefied. So from then on al-Mansur paid his officials in pure gold and in dinars of proper weight only. At the gate of his palace 1700 smiths were daily engaged in striking dinars.'[5]

However, on Mawlay Ahmad's death Morocco was split in two by a struggle for the succession, and sank into a period of disorder which was to end only with the emergence of a new Sharifian dynasty, that of the 'Alawids, during the 1660s. In these circumstances the Sudanese garrison could not be reinforced, and the Moroccans already in the Sudan became correspondingly independent, marrying Sudanese wives, electing their own pashas, and allowing the tribute to fall to negligible proportions. Thus, the former colonial troops gradually became an indigenous ruling class. As such, the Moroccans, or the *arma* (musketeers) as they were locally known, ruled the Niger bend for two centuries. To the class of learned Muslim clerics which supplied the chroniclers of this period the government of the *arma* appeared a sad contrast to that of the Askiyas of sixteenth-century Songhay. Many of the leading scholars of Timbuktu were deported to Marrakech, and the Sankore mosque never recovered its position as the intellectual capital of the Sudan. Dangers constantly threatened from the peripheral peoples, such as the Mossi to the south and the Fulbe to the west. A remnant of independent, pagan Songhay sur-vived in Dendi, downstream to the east. The Iwillimidden Tuareg of Adrar of the Ifoghas soon closed off the eastern desert route from Gao to Takedda and the copper-mines. Nevertheless, the main northern route to the Taodeni salt-mines and Morocco remained open, and the

[5] Al-Ifrani, *Nazhat*, cited and tr. N. Levtzion, in *Cambridge History of Africa*, vol. IV (Cambridge, 1975), pp. 150–1.

arma, by careful policing of the waterway from Jenne to Timbuktu, continued to take handsome profits from the salt coming south and the gold and slaves passing to the north.

Indeed, there can be no doubt that when the 'Alawid dynasty seized power in Morocco, it led to a considerable expansion of the trans-Saharan trade. The 'Alawids, like their predecessors, were Sharifs from the desert fringes, very conscious of the value of black man-power and Sudanese gold. Sultan Mawlay Ismail, who consolidated their regime during a reign which lasted from 1672 to 1727, built up his power almost entirely through his black slaves, whose numbers reached 150,000. Mawlay Ismail conscripted into his own service many black slaves already in Morocco, but he imported many more both from the Timbuktu pashalik and from his own slave-raids across the western desert to the upper Senegal. The blacks, both men and women, were settled around his capital at Meknes. They supplied his army, his garrisons around the country, his palace servants, his skilled artisans and the agricultural labour necessary to feed his court and capital. In the early eighteenth century the French, who by this time had supplanted the Portuguese on the Senegal, noted the presence of Moroccan raiding parties on both banks of the river, while upstream in Galam their advanced posts collected accounts of the 'Moors' of Timbuktu, living in their forts beside the Niger and trading blocks of salt for gold and slaves. The later eighteenth century probably saw a change at least in the volume of the trans-Saharan slave-trade. On the death of Mawlay Ismail, the slave soldiers took charge of the govern-ment, causing chaos and disorder for more than thirty years. They were finally mastered only by Ismail's grandson, Sidi Muhammad (1759–90), who returned to the ancient system of using Arab levies. Certainly by 1795, when Mungo Park finally penetrated to the upper Niger, the trade in salt and gold was still in vigour, but the slave-trade was now mostly with the Europeans at the Atlantic coast, where guns were the most valued import.

WESTERN WEST AFRICA AND THE ATLANTIC SLAVE-TRADE

We have seen that in western West Africa the opening of the Atlantic coastline by the Portuguese had resulted by the middle of the six-teenth century in the diversion of perhaps a quarter of the long-distance trade in gold and slaves into the new maritime channels. The gold which had taken a new direction had been almost exclusively that of the Akan country, which had thus far been an importer rather than an exporter of slaves. The slaves who had been shipped overseas to

85

13*a*   Western West Africa (2): African states and peoples, Senegal to Asante; European trade in slaves (western half) 13*b*   (eastern half)

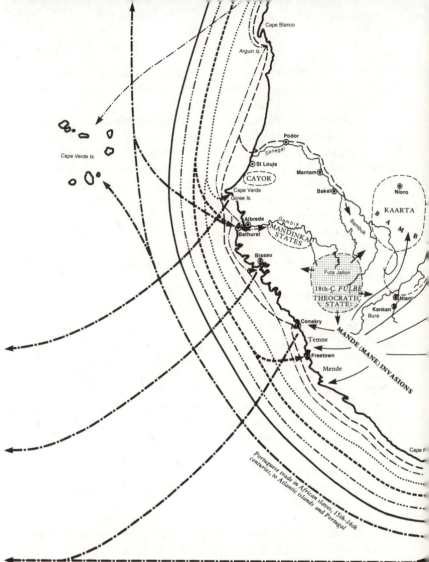

Cape Blanco

Arguin Is.

Cape Verde Is.

Podor

Senegal

St Louis

Mantam

CAYOR

Bakel

Nioro

Cape Verde

KAARTA

Goree Is.

Bambuk

B

Albreda

Gambia

Bathurst

MANDINKA
STATES

A

M

B

Bissau

Futa Jallon

(18th-C. FULBE
THEOCRATIC
STATE)

Niani

Kankan
Bure

Conakry

MANDE (MANE) INVASIONS

Temne

Freetown

Mende

Cape P

*Portuguese trade in African slaves, 15th–16th
centuries, to Atlantic islands and Portugal*

*European trade in African slaves, c. 1530 to abolition – to Brazil, West
Indian islands, Southern Colonies (States) of America*

European trading activities:

▦ Futa Jallon Fulbe expansion, 18th century

—·—·— Portuguese – from mid-15th century

············· Dutch – from early 17th century

▦ Asante expansion, 18th century

——— French – from mid-17th century

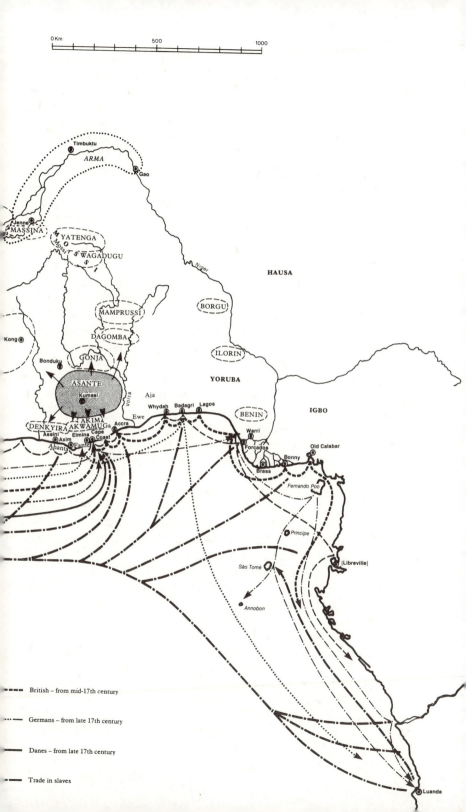

Scale:
0 Km — 500 — 1000

Timbuktu
ARMA
Gao
Jenne
MASSINA
YATENGA
MOSSI
WAGADUGU
Kong
MAMPRUSSI
Bonduku
DAGOMBA
GONJA
ASANTE
Kumasi
DENKYIRA
AKIMI
Assini
AKWAMU
Axim
Ahanta
Elmina
Cape
Coast
Fante
Ga
Accra
Ewe
Aja
Whydah
Badagri
Lagos
BENIN
Warri
Forcados
Bonny
Brass
Old Calabar
Niger
HAUSA
BORGU
ILORIN
YORUBA
IGBO
Volta
Fernando Poo
Principe
São Tomé
Annobon
[Libreville]
Luanda

---- British – from mid-17th century

─·─· Germans – from late 17th century

──── Danes – from late 17th century

─··─ Trade in slaves

Portugal and the Atlantic islands had been taken from Senegambia and the rivers to the south of it, or else, and predominantly, from lands to the east of the Gold Coast. From about 1530 the New World had begun to be a destination for African slaves, but for almost a century after this the numbers exported there remained very small – perhaps 2,000 a year in all – and, so far as western West Africa was concerned, Morocco continued to be by far the most important market. It was only with the development of plantation agriculture in Brazil and the West Indies during the 1630s that the trans-Atlantic slave-trade began to be a big business worth the active competition of the new maritime powers of northern Europe. The first of these nations to enter the West African trade were the Dutch, who had already supplanted the Portuguese in the Indian Ocean and who in 1621 had founded a West Indian Company to plant coffee and sugar in the Caribbean. During the 1630s the Dutch occupied the Portuguese plantations in Brazil. By 1642 they had ousted the Portuguese from all their coastal bases in West Africa, including their headquarters at Elmina on the Gold Coast. During the 1650s and 1660s French, British, Danish, Swedish and German companies were formed to develop tropical plantations and to promote the shameful trade in African slaves which appeared to be the only means of providing the necessary manpower. By the second half of the seventeenth century the trans-Atlantic slave-trade had escalated to some 20,000 a year, almost ten times its sixteenth-century level. The eighteenth century saw a further threefold increase, to close on 60,000 slaves a year from Africa as a whole.

To the total figure of slave exports by sea it is likely that the contribution of western West Africa was of the order of one-third. Different parts of the area were differently affected at different periods, however, and here as elsewhere there is an obvious correlation between the processes of conquest and territorial expansion among the indigenous African states, many of them in the far interior, and the supply of slaves at particular points along the coast. We have seen that during the first century of the Portuguese outreach the main sources of slaves were the Wolof states south of the Senegal and the Mandinka states on both sides of the Gambia, all of which were in course of consolidation at this period. During the second century of the trade, from about 1530 till about 1630, when most slaves were exported under the *asiento* system to the silver-mines in Mexico and Peru, the main area of supply seems to have been the river estuaries of modern Guinea, Sierra Leone and Liberia, where the hinterland was at this period subject to a series of invasions by warlike groups of

Mande origin, who carved out a score of little states among the ill-defended 'West Atlantic' peoples. The best-known among these invaders were the Mane, who originated in some part of the Mali empire and travelled as a plundering horde through much of modern Ivory Coast and Liberia before settling, about 1545, in Sierra Leone, where they gradually broke up as their sections conquered and colonised different ethnic groups. The Mane migration was certainly not due in any way to the Europeans. Its warriors were armed with bows and arrows, not with guns. Yet the existence on the Sierra Leone rivers of a ready market for their war captives caused a mutation in the Mane mode of military dominance which turned them into the main suppliers of the Atlantic slave-trade for the best part of a century.

During the second half of the seventeenth century, however, while the slave-trade was growing rapidly elsewhere, in Sierra Leone it almost died out. The various Mande conquerors had become absorbed into the local societies, and there was no more occasion for slaving expeditions until, in the early eighteenth century, a revolution occurred among the Fulbe of Futa Jallon, a little further inland. Here, in 1726, the Muslim Fulbe declared a jihad against their pagan Djallonke neighbours, driving them from their highland plateau and forming a powerful and aggressive theocratic state which for the rest of the century conducted regular slaving wars against all the neighbouring peoples and traded their captives in huge numbers to the Europeans at the coast. As earlier with the Mane, the origins of the disturbance had nothing to do with the Atlantic trade, but once the process of conquest had begun, it was no doubt carried much further than it would otherwise have been by the fruits of the trade, in this case mostly fire-arms. A similar situation developed during the same period along the banks of the upper Niger, where Mande warlords, armed with guns from the Gambia trading posts, built up the so-called Bambara kingdoms of Segu and Kaarta.

The most spectacular developments in the agglomeration of political power resulting from the intensification of European commercial activity in the seventeenth and eighteenth centuries occurred in the hinterland of the Gold Coast. Here, the initial attraction for the Europeans was the gold of the Akan forest, mostly situated between 100 and 250 kilometres from the coast. Some of it was still traded inland to Timbuktu and Hausaland. The rest found its way to the coast by a score of routes, and once the Portuguese monopoly had been broken in the 1640s, Dutch, British, Danes and Germans pressed in to build fortified trading settlements at almost every fishing village along a 350-kilometre stretch of palm-fringed, surf-beaten 89 shore. The coastal peoples – Nzima, Ahanta, Fante, Gwang and Ga – soon joined in the competition, aligning themselves with one or other of the forts, and each striving to attract the upcountry caravans into their own sphere of patronage. In these circumstances larger concentrations of power could occur only in the interior. It was at the heart of the forest region that political opportunities were greatest. Here were the sources of gold. Here lay the option of trading both to the north and to the south.

In the seizing of these opportunities it would seem that the Atlantic trade, as reorganised by the northern Europeans during the seventeenth century, played a major part. Where the Portuguese had traded slaves for gold (see p. 77 above), the Dutch, the British and the Danes traded guns. As a result, states of the gold-producing belt – in the west Denkyira, in the east Akim and Akwamu – were helped on the path to rapid territorial expansion, in the course of which the Gold Coast became a large supplier of slaves for export. Akwamu, in particular, soared from very small beginnings in the eastern forest hinterland to dominate all the trade routes from Accra to the Volta. The Ga state of Accra was conquered between 1677 and 1681, and Akwamu armies rampaged across the coastlands of modern Togo and Bénin (Dahomey), capturing and enslaving tens of thousands of the Ewe and Aja peoples, and creating a series of colonial provinces among the conquered. Further west, Denkyira, though never reaching the sea, conquered and made tributary most of the Akan peoples living to the north of the Fante and Ahanta of the coastal states, thus dominating all the trade routes between Cape Coast and Axim. From each of these expanding empires a steady supply of war captives was delivered to the European forts and waiting slave-ships.

At the very end of the seventeenth century, however, both Denkyira and Akwamu were succeeded by Asante, in origin a group of small states formed by migrants and refugees from the earlier empires to the south. At some time about 1680 these formed a confederation based upon Kumasi in the very centre of the forest region, astride the economic watershed between trade routes running to the north and the south. Asante gathered in the political experience of almost every state founded among the Akan peoples. The founding ruler (Asantehene), Osei Tutu, had been educated at the courts of both Denkyira and Akwamu. His chief priest, his military leaders and his fire-arms all accompanied him from Akwamu. Starting as a tributary of Denkyira, Asante fought a war of independence between 1698 and 1701, which left it in control of the main gold-bearing regions. From there it went from strength to strength. By 1724 it had reached the savanna to the north. In 1741–2 it conquered Akim, which had already super-seded an exhausted Akwamu. Its lands thus reached the eastern seaboard. In 1744–5 its northern armies defeated and made tributary the large savanna states of Gonja and Dagomba. Here the musketmen of the forest triumphed over the armoured cavalry of the Muslim Sudan. It was a turning-point in West African history.

During the second half of the eighteenth century Asante consoli-dated its vast and destructive conquests into one of the largest and most sophisticated imperial systems ever constructed without the aid of literate skills. It was based upon a careful distinction between a highly centralised metropolitan region, of which the population was deliberately built up into a dominating position by forced deporta-tions from the conquered areas, and an outer circle of dependent provinces held under strict military and fiscal control. A network of well-kept roads radiated from the capital, with designated resting-places for the caravans passing to and fro on military, commercial and diplomatic business. All high officials were required to present them-selves regularly at the royal court, and something like a regular career structure emerged in the army and the civil service. In 1819 a proud Asantehene told a European visitor that it was not his practice to make war 'to catch slaves in the bush like a thief'. This remark reflected a state of satiety in which Asante had long ceased to feel the need of territorial expansion. There was by then no problem about the dis-posal of war captives, and the country's mineral wealth sufficed for its necessary purchases of foreign arms. Asante, like other full-grown West African empires, had almost ceased to be a slave-trading power. Yet, without the Atlantic slave-trade of the eighteenth century, Asante might never have emerged from the obscurity of its forest heartland.

We have seen that in western West Africa, with its immense stretch of coastline curving round from the Senegal to the Volta, the opening of the Atlantic was a factor of great significance in causing the peoples who lived within 200 or 300 kilometres of the ocean to realign their economic and political systems away from the old centres of power in the savanna belt and towards the opportunities offered by the new maritime contacts with the outside world. Even so, the process was a slow one. The trans-Saharan routes remained open, and the cultural and religious ties with the Islamic world remained paramount. In eastern West Africa, from the Volta to the Cameroun highlands, the coastline was much shorter in relation to the hinterland. Moreover, although the ocean trade, as it developed, greatly affected the lives of some of the southernmost peoples, there were others living quite close to the coast who were scarcely affected by it until after the end of our period. In the region as a whole, societies were stabler and more self-sufficient than in the west. In so far as there was a tendency towards consolidation into larger political units, particularly in the southern savanna and along the fringes of the forest, the momentum for it was provided mainly by the southward spread of cavalry warfare and social stratification already developed in the north. Even at the very end of our period, it was a movement of Islamic reform and reorganisation originating in the northern savanna which carried the religon of the Prophet across the southern savanna and deep into parts of the forest belt.

THE SOUTHERN PEOPLES AND THE ATLANTIC TRADE

The first of the southern peoples to encounter the new influences from the outside world were the Edo of Benin and their waterside neighbours, the Itsekiri and the Ijo. This was in the third quarter of the fifteenth century, at a time when Benin had already enjoyed a long history as a compact city state in the forest region to the west of the Niger delta, and when it had already begun to embark upon a course of military conquest which was to make it, by the end of the sixteenth century, the overlord of all the southern Edo, as well as of many of the eastern Yoruba and the western Igbo. The origins of the process are intriguing but obscure. At a time of dissension among the ruling factions in the thirteenth century, the city state had accepted a dynasty from Ife, traditionally the most ancient and ritually prestigious of the Yoruba cities, but this did not at once set Benin on the road to expansion. The new dynasty – despite its possession of state swords, a stable of stall-fed horses for use on ceremonial occasions and a guild of royal brass-casters able to portray its gods and heroes in a manner fitting for the palace shrines – took some two centuries to establish its ascendancy in the capital city. It was only in the mid-fifteenth century, a mere generation before the arrival of the Portuguese, that the throne was seized by a usurper, Eware, who became the first great conquering Oba, subjecting the Yoruba and Igbo towns in a wide circle to the north of Benin City. Alan Ryder, the historian of Benin, puts forward the interesting suggestion that Eware was responding to a general enlargement of scale that was taking place among the great states of the region – especially in Igala and Nupe.[1] At all events, during Eware's reign Benin developed something like a standing army, and its metropolitan area became a regular recipient of war captives, which transformed the character of the state. The established citizens became courtiers and warriors, traders and skilled craftsmen, commanding large numbers of slaves, who grew the food and carried it to the metropolis, and who transported the raw materials and the finished products of the important regional trade. When the Portuguese reached the Gold Coast, they found that cloth, and probably also slaves, were already being imported there from Benin, and it is likely that the Akan chiefs, anxious to buy more slaves to dig for gold, suggested that the Portuguese with their superior shipping should supplement the canoe traffic passing perilously through the creeks and coastal waters.

The Portuguese reached Benin in 1486, during the reign of Eware's son, Ozolua. By this time they were planning to colonise and establish sugar plantations on the uninhabited islands of São Tomé and Principe, so their interest in a local supply of slaves was increased. Ozolua, a conqueror like his father, welcomed the newcomers, selling them slaves and cloth for the coastal trade, and peppers and a little ivory for the European market, in exchange for copper and brass for his metal industries, coral for his own ceremonial dress, and glass beads and European textiles with which to reward his aristocracy. Individual Portuguese accompanied the Oba on his military expeditions and excited his interest in fire-arms. It was explained to him that these

[1] *Benin and the Europeans 1445–1897* (London, 1969), p. 8.

TUAREG

TUAREG

Songhay expansi

Tondibi

Gao

SONGHAY

Timbuktu

Kukya

S
exp

Mossi

Y A T E N G A

M O S S I P E O P L E

WAGADUGU

Niger

Jenne

Segu

Dyula

GURMA

Bobo-Dioulasso

Hausa

Kankan

White Volta

DAGOMBA

Kong

Dyula

S   l   a   v   e   n   g

r   Black Volta   i   d   Yendi

GONJA

Dyula

Begho

Mono

DAHOMEY

Abo

Ali

Asante expansion

Tafo

AJ

Kumasi

Wydah

ASANTE

Volta

Ewe

AKAN

Tano

DENKYIRA

AKWAMU

AKWAPIM

Accra

Pra

FANTE

Axim

Elmina

Cape Coast

PORTUGUESE, LATE 15TH–16TH C.

DUTCH, ENGLISH AND FRENCH, 17TH C.

- - - - -   Portuguese maritime slave routes

- - - -   Trade routes

····   Dutch, English and French maritime slave-trading

───   Territorial expansion

ASANTE   States or kingdoms

───   Slave-raiding and slave-trade routes

AKAN   Ewe   Peoples

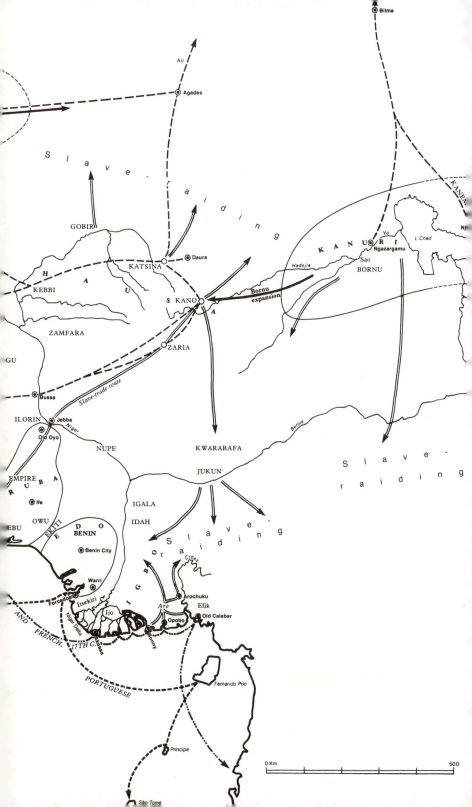

weapons could only be supplied to Christian allies of the Portuguese, and in 1514 he sent an embassy to Lisbon requesting both clergy and cannon. King Manuel sent the clergy and a letter promising that

When we see that you have embraced the teachings of Christianity like a good and faithful Christian, there will be nothing in our realms with which we shall not be glad to favour you, whether it be arms or cannon and all other weapons of war for use against your enemies; of such things we have a great store, as your ambassador Dom Jorje will inform you.[2]

But it was not to be. The priests sickened and soon withdrew. Ozolua died unbaptised, and his successor, Esigie, continued to expand the frontiers of Benin without European arms but with conspicuous success, defeating the great inland state of Igala and carrying his conquests westward along the coastal lagoons to the island of Lagos. As Benin grew more powerful, it also grew more indifferent to the European trade. Higher prices were demanded for slaves, and the sale of male captives was forbidden from the metropolitan districts. The Portuguese, now firmly established on São Tomé and Principe, found it easier to do business with the peripheral regions, especially those to the east around the Niger Delta, where the military outreach of Benin was proliferating under a series of Edo princelings who were founding little states among the western Igbo too remote to be controlled from the metropolis.

Throughout the Delta region the coastline was masked by a belt of swamp and mangrove, intricately dissected by rivers and lagoons. Even the patches of dry land were sterile and uncultivable, and the Ijo inhabitants of the coast had from time immemorial lived by fishing and by boiling salt, trading the produce of the brackish waters for the oil, yams, meat and iron tools of the Igbo people of the lush, forested interior. Even the earliest of the Portuguese accounts, that of Pereira in 1505, describes the great canoes, six feet wide in the beam and large enough to carry eighty men, which came down the rivers from 400 to 500 kilometres inland, bringing vegetables, cows, goats, sheep and slaves. 'They sell all this to the natives of the village [in this case probably Bonny] for salt, and our ships buy these things for copper bracelets, which are here prized more than brass ones, a slave being sold for eight or ten of such bracelets.'[3] Such was the system already established that it needed only enlargement to meet the needs of the Atlantic traders as they came to the Delta in greater and greater

[2] Cited in ibid., p. 47.

96   [3] T. Hodgkin, *Nigerian Perspectives*, 2nd edn (London, 1975), p. 123.

numbers. There can be little doubt that the military pressure of Benin upon the western Igbo, and that of Igala on those living further to the north, must have fuelled the flow of captives, especially during the sixteenth and early seventeenth centuries. However, it is certain that the decentralised pattern of Igbo society itself was also favourable to the trade in men. Living in stockaded villages amid their forest plantations, communities of three to five thousand people regarded even their closest neighbours as foreigners. Kidnapping of individuals by one community from another was a recognised hazard of life. Only a few specialists – smiths, diviners and long-distance traders – could travel abroad with reasonable security, and it was through such professional networks that kidnapped slaves passed into the international trading circuit.

So long as the Portuguese monopoly lasted, the trade seems to have been limited to the rivers actually connecting with the main Niger, roughly from Akassa to Bonny, and the number of slaves exported each year was probably less than 5,000. With the advent of Dutch and British traders in the later seventeenth century, however, the system was extended eastwards to the Cross River, where the Efik of Old Calabar assumed the role of middlemen played further west by the Ijo. The slaves exported down the Cross River were still mostly Igbo, and here kidnapping reached its most highly organised form under the priests of an oracular cult based at Arochuku, on the Igbo–Efik border. During the eighteenth century Aro priests and their henchmen, armed now with guns, spread out widely over eastern and central Igboland and became the main inland suppliers of slaves to all the ports from Old Calabar to Bonny. It may be that during this century alone the Igbo sold nearly a million of their own people into slavery – none of them directly to Europeans, but to African middlemen who organised overland and river transport and who brought back into the interior imports that were genuinely valued in exchange: iron, copper, hardware and cloth. Probably no Igbo village community would have sold its own members for such commodities, but members of other village communities were seen in a wholly different light. The Igbo in fact behaved like a vast assembly of tiny nations. On this premiss, their participation in the trade was no more immoral than that of larger nations which raided their weaker neighbours. Nevertheless, the practical effect was to make Igboland a more prolific and enduring source of slaves than any other comparable area of Africa.

To the west of Benin, the so-called 'Slave Coast', extending from Lagos to the Volta, acquired its evil name only in the late seventeenth century. Here, as every modern air traveller between Lagos and Accra can observe, the coastline is a narrow beach, pounded by heavy surf on one side and separated from the mainland by a wide stretch of marsh and lagoon on the other. Rivers flow to the lagoon, which empties into the sea only at Lagos. Elsewhere ships must ride at anchor and small boats must face the perils of the surf. It is no wonder that the Portuguese sailed by, noting that it was a coast where there was no business to be done. Behind the lagoon, however, lay a unique region of coastal West Africa, where for meteorological reasons there was a break in the forest line and the savanna reached down to the coast. Here was the home of the Ewe and Aja peoples, the former living in independent village communities like the Igbo, the latter just beginning to experience the more ambitious state-building activities of small dynasties on the western Yoruba pattern.

As we saw in Chapter 6, the isolation of the Ewe was brutally shattered by the eastward conquests of the Akan state of Akwamu in the 1670s and 80s, when thousands of captives were sold on the beaches of every fishing village from the Volta to Whydah. During the eighteenth century the Ewe passed into the raiding sphere of Asante, and many Ewe captives were resettled in the heartlands of the empire around Kumasi. Meanwhile, the Aja were being drawn into a more direct and long-lasting connection with the Atlantic trade, most of which passed across the beaches of Allada and Whydah. Here, at least three new factors came into play almost simultaneously. The first was the Akwamu expansion, the captives from which were exported through the Aja coastal states. The second was the expansion from the north-east of the great Yoruba state of Oyo, which swept with its newly developed cavalry forces around the western fringes of the Nigerian forest belt, conquering the Egba and Egbado Yoruba and reaching the coast between Badagri and Porto Novo, on the eastern frontier of Ajaland. The third factor was the emergence, between the two great powers of Akwamu and Oyo, of the inland Aja state of Dahomey. In origin no more than an offshoot from the coastal state of Allada – a branch of the ruling dynasty, which set out with a few hundred followers to conquer the stateless inhabitants of the Abomey plateau – Dahomey developed along centralised, military lines, and by the late seventeenth century was in command of the slave-raiding areas in the hinterland of the coastal states. Though itself frequently raided by the cavalry forces of Oyo, it was able to keep its inland autonomy by paying tribute when necessary, and even to expand its territory to the coast by conquering Allada and Whydah between 1724 and 1727. As in the Akan region further to the west, it was the enlargement of the successful military states at the expense of their weaker neighbours that supplied the tragic flow of captives to the seacoast and the New World. During the period of almost continuous warfare from 1680 till about 1730 the export of slaves through Allada and Whydah reached some 20,000 slaves a year. Thereafter, with a single, strong power in control of the beaches, the trade became a royal monopoly, and the supply fell to a quarter of its previous level as Dahomey, having satisfied its territorial ambitions, was concerned only to maintain supplies of European fire-arms and court luxuries and to provide the quota of these items required for its tribute payments to Oyo. It is significant that in the Dahomean savanna the cavalry of Oyo was able to maintain its ascendancy over the imported musket.

CITIES AND STATES OF THE SOUTHERN SAVANNA

Behind the coastal belt and its immediate hinterland lay a wide stretch of open or lightly wooded country which, taken together with its forest fringes to the south and the forest galleries along its rivers, constituted the most varied and the best-endowed environment of eastern West Africa. Here were sufficient rain for yams and oil-palms and sufficient sunlight for cereals and cotton. Here were dense populations with an ancient tradition of urban settlement. Towns might be quite small, but they were the centres of religious and political life, and also of varied and highly specialised industries: weaving and dyeing, woodwork and carving, metalwork and leatherwork, in places even glass-founding and brass-casting. Most extended families had an urban base, from which some of their members went out to cultivate the surrounding farmlands at certain seasons. Towns were defended against the attacks of their neighbours by mud walls and deep ditches. Nevertheless, the system of exchange was highly developed, with regular markets and a currency based on sea-shells described by Pereira as somewhat larger than those in use in the contemporary Kongo kingdom – 'They use them to buy everything, and he who has most is richest.'[4]

The origins of this urban culture certainly go back to the early centuries of the present millennium and may have been influenced by the civilisation of early Chadic-speaking communities in pre-Islamic Hausaland or Bornu. The intermediate stage, involving connections with the long-distance trading system of the western Sudan, probably dated from the eastward expansion of the Dyula trade in the

[4] Ibid., p. 121.

fourteenth century. A third phase, which seems to have predominated around the beginning of our period, was the southward spread of cavalry warfare and slave-raiding from the Hausa region immediately to the north. In the Kano Chronicle we see the kings of the early fifteenth century engaged in perennial slave-raiding with the Kwararafa, or Jukun, of the Benue valley, in which the Hausa supplied horses and armour to the Jukun in exchange for slaves captured by the Jukun still further to the south. Zaria at the same period seems to have been involved in a similar exchange with the Nupe. The theatre of cavalry warfare was moving south. In the late fifteenth century Nupe was being reorganised into an aggressive, centralised state by a new dynasty from Igala, itself already a powerful state dominating the region to the south of the Benue–Niger confluence. Igala, as we have seen, was already pressing upon northern Igboland, and by the early sixteenth century was engaged in major warfare with Benin. Meanwhile, under its new dynasty, Nupe was raiding into Yorubaland and, some time around 1535, actually occupied the northern Yoruba state of Oyo, forcing its dynasty to evacuate the capital and take refuge in the neighbouring Bariba state of Borgu. The exile lasted some eighty years, and was followed by a reconquest in which horses and cavalry techniques, and no doubt many other northern influences acquired in Borgu, were applied to the reconstruction of a new, centralised and expansive Oyo state, which was destined in the seventeenth and eighteenth centuries to incorporate or make tributary all the forest-free parts of Yoruba and Ajaland.

In their origins all of these important developments were quite independent of the activities of Europeans on the Atlantic coast. Here and there, as we have seen, there are indications that captives taken in the later and more peripheral stages of these wars were exported overseas, but it would seem that the main impetus of conquest was only incidentally concerned with the slave-trade in any external direction. The new cavalry forces were dependent on the northern savanna for a continuous supply of horses, and these were no doubt purchased mainly with slaves. The main object of the new states, however, was to produce concentrations of wealth and power by imposing taxation and tribute over wide areas, and also by the forced transfer of population into the neighbourhood of the new metropoles for agricultural and industrial as well as military reasons. It had long been the practice of the great Hausa city states to settle communities of slaves in agricultural villages around the urban areas. Benin strictly limited the sale of slaves from its metropolitan region to Europeans, because their labour was needed at home. The compulsory resettlement on somewhat more privileged terms of skilled men, especially blacksmiths, from conquered communities had been practised by many African states, including the empires of the western Sudan. Again, at the highest level, slaves, and especially eunuchs, often became the intimate servants and trusted officials of courts and kings, since they lacked family connections which could lead to a conflict of loyalties. More generally, within West African societies the slave status of one generation of captives slid easily into a mere difference of class or caste among their descendants. Servile origins were long remembered, but seldom alluded to. It was taken for granted that the descendants of forced migrants would assume, for military purposes, the patriotism of their new countries.

Unfortunately, too little is known of the traditional history of most of the southern savanna states for us to appreciate fully the significance of the enlargement of scale that took place in our period. In Benin it is clear that the spread of cavalry warfare cannot have been a serious factor, since horses were almost useless in a forest environment. Here, as also in Igala, competition for control of the developing trade of the Niger waterway may have been the critical issue. In Kwararafa and Nupe, the military collection of tribute from a large number of very small, formerly independent city states seems to have been the dominant theme. And the same motive can be seen much more clearly in Yorubaland, where an older centre of wealth and prestige based in the forest margin was forced into decline by the competition of a new centre based far out in the savanna, in the northernmost corner of the language area, with significantly fewer natural resources – the neighbourhood of Old Oyo is today practically uninhabited. The older system was one of city states acknowledging the historical and religious pre-eminence of Ife, but each practising a real autonomy, and this system continued through our period in those states, such as Ife itself, Ekiti, Owu and Ijebu, which enjoyed the protection of the forest. The new system was based squarely on the military hegemony of Oyo, which demanded regular tribute from all within reach of its powerful armies. This hegemony was built up entirely within the seventeenth and eighteenth centuries. It consisted of four concentric areas: first, the metropolitan area, which would have corresponded more or less with the ancient city state as it existed before the Nupe conquest; second, the immediately neighbouring Yoruba states, the first to be conquered by Oyo and situated so close that their traditional rulers could be recognised as brother kings; third, a peripheral Yoruba region situated to the southwest in Egba and Egbado, where Oyo suzerainty was enforced by resident commissioners (*ajele*); and fourth, an outer periphery, mostly in Aja country, from which tribute was exacted under the threat of far-flung military expeditions. The system reached its peak around the middle of the eighteenth century, when even so strong a dependency as the kingdom of Dahomey was regular in its tribute payments. During the later eighteenth century the army was neglected, perhaps, as Akinjogbin suggests, because the rulers had found an easier road to wealth by acting as middlemen in a newly developed long-distance slave-trade between Hausaland and the Atlantic coast, which crossed the Niger at Jebba and reached the sea at Porto Novo on the Lagos lagoon. In the longer term, this was to prove a disastrous change of emphasis, when the Oyo empire broke up under the impact of the Fulbe jihad in the early nineteenth century.

For most of our period the states of the southern savanna remained very little influenced by Islam. The *alafins* of Oyo, the *etsus* of Nupe, the *attas* of Igala, the *obas* of Benin, and the *akus* of Kwararafa were all, in ceremonial and ritual matters, old-style 'divine kings' – not in the sense that they enjoyed absolute powers, but in the sense that they were regarded as the principal points of contact with the unseen world. They inhabited the innermost courtyards of palace cities, surrounded by hundreds of wives and thousands of officials and slave servants. They ate alone. They were seen in public once or twice a year. They were subject to ritual murder or suicide. They were buried together with sacrificial victims. In all these ways, and in everything implied by them, the states of the southern savanna were two or three centuries behind those of the north. They were less aware of the outside world. They were less adaptable to change. Nevertheless, when these systems at last yielded, it was, with the exception of Benin, to influences from the Muslim north and not to any emanations from the Atlantic trading frontier to the south.

ISLAMIC STATES OF THE NORTHERN SAVANNA

To the north of Borgu, Nupe and Kwararafa there stretched the open lands of the northern savanna, merging with the desert in the north, and occupied at the beginning of our period almost exclusively by Chadic-speaking peoples – in the west and centre the Hausa, in the east a series of smaller groups known collectively as the Sao, of whom the Budduma and the Kotoko are today the main survivors. All these were characteristically dwellers in walled settlements, which grew by agglomeration into towns. However, it was only in central Hausaland that a handful of such towns – Kano, Katsina, Zaria (Zazzau), Daura and Gobir – had grown into metropolitan cities, each governing and taxing the smaller settlements within a radius of 50 or 60 kilometres, waging occasional warfare against each other and conducting more regular slave-raids into the peripheral areas, especially towards the south. With slave settlers available for agricultural production, urban industries had developed, and in the fourteenth century Dyula traders from southern Mali, accompanied by Islamic teachers, had entered the region from the west. In the fifteenth century came regular camel caravans from the north, through Aïr, bringing salt from Bilma, horses from Barbary, swords and coats of mail from Europe, and the all-important idea of heavy-armed cavalry warfare from the Turkish armies of the Middle East. It was with application of this new military technology that the Hausa cities began to raid deep into the southern savanna, augmenting their own populations with a large servile class and supplying the needs of the trans-Saharan trade. It was the south-ward spread of this technology that was in turn to be the main cause of the political reorganisation of the southern savanna which we have just examined.

The great difference between the city states of Hausaland and the new centres of power in the southern savanna was that in Hausaland political and economic development went hand in hand with the conversion of the ruling classes to Islam. This was an influence which came with the Dyula traders from the west, and it came from Mali rather than Songhay. Even at the material level, it was very likely under Dyula influence that the Hausa developed their excellence in industries like weaving, dyeing and leatherwork, for one of the first signs of grace expected in Muslim converts was that they should distinguish themselves from 'naked pagans' by the decency and clean-liness of their dress. So the agricultural slave villages were put to growing cotton and indigo, and Hausa robes and sandals were loaded on to the long-distance caravans. More important, however, was the influence of Islam on law and government, with the balancing of the military caste by one composed of clerics, many of them immigrants attracted by the patronage of the rulers, with their knowledge of distant countries, their literacy and their expertise in an international system of law and justice. The rulers of Katsina, Kano and Zaria all became converts to Islam during the middle years of the fifteenth century. Muhammad Rumfa, *sarki* of Kano from 1463 till 1499, is remembered in the Kano Chronicle as the great *mujaddid*, defender of the faith, who sought the advice of the celebrated jurist al-Maghili of Tuat in converting the old Hausa institutions of kingship into those of a Muslim sultanate. Under its first Muslim rulers Katsina became for a time a veritable holy city, the *ribat* of Hausaland, a fortified place of devotion and study, attracting holy men and scholars from Egypt and North Africa.

These growing Islamic connections probably helped Hausaland to keep its independence when, in the sixteenth century, it faced inter-ference from the great Muslim powers to the west and the east. The earliest incursion came from Songhay, probably in 1515, when the Askiya Muhammad led a marauding expedition through the ter-ritories of Zaria, Katsina, Kano and Gobir, and on to the capital of the Aïr Tuareg at Agades. The motive seems to have been booty rather than conquest (see Chapter 6, p. 81), but the kings of Zaria, Katsina and Gobir all lost their lives, and it was said that as many as half of their subjects were marched away into slavery. Kano, however, was able to withstand a siege for long enough to make terms. And at the end of the campaign Muhammad's western Hausa allies, disappointed with their share of the booty, broke off the Songhay connection and built up the city state of Kebbi on the central Hausa pattern, which was henceforward to prove an effective bastion against Songhay attacks.

Much more significant was the threat to Hausa independence which came from the east, from Bornu. This was no simple matter of long-distance raiding. It led to the permanent occupation and settle-ment of eastern Hausaland and the neighbouring Chadic-speaking territories by Kanuri people from the ancient empire of Kanem to the north-east of Lake Chad. In its origins, this was an act of retreat by the Magumi dynasty of Kanem from the breakdown of its authority in the east (see Chapter 8, p. 109). At some point in the 1390s Mai 'Umar ibn Idris abandoned the former capital at Njimi, and in the words of the traditional king-list, 'He took out his armies and all his possessions and his people into Kaga, and down to this day none of our rulers have ever returned to Kanem to re-establish their residence there.'[5] How-ever, resistance to the newcomers by the Chadic-speaking peoples of Bornu was fierce and prolonged. Four successive *Mais* died fighting against the Sao, and it was not until the last quarter of the fifteenth century that conditions were settled enough to permit the building of a new capital at Ngazargamu, some 200 kilometres up the River Yo from its mouth on the north-west shores of Lake Chad.

In the early sixteenth century Leo Africanus painted the picture of Bornu as a military state, depending for its revenues on the slaves brought in by the annual dry-season campaigns of its 3,000 armoured knights, who were accompanied to war by vast numbers of con-

---

[5] Dierk Lange, *Le diwan des sultans du [Kanem–] Bornu: chronologie et histoire d'un royaume africain* (Wiesbaden, 1977), p. 76.

scripted peasants armed with spears and bows. The regular slaving grounds were in Sao territory to the south of Lake Chad. However, a strong military power with few resources and no industries could not overlook the attractions of booty and tribute that might be taken from the prosperous city states of Hausaland. Kano, only 400 kilometres up the Hadejia valley from Ngazargamu, was well within range and suffered several attacks. On one occasion, around 1561, the Bornu army penetrated as far west as Kebbi, almost 900 kilometres from its base. The general impression that emerges of these campaigns is that the Hausa cities themselves survived because of their defensive walls, but also perhaps because their inhabitants were fellow Muslims. The pagans of the countryside, however, especially those of the dependent slave villages, were fair game for the Bornu soldiery. The Hausa states were not extinguished, but they were gravely weakened, so that, for example, by the early seventeenth century the southern savanna state of Kwararafa was daring to mount expeditions against Kano, a situation that would have been unthinkable a hundred years earlier.

Bornu reached the peak of its power and prestige between the middle of the sixteenth and the end of the seventeenth century. Although most of Kanem remained independent under the Bulala dynasty, the western part of the country around the old capital at Njimi had been reconquered, and with it control of the great caravan route to the north, as far as the salt-mines of Bilma. Bornu was thus the neighbour of Ottoman Tripoli, and it was in regular diplomatic touch with Morocco and Egypt. After the break-up of Songhay following the Moorish conquest, Bornu was probably the most powerful state in Black Africa. Unlike the Askiyas of Songhay, the Mais of Bornu had been wise enough to initiate the slave bodyguard, which was the kernel of their infantry, in the use of fire-arms. These were imported from Tripoli (see Chapter 5, p. 72) along with 'Turkish' military instructors by Mai Idris Aloma (?1569–1600), whose biographer classed fire-arms high among the benefits which God in his bounty had conferred upon the sultan. They were probably not of much importance in the little wars against weaker neighbours by which Bornu made its living. However, they strengthened the monarchy in its relations with its own powerful subjects, and their greatest significance was perhaps as a deterrent against long-distance adventures like that of Morocco in Songhay. Against an army accustomed to the sight and sound of fire-arms, a surprise victory like that of Tondibi would have been impossible.

The ascendancy of Bornu established by Idris Aloma continued through most of the seventeenth century. Essentially it consisted in the military power to exact tribute from the neighbouring states, but it was reflected also in a cultural and religious hegemony which resulted from a closer relationship with the central currents of Islam. Hausaland had been converted from the west, and remained, especially after the fall of Songhay and the decline of Timbuktu, on the periphery of an outer province of the faith. Its rulers did not go on pilgrimage or surround themselves with scholars and theologians. In Hausaland the most active clerics were increasingly to be found among the Fulbe nomads, who did not belong to the official establishment and would one day take the lead in overthrowing it. The Islam of Bornu had in contrast come from Kanem, where it had been the religion of the state since the eleventh century. In Bornu it was thus the religion of the Kanuri, the conquering immigrants, who saw themselves as warriors of the faith in a pagan land. There had been a long tradition of royal pilgrimages in Kanem which, following the tribulations of the conquest, reasserted itself in Bornu. Idris Aloma returned from pilgrimage to build mosques of brick in the principal towns of his kingdom, and to appoint religious judges (*qa'ids*) to administer justice according to the *shari'a* law. His grandson, Mai 'Ali, who reigned in the later seventeenth century, made three pilgrimages, and was accompanied on each by thousands of his subjects. Between his many military campaigns he presided over a court famous for the high standard of its legal and theological disputations.

During the eighteenth century the military ascendancy of Bornu slowly faded, although the religious ascendancy survived. There were no dramatic defeats. Armies could still be sent to the walls of Kano, as of old, but the actively developing parts of Hausaland were now in the west, in Zamfara and Gobir, and they were beyond the effective range of Bornu – as were their trade routes, which passed northwards through western Aïr and Agades. It was in the desert marches of northern Gobir that the Fulbe leader, Usuman dan Fodio, in 1804 launched his great jihad for the overthrow of the Hausa states. The kings of central Hausaland – Katsina, Zaria and Kano – then appealed for help to their overlord the Mai of Bornu, who was by then blind and senile and unable to take decisive action even against the Fulbe rebels of his own country. Nevertheless, the Fulbe did not conquer Bornu, which was saved by a warrior cleric from Kanem, Muhammad al-Amin al-Kanemi, who proved himself a match for Usuman dan Fodio. A full circle thus turned in Africa's most ancient empire, with Kanem coming to the rescue of Bornu.

8 From the Niger to the Nile

Until the eve of our period the vast region lying between the Niger drainage system and that of the upper Nile remained the most isolated section of the whole Sudanic belt. Its main geographical feature was the inland basin of Lake Chad, which stretched in a great plain for more than a thousand kilometres to the east of the lake. Bounded by the Tibesti massif in the north, by the highlands of Ennedi and Darfur in the east and by the Ubangi–Shari watershed in the south, it had no natural line of communication with any part of the outside world. Save for the route through Kanem to the Fezzan, the desert crossings to the north were exceptionally severe. To the east, the Christian kingdoms on the upper Nile posed until the fourteenth century an effective barrier to migration, trade or pilgrimage routes passing south of the desert.

In these circumstances it was natural that the external relations of the region should have developed mainly through Kanem, with the principal line of access running north-westwards through Kawar to the Fezzan. Here, as elsewhere, the most essential resource lacking from the Sudanic latitudes was salt, of which a copious supply existed at Bilma in Kawar. The earliest descriptions we have of the region show Zaghawa camel-breeders trading salt for slaves with Kanem on the one hand and with Ennedi and Darfur on the other. As the kingdom of Kanem expanded from the eleventh century onwards, it embraced much of the northern half of the Chad basin with its Nilo-Saharan-speaking peoples like the Teda and the Daza, but made comparatively little impact on the Central Sudanic-speakers like the Sara and the Bagirmi who inhabited the marshy country further to the south. Of the Central Sudanic-speakers only the Kuka living around Lake Fitri had a ruling group, the Bulala, which might have come from Kanem.

Further to the east, in the mountains of the Chad–Nile watershed, linguistically unclassified, and perhaps very ancient, populations, like the Maba of Wadai and the Fur of Jabal Marra, lived in total independence of Kanem, with Eastern Sudanic-speakers like the Daju in their midst and to the south. In all these eastern and southern parts of the region the influence of Islam was at the beginning of our period still

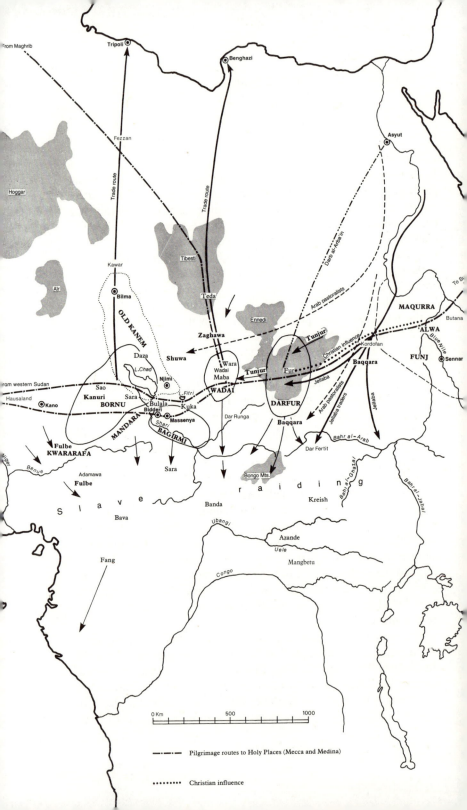

From Maghrib

Tripoli

Benghazi

Asyut

Fezzan

Trade route

Trade route

Hoggar

Air

Kawar

Bilma

Tibesti

OLD KANEM

Teda

Ennedi

Zaghawa

Daza

Shuwa

L. Chad

Njimi

Wara

Wadai

Maba

WADAI

Tunjur

Tunjur

Fur

Christian influence

Darb al-Arba'in

Arab pastoralists

MAQURRA

To Su

Butana

ALWA

Blue Nile

FUNJ

Sennar

Kordofan

Baqqara

from western Sudan

Hausaland

Kano

Sao

Kanuri

BORNU

Sara

L. Fitri

Kuka

Bulala

Bidderi

DARFUR

Jellaba

Jellaba traders

Arab pastoralists

MANDARA

Massenya

BAGIRMI

Shari

Dar Runga

Baqqara

Dar Fertit

Bahr al-Arab

Jellaba

Fulbe

KWARARAFA

Niger

Benue

Adamawa

Fulbe

Sara

Bongo Mts.

s l a v e

r a i d i n g

Bahr al-Ghazal

Bahr al-Jabal

Bava

Banda

Kreish

Fang

Ubangi

Uele

Azande

Mangbetu

Congo

0 Km   500   1000

quite negligible. At least in Darfur, and possibly still further to the west, there may have been outposts of Nubian Christianity: at all events the Christian kingdom of 'Alwa was probably felt as a closer neighbour than the Muslim state of Kanem.

THE COMING OF THE ARABS

The situation in the region was, however, radically changed by the fall of the Christian kingdoms on the Nile. As we saw in Chapter 3 (pp. 36–8), the Arab penetration of the northern kingdom of Nubia began in the late thirteenth century. By the mid-fourteenth century bedouin Arabs had bypassed the Dongola reach and spread across northern Kordofan and Darfur into the Chad basin. In 1391 Mai Abu Amr Uthman of Bornu wrote to Sultan Barquq of Egypt complaining of the devastation committed by these Arab migrants in the old centre of his kingdom, in Kanem. Without doubt, the arrival of these newcomers had upset the whole pre-existing balance of power around Kanem's eastern frontier. In the highlands of Darfur and Wadai warlike Arab pastoralists had settled in pockets between the agricultural Daju, Fur and Maba. Further west, they had made common cause with the Bulala and Kuka around Lake Fitri, joining them in raids against Kanem, which had caused the retreat of the Kanem dynasty west-wards into Bornu. In the early sixteenth century Leo Africanus reported the existence, to the east of Bornu, of a large and powerful kingdom of 'Gaoga', the ruler of which traded directly with Egypt, sending slaves and ivory northwards in exchange for horses, arms and armour. This account is best understood as referring to a greatly expanded kingdom of the Kuka (Gaoga) and Bulala during the cen-tury following the Arab penetration of Kordofan, Darfur and the Chad basin. Certainly, we know that the fifteenth- and sixteenth-century kings of Bornu were constantly at war with the Bulala, by now a strong cavalry power which had occupied much of the territory of old Kanem. The special interest of Leo's account is the implication that the Bulala kingdom was a major slave-raiding state with a direct trans-Saharan link to Mamluk Egypt, running in parallel with Bornu's route to the Fezzan. If so, the Arab breakthrough in Nubia must be seen as the precursor of a whole new range of impetus in slave-raiding and empire-building in the region to the east of Lake Chad.

In Darfur and Wadai, the Arab migrations of the mid-fourteenth century were accompanied by the advent of new ruling groups called Tunjur, who displaced earlier dynasties of Eastern Sudanic Daju

15 From the Niger to the Nile (1): the savanna lands

origin. The Tunjur were outsiders, Arabic-speakers yet not Muslims, claiming a relationship with the bedouin Arab tribe of the Banu Hillal, yet more probably connected with the veil-wearing, eastern Berber camel-nomads and horsemen of northern Kordofan and Darfur, who had lived close enough to the Arabs to have adopted their language, though not yet their religion. At all events, it is clear that the raison d'être of the Tunjur hegemony in Darfur and Wadai was the long-distance slave-trade with Egypt. The headquarters of both states were established at the head of new desert routes to the north-east, which converged into the famous Darb al-Arba'in, or Forty Days' Road, leading to Upper Egypt via the oases of Atrun and Kharga. At the same time, both capitals were situated on the northern edge of well-populated highland country, with rich volcanic soil irrigated by streams and rivers draining south-westwards to the Shari and south-eastwards to the Bahr al-Ghazal. The sites associated with the Tunjur, especially those at Uri in Darfur and Kadama in Wadai, were walled citadels built in stone or brick, with 'audience platforms' prominent in their central enclosures. The Tunjur practised a form of ritual kingship which they may have inherited from their Daju predecessors, and much of which we know survived into later, Muslim times. From their immediate Fur and Maba subjects they probably demanded little but tribute in the shape of labour, food and drink for their capitals and their standing troops. But every year the supplies of horses and armour came south from Egypt, and every year in the dry season they were employed in long-distance raiding against the less well-defended populations further to the south. It was the pattern long familiar from Kanem, but now enacted later in time and on a more easterly stage.

Somewhere around the middle of the sixteenth century the Bulala began to be eclipsed by the rising power of a new state, that of the Central Sudanic-speaking Bagirmi, with its capital at Massenya, some 250 kilometres to the south-west of Lake Fitri, on a tributary of the Shari. Along with Wadai and Darfur, Bagirmi was henceforward in the front line of cavalry states pressing southwards year by year on the less organised Central Sudanic and Eastern Nigritic peoples of northern Cameroun, southern Tchad and the Central African Republic. On its western frontier it also raided the Chadic-speaking areas to the south of Bornu, thus attracting on occasion Bornu armies into its own territory. In general, however, it is clear that the trade of Bagirmi followed the same lines as that of the Bulala kingdom, either north-wards to the Fezzan or north-eastwards to Egypt. The Shuwa Arabs of the central Chad basin, who had played so important a role in the fifteenth-century expansion of the Bulala kingdom, were probably no less influential in the emergence of Bagirmi.

THE ACCEPTANCE OF ISLAM

If the first result of the Arab breakthrough into northern Central Africa was the establishment of direct trade with Egypt fed by the opening of a new slave-raiding frontier from Darfur to Bagirmi, the second result, which followed about a century after the first, consisted in the cultural integration of the region with the rest of Muslim Africa. Whereas the first development was primarily based on a traffic running north and south, the second was much more concerned with communications and influences running east and west. In this case the vital external event was not so much the fall of Christian Nubia as the emergence during the early sixteenth century of the strong Muslim kingdom of the Funj (see pp. 39–41) in its place. For West African Muslims, particularly for the poor who needed to work their passage by farm labour or the exercise of a craft, the existence of a Muslim state in the Nilotic Sudan created the possibility of making the pilgrimage without crossing the Sahara. On the other hand, to Muslims of the Maghrib, accustomed to desert travel and the care of camels, the rise of the Funj state opened new routes avoiding the expenses of Egypt and other centres of Ottoman rule. Maghribi pilgrimage caravans habitually travelled through the desert fringes in preference to the settled lands near the coast. Many passed through the Fezzan, and some of these now turned south-eastwards to the Tibesti highlands, across the northern part of the Chad basin to Wadai, and on through Darfur, Kordofan and the Butana to the Red Sea port of Suakin.

The West African pilgrims coming from the lands south of the Niger bend opened up routes across Hausaland to Bagirmi and on through Wadai. In doing so they were helped by the existence across most of the Sudanic belt of pockets of Fulbe pastoralists – people who travelled widely and could act as intermediaries with the local farming communities, and who were accompanied by Muslim clerics prepared to act first as advisers and then as missionaries to pagan rulers. An excellent example is provided by the tradition of a Fulbe cleric, Ould Dede, who set out on the pilgrimage around A.D. 1500 perhaps from as far afield as the Senegal, hoping to find his father who had departed some years previously and had never returned. On reaching Bagirmi he learned that his father had died and been buried at a place called Bidderi. Ould Dede thereupon decided to remain there and to build a shrine for pilgrims at the site of his father's tomb. This shrine at

Bidderi became a religious centre of great influence for the spread of Islam along the southern frontier of the faith in tropical Africa. When in the early seventeenth century a Muslim prince finally gained the throne of Bagirmi, it was with the help of the Fulbe clerics of Bidderi, who thereafter guided him in modernising his government, in organising Muslim courts and in building a walled palace at Massenya worthy of a Muslim sultan.

At about the same time as the religious revolution in Bagirmi, the Tunjur dynasty of Wadai was replaced in a coup d'état by a Muslim cleric, 'Abd al-Karim, a Nubian Arab from the northern part of the Funj kingdom who had travelled widely in the Hijaz and perhaps also in Morocco and who may even have studied for a time at the religious centre at Bidderi. 'Abd al-Karim's military support in Wadai came first of all from the Shuwa Arabs, who had been living for some two centuries in the more arid northern parts of the country, and who were probably feeling the need to expand from the desert margins into the lands of the Maba cultivators. Nevertheless, it is apparent that there was a ground swell of enthusiasm for Islam at this time in Wadai, as in other parts of northern Central Africa, which no doubt proceeded from a genuine respect for the lives and teaching of the 'holy men' who were spreading into the region from North and West Africa. Such men were usually tireless in preaching the necessity for Muslims to live under Muslim rule, and among their followers considerations of self-interest could go hand in hand with a real concern for justice and public morality.

After defeating the last of the Tunjur rulers – according to one tradition, by the stratagem of tying branches to the tails of his camels and so raising enough dust to suggest a very much larger host than in fact he had – 'Abd al-Karim established his capital in the mountain-enclosed defile of Wara, where it was to remain until the nineteenth century. Around the brick-built palace and mosque a large town grew up, which was regularly visited by traders and clerics from many regions, but especially from Funj and Upper Egypt. At the centre of the state, 'Abd al-Karim and his successors maintained many of the rituals of pre-Islamic divine kingship. The sultan's food and drink were carried into the palace secretly, and he ate alone. When in audience he was seated behind a curtain, and his words were relayed by a spokesman. His authority was symbolised by royal drums and a royal fire, from which all other fires had to be rekindled at the new year. Elaborate sacrifices were made to the royal ancestors. Beyond the capital, the sultan was represented by four provincial governors and by some thirty great military feudatories with landed estates from which they had to raise both cavalry and foot-soldiers. Tribute was paid by cultivators in foodstuffs; by pastoralists in camels and horses, cattle and sheep; by hunters in ivory and honey; by smiths in tools and weapons; and by other craftsmen in the products of their trade. Muslim territory was considered to stretch for some 300 kilometres to the south of the capital, to Dar Runga in the northern foothills of the Ubangi–Shari watershed plateau, but all round the southern border-lands pagan tribes were required to pay tribute in slaves on pain of military raiding in default. The external necessities of the kingdom, chiefly horses, fire-arms and other weapons, armour, and cotton textiles, were paid for in ivory and slaves.

Darfur, which was to be by the end of our period the largest and most powerful of the states of northern Central Africa, passed under Muslim rule a little later than Wadai and Bagirmi, probably about the middle of the seventeenth century. Here, the old Tunjur dynasty had long been displaced by kings of the Kayra clan, who were Fur from the central mountain massif of Jabal Marra. The early history of the Kayra dynasty is not well known. It begins with the almost legendary figure of Sultan Dali, who may have ousted the Tunjur some time in the late fifteenth century. But his successors during the following century and a half are remembered by little more than their names, and even so with considerable uncertainty about their order. It would seem that during this period the kingdom was confined to the Jabal Marra and its northern approaches. The first Muslim ruler, Sulayman Solong, though the son of a Kayra prince, had an Arab mother from Wadai, and was probably in some sense a military usurper. Certainly, his reign was mainly one of warfare and conquest, in which Darfur established its dominance over the surrounding Arab nomads – both the camel-pastoralists of the deserts of the north and the cattle-owning Baqqara Arabs living to the east and south-east of the Jabal Marra range. It was traditionally reported that Sulayman Solong extended his boundaries eastwards beyond the Nile to the Atbara. Since his reign corresponded with the high period of the Funj, the claim cannot be taken literally, but it may indicate that his caravan leaders were prominent on the routes passing across northern Kordofan towards the Red Sea port of Suakin.

It is clear that the Islamisation of Darfur did not proceed very far during the reign of Sulayman, or even during that of his son Musa. However, his grandson, Ahmad Bukar, was remembered not only for successful wars against Wadai based upon the effective use of imported fire-arms, but also for the building of schools and mosques, and for his policy of attracting Muslim settlers from other lands. 113

These included people from the Funj kingdom and Egypt, but also many others from Bornu, Bagirmi and other places to the west. Pilgrims from the western Sudan, known collectively as Takarna, or people of Takrur, stopped for long periods on their way to and from Mecca: some became permanent settlers and catered for those who passed through. Those who came to trade in Darfur were mostly Jellaba – Arabic-speakers from the Nubian reaches of the Nile – and they were attracted above all by the rich trade in ivory and slaves from the indeterminate southern borderlands of the country.

To the south of Jabal Marra and beyond the valley of the Bahr al-Arab, in the broken, hilly country of the Nile–Congo watershed, was the region known as Dar Fertit, inhabited by Kreish and other peoples speaking the eastern group of Central Sudanic languages. According to the Scottish traveller W. G. Browne, who visited Darfur during the last decade of the eighteenth century, the peoples of Dar Fertit had within the period of living memory enjoyed both political independence and material prosperity. Their country was well watered and rich in iron- and copper-ore. There were excellent black-smiths producing tools and weapons of the highest quality. Copper from the many small mines of Hofrat en-Nahas was cast into ingots and exported through Darfur and Wadai, where it had doubtless played an important part in the process of political centralisation and state-building, for the sacred drums which were the principal insignia of both kingdoms were of copper. By the time of Browne's visit, however, the people of Dar Fertit had been reduced into vassalage and forced to pay tribute, mainly in slaves. The Darfur sultan sent out annual tribute-collecting expeditions, called *salati*, which were in effect little more than slave-raids. Meanwhile the Jellaba traders, operating their own *salati* under licence from the sultan, ranged even further afield than the official expeditions, especially over the swampy plains of the upper Bahr el-Ghazal, which supported great herds of elephant. By the late nineteenth century Dar Fertit was to become practically depopulated, the survivors from a century of slave-raiding having retreated far to the south.

THE PEOPLES OF THE SOUTH

It is obvious that by the end of our period the three Muslim states of Bagirmi, Wadai and Darfur had established a real and irreversible ascendancy over the pagan peoples living on their southern frontiers. It was an ascendancy based on the horse, the musket and control of communications with the outside world. It was not, however, an

16 From the Niger to the Nile (2): the backlands of the central Sudan

ascendancy of superior men over inferior men, and if we are to understand developments in the southern half of the region, we have first of all to discount all the partisan contempt of Muslim chroniclers for the pagan victims of Muslim aggression.

The peoples living along the highlands of the Ubangi–Shari watershed, from the Adamawa massif in the west to the Bongo mountains in the east, were some of the most skilled and resourceful in black Africa. Linguistically, most of them belonged to the Eastern Nigritic sub-family of Niger–Congo – that is to say, their basic affiliations were with West African peoples, and especially with the northern members of the Benue–Niger sub-family, rather than with the

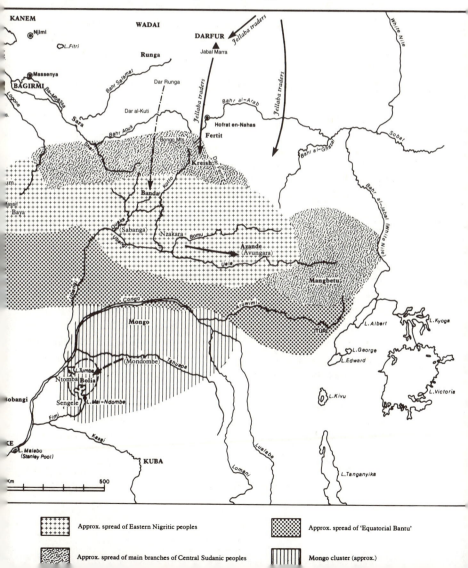

Approx. spread of Eastern Nigritic peoples

Approx. spread of main branches of Central Sudanic peoples

Approx. spread of 'Equatorial Bantu'

Mongo cluster (approx.)

Central Sudanic peoples who surrounded them to the north and the east, or the Bantu peoples on their southern frontier. In all probability the backbone of the Eastern Nigritic infiltration into northern Central Africa had been established well before the beginning of our period. In the west of the region, the Mbum, the Baya and the Wute have shifted their position only a little to the southward within recent times, and that only in retreat from the Fulbe expansion into Adamawa in the early nineteenth century. In the centre of the region, the Banda have moved south from an earlier position in Dar Runga and the western foothills of the Bongo massif to occupy the land between the Ouaka and the Kotto tributaries of the Ubangi. This was, no doubt, a movement of retreat from the slaving frontiers of Bagirmi and Wadai, but it did not basically change the ethnic composition of the area, which was already occupied by an earlier layer of Eastern Nigritic people remembered in tradition as the Sabanga. It was probably from the same layer as the Sabanga that there emerged the Nzakara people, who occupied the country around the confluence of the Uele and the Bomu, and also, somewhat later, the conquering group called the Avungara, who in the late eighteenth and early nineteenth century were to weld nearly a million Central Sudanic and Bantu people living around the headwaters of the Uele and the Bomu into the Zande nation. South of the upper Uele, in the north-eastern corner of the Ituri forest, the Central Sudanic Mangbetu were to build a comparable hegemony out of Eastern Nigritic, Central Sudanic and Bantu elements.

On the whole, therefore, it may perhaps be said that the main positive result of the attrition by the Muslim states in the north of the region was to cause a consolidation of political structures in the pagan areas to the south. If so, however, it was not a simple process of challenge and response. Around the southern periphery of the Muslim states there were those who accepted the role of tributary slave-hunters for their powerful neighbours. Such were the Runga to the south of Wadai and the Fertit to the south of Darfur. Beyond the tributaries was the area of active raiding, which tended to become depopulated as some of its inhabitants were seized and exported while others retreated out of range of the raiders. Thus most of the Banda drifted south into the country of the Sabanga and the Nzakara, while the majority of the Kreish drifted south-east along the line of the Nile–Congo watershed into the country of peoples like the Momvu and the Lese. Those living in the direct path of these migrations tended to be absorbed by them, joining one or other of the many small Banda or Kreish chieftainships. Some, however, moved away, and paid the price of independence by making themselves the rulers over others. It is in this kind of way that we have to see the origins of the Zande and Mangbetu hegemonies – the first as an indirect consequence of the pressure of Wadai upon the Eastern Nigritic Banda, the second perhaps as an indirect consequence of the pressure of Darfur upon the Central Sudanic Kreish.

If there was any significant transfer of political ideas from the north of the region to the south, it was certainly more apparent in the Mangbetu system than in the Zande one. The Mangbetu kingship was of the heavily ritualised kind, with vast palace installations and a tremendous display of royal insignia, above all in burnished copper. 'The midday rays of the equatorial sun', wrote George Schweinfurth during a visit to the capital of Munza, the fourth Mangbetu ruler, in 1870, 'shed a blinding light over this concentration of red-gleaming metal, and a glow as of burning torches flickered on each ceremonial spear-blade, the serried rows of which provided a gorgeous background for the ruler's throne.'[1] The copper was surely that of Hofrat en-Nahas, paid for with the ivory of the northern Ituri forest. Schweinfurth noted that Munza was the middleman for the exchange of northern and southern produce over a region much wider than his own kingdom. The Zande 'empire' represented in contrast the very pragmatic translation of an essentially military organisation into political terms. The Avungara chiefs lived without display in compounds little larger than those of their subjects. All independent rulers were descendants of Ngura, the leader of the original conquering horde, but despite the close family feeling it was accepted that there would be segmentation of authority in every generation, mostly arising from the expansion of the hegemony at its peripheries. Under the royals there functioned a class of tribute-collecting officials, often descended from members of the original horde. At the level of village chiefs, the petty rulers of the conquered peoples were often left in position. The most remarkable feature of Zande rule, however, was the system of assimilation practised upon the young. Boys were removed from their parents at puberty and assigned as servants and later as armed retainers to the Avungara rulers or to members of the Zande-speaking aristocracy. When they eventually returned to their villages to marry, they felt themselves to be Zande like their former masters, and so in three or four generations a new nation was built up, more effectively and certainly more lastingly than by the Mangbetu method.

The influences of Eastern Nigritic or Central Sudanic peoples possibly spread even further south, deep into the forests of the great

[1] Cited in D. Westermann, *Geschichte Afrikas* (Cologne, 1952), p. 171.

bend of the Congo river. Here lived the Mongo group of Bantu peoples, who, like many of their southern neighbours, once had a matrilineal social system. In time this changed partly to a patrilineal pattern, a reaction, it seems, to the introduction of a more complex mode of exchange, in particular the acquisition by the Mongo of iron or copper money, which probably came from the people of the savanna to the north. Not only did the Mongo experience a social transition, but some groups of them at least developed politically. The Bolia, Ntomba and Sengele sections of the Mongo moved from their homes on the banks of the Tshuapa, very likely because of the pressure of population, to the dense forests around Lake Mai-Ndombe. 'The whole political structure of the Bolia', writes Jan Vansina, 'is associated much more closely with divine Kingship and the emblems of it than is the case in other Central African Kingdoms.'[2] The Bolia traditions say that the sacred symbols of kingship, a lump of kaolin and a piece of ant-hill, were carried in their migrations from their more northern homelands. It is possible that these were local adaptations of the idea and emblems of divine kingship so widespread in the Sudanic zone.

If the social and political transformations undergone by the Bolia and other Mongo peoples are linked to the southward movement of Eastern Nigritic and Central Sudanic groups in the savanna and hills to the north of the Congo basin, then they are part of a historical process that has been less studied than that of any region of Africa. By the eighteenth century, the indirect influences of the European trading activities on the Loango coast north of the Congo estuary were beginning to reach the people of the southern borderlands of the Central African savanna. The Vili kingdom of Loango transported European goods (in exchange for slaves) overland from the coast to the Congo river north of Lake Malebo (Stanley Pool). Much of this trade bypassed the Teke kingdom of the lake area, and was continued up the Congo by the canoes of the Bobangi 'peoples of the river'. These lived along the stretch of the river north of Lake Malebo to the Ubangi confluence, and had been pushed steadily southwards by pressure from the savanna groups, such as the Abandiya and Banda. The Bobangi became by the nineteenth century the middlemen par excellence of the complex Congo trading system, and it was by means of Bobangi canoes plying the great river and the equally large northern Ubangi tributary that the borderland peoples of the northern savanna first came into contact with the coast-based commercial network of

[2] *Kingdoms of the Savanna* (Madison, Wisc., 1966), p. 99.

the European companies. The Muslim states to their north, and Azandeland on the Nile–Congo divide, had their first experience of foreign imperialism when Egypt conquered the Nilotic Sudan early in the nineteenth century.

Between northern Central Africa on the west and the Ethiopian highland region to the east lay the great basin of the upper Nile. At its centre, extending for near 500 kilometres on either side of the White Nile, was the Sudd – a vast, swampy region most of which lay under water for half of every year. The Sudd set a natural limit to the southward expansion of the great states of the middle Nile – first Meroe, then the Christian kingdom of 'Alwa, then the Muslim sultanate of the Funj. The Sudd was inhabited by Western Nilotes (sometimes called Rivers and Lakes Nilotes) speaking the Dinka, Nuer and Lwo languages. Though practising some agriculture, these were primarily fishermen and pastoralists, who congregated during the wet season on the low ridges which rose above the flood waters, and during the dry season spread out with their cattle to take advantage of the floodland grazing. Beyond them to the east and the south, the drier peripheries of the upper Nile basin were inhabited by another set of Nilotic-speaking peoples, known as Paranilotes, or Highland and Plains Nilotes, who were the easternmost of all the Sudanic peoples.

Until the early part of the present millennium, all these Nilotic-speaking peoples seem to have lived to the north of the Imatong mountains, within the modern frontiers of the Sudan Republic or in the lowland margins of south-western Ethiopia. Northern Uganda was occupied mainly by Central Sudanic-speakers, with Bantu to the south of them. Northern and central Kenya was occupied by Cushitic-speakers, who made a deep wedge into the northern frontier of the Bantu world, separating the North-Eastern Bantu of eastern Kenya from the Interlacustrine Bantu around Lake Victoria. During the present millennium, however, and perhaps mainly from the thirteenth or fourteenth century onwards, there occurred a great expansion of Nilotic peoples to the southward. In northern Uganda, Central Sudanic languages were reduced into a few pockets, all to the west of the White Nile. In Kenya, Cushitic languages were eliminated from the western highlands and the Rift Valley. Only in north-central Tanzania did a handful of Southern Cushitic languages survive as remnants, surrounded by Bantu languages to the west and south and by Nilotic languages to the north and east. Moreover, there is ample

17   The upper Nile basin and the East African plateau (1): language distribution, c. 1200

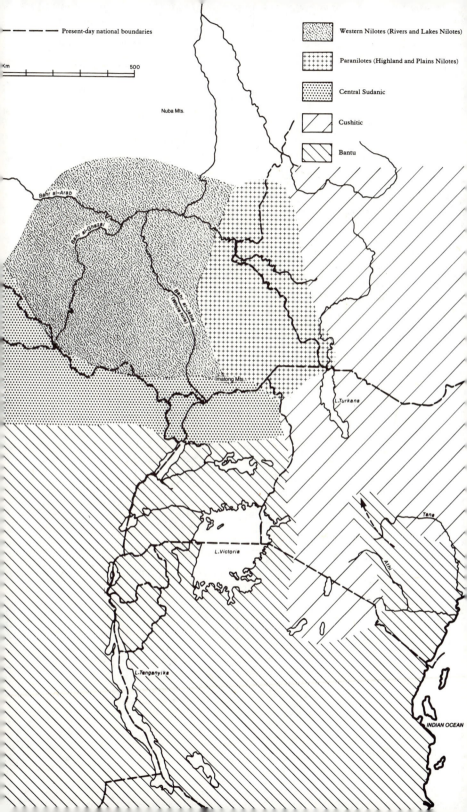

— — — Present-day national boundaries	

	Western Nilotes (Rivers and Lakes Nilotes)
	Paranilotes (Highland and Plains Nilotes)
	Central Sudanic
	Cushitic
	Bantu

Km   500

Nuba Mts.

Bahr al-Arab

Bahr el-Ghazal

Bahr al-Jebel (White Nile)

Imatong Mts.

L.Turkana

Tana

Athi

L.Victoria

L.Tanganyika

INDIAN OCEAN

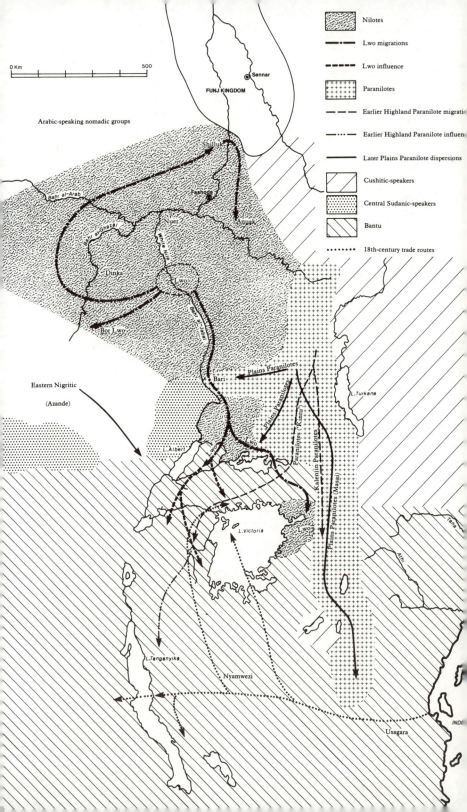

Nilotes	
Lwo migrations	
Lwo influence	
Paranilotes	
Earlier Highland Paranilote migration	
Earlier Highland Paranilote influence	
Later Plains Paranilote dispersions	
Cushitic-speakers	
Central Sudanic-speakers	
Bantu	
18th-century trade routes	

0 Km   500

FUNJ KINGDOM

Sennar

Arabic-speaking nomadic groups

Shilluk

Fashoda

Anuak

Bahr al-Arab

Bahr al-Ghazal

Nuer

White Nile

Dinka

Lwo

Bahr al-Jabal

Bor Lwo

Bari

Plains Paranilotes

Eastern Nigritic

(Azande)

Plains Paranilotes

Paranilotes (Kenu)

Kalenjin Paranilotes

Plains Paranilotes (Masai)

L.Turkana

Lwo

L.Alberi

L.Victoria

Lwo

Tana

Athi

L.Tanganyika

Nyamwezi

Usagara

INDI

evidence of Nilotic influences spreading far to the south of Nilotic language frontiers.

We do not know the reasons for this long, slow overspill of Nilotic populations from the upper Nile basin on to the East African plateau. One reason may have been zoological, in the sense that the Nilotic peoples were strongly pastoral, and it may have been the increase of herds rather than that of people which provided the main dynamic of expansion. Another reason may have been climatic, in that we know that there were great variations in the Nile flood, which may have had their most catastrophic effects in the Sudd region, where the waters were most dispersed and most subject to evaporation. Another reason may have been agricultural, in that some Nilotes may have developed hardier cereals and a more effective pattern of mixed farming than their southern neighbours, so that they were able to infiltrate the drier areas which had not previously been used for food-production. A fourth reason may have been technological, in the sense that the Nilotic peoples had become better armed and more practised in warfare than their neighbours to the south. What we do know is that in Uganda, Rwanda, Burundi, eastern Zaïre and north-western Tanzania a uniform Early Iron Age culture, which had lasted for more than a millennium, was succeeded by a later Iron Age culture, employing a totally distinct pottery tradition and practising a pattern of farming which used much more of the land area than the Early Iron Age people had done. In western Kenya this later Iron Age culture, associated with an essentially similar pottery tradition of northern origin, was introduced directly into a region apparently unaffected by any kind of Early Iron Age culture, where mainly pastoral, Cushitic-speaking farmers had continued to use neolithic equipment until after the beginning of the present millennium.

THE EARLY PARANILOTES AND THEIR IMPACT

The archaeological evidence for this transition in western and central Kenya has been neatly surveyed by John Sutton,[1] who shows that the first main Iron Age culture practised in this region was that associated with the hillside hollows, frequently lined with dry stone walling, which are commonly known as 'Sirikwa holes'. These were the stock-pens of Paranilotic Kalenjin peoples, who occupied the whole area of the western highlands and the adjacent parts of the Rift Valley until they were dispossessed by the Masai in the eighteenth century. The starting-date of their occupation is uncertain. Radiocarbon dates

[1] *The Archaeology of the Western Highlands of Kenya* (Nairobi, 1973).

18   The upper Nile basin and the East African plateau (2): language distribution, *c*. 1800

for sites with stone equipment in this region have been found for a period as recent as the sixteenth century, but the beginnings of Kalenjin occupation are likely to have been several centuries earlier, at a period corresponding with the earliest Paranilotic incursions into north-eastern Uganda. Here, later Iron Age pottery was certainly in use by the fifteenth century, and genealogical evidence for population disturbances in the north-eastern part of the country would indicate a period a century or two earlier than that.

In western Kenya the distribution of later Iron Age sites would suggest that the Paranilotic immigrants were mixed farmers who tilled the higher and moister slopes of the western highlands, using the deep, rich soils around the forest margins, but sending out their young men and boys to pasture the herds on the lower, drier grass-lands of the Uasin Gishu plateau and in the central section of the Rift Valley. The large proportion of Cushitic loan-words surviving in their language would suggest that the Kalenjin mixed with and absorbed their Stone Age predecessors, while their social organisation into age-sets and their adoption of certain Cushitic customs and taboos, such as the prohibition against eating fish, would indicate that cultural influence worked both ways. It is to be hoped that one day we shall know much more about this early Paranilotic infiltration into eastern East Africa, for its potential significance is very great. We need much more chronological evidence and, in particular, we need evidence about the southward spread of the pattern of mixed farming which resulted from the mingling of Paranilotes and Cushites in western Kenya. Geography would suggest that a way of life based around expanding herds of cattle would spread more easily through the dry uplands of central Tanzania and north-eastern Zambia, which were still at the beginning of the present millennium populated mainly by hunters and gatherers, than through regions further to the west where agricultural populations had long been established. For the present, our lack of evidence forbids us to do more than pose the question.

What is certain, however, is that the later Iron Age culture associated with the Paranilotic Kalenjin in western Kenya had its counterpart in Uganda and other areas to the west of Lake Victoria. As in the east, its archaeological hallmark was a coarse, poorly fired, roulette-decorated pottery, which here ousted the smooth, delicate, handsomely grooved and bevelled Urewe ware of the Early Iron Age. Not only did a new pottery style supersede the old, but it was used in areas where no pottery had been used before, because they were too arid for the methods and the crops of Early Iron Age food-producers. Right

124

19   The upper Nile basin and the East African plateau (3): later Iron Age immigrants (Highland Paranilotes)

across Uganda, from north-east to south-west, and southwards through eastern Rwanda and Burundi, there runs a corridor of dry grassland, well suited to cattle-raising but hardly at all to agriculture, and within this corridor the later Iron Age rouletted pottery has been found in abundance. It would seem highly likely that fairly specialised pastoralists moving in from the direction of the Paranilotic homelands were the first food-producing inhabitants of these dry areas. These would have been the ancestors of the specialised pastoralists later known as Hima in western Uganda and Tutsi in Rwanda and Burundi. In so far as they remained in the grassland belt, their peculiar way of life and their milk diet would have encouraged a large measure of endogamy and the persistence of a characteristic pastoral physiognomy. But of course there would always have been blurring around the edges, where pastoralists and cultivators interacted, and at least in the field of language it would seem that the speech of Early

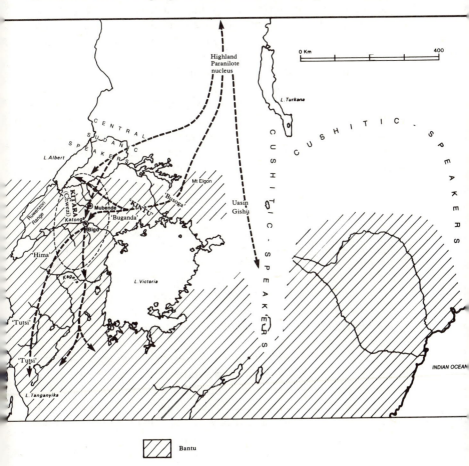

Bantu

- - - - Probable lines of Highland Paranilotic migrations

Iron Age cultivators often triumphed over that of later Iron Age immigrants. At the time of Paranilotic expansion much of northern Uganda was certainly occupied by Central Sudanic-speakers, and it may well have been as Central Sudanic-speakers that the first specialised pastoralists passed into the Bantu sphere. But, if so, it would seem that they soon adopted the Bantu speech of the Early Iron Age food-producers already settled in the land.

In fact, we can be sure that the later Iron Age immigrants into Uganda included many who were by no means specialised pastoralists. The distribution of later Iron Age pottery covers every type of soil, vegetation and rainfall, from the lush islands and coastline of Lake Victoria to the cold, high valleys of the Ruwenzori range and the mountains of western Rwanda. Moreover, the earliest layers of oral tradition preserved in the eastern part of the region – between Mt Elgon and the northern shores of Lake Victoria – paint a convincing picture of primarily agricultural immigrants coming from the northeast and settling in country already occupied by Bantu farmers and fishermen. The stereotypic figure of such traditions is called Kintu, and everywhere from eastern Busoga to central Buganda he appears as the leader of incoming migrants, whom he settles by agreement with the local clan-heads, dividing the territory between the clans of the migrants and those of the existing residents. Everywhere Kintu stands for the founding father of a small monarchical state, welding clan-heads into his service by installing them in ceremonial positions around his court and by marrying their daughters. Everywhere, likewise, Kintu is a culture hero, who introduces new crafts and new crops which improve the quality of life. Having carried out his mission in one area, he leaves a regent in charge and moves on to repeat it in another, performing incredible feats of statesmanship and procreation. Differences of language are never mentioned in the traditions, and it may be that the immigrant element in the Kintu states had already been Bantuised before reaching Lake Victoria. If not, the nature of the accommodation between newcomers and existing residents would seem to have favoured assimilation, the newcomers transmitting their material culture but losing their former languages. The political systems seem usually to have represented a compromise between new and old.

It is clear from traditions that the Kintu states were small, comprising a few hundred square kilometres and a few thousand subjects. The first evidence of a larger state comes from the western grasslands, from Lake Albert south to the Kagera. This was the state of Kitara, established by a pastoral dynasty of the Chwezi clan at a period established both by archaeology and traditional genealogies to around the middle of the fifteenth century. The first capital of the Chwezi kingdom was traditionally at Mubende, on a striking hilltop midway between Lake Victoria and the Ruwenzori. The second and final capital was 60 kilometres further south, in the famous earthwork site of Bigo. Although insignificant by comparison with the defensive systems of West African city states, Bigo is the largest earthwork in eastern or southern Africa. An inner trench 2 kilometres in circumference encloses a typical royal residence. An outer trench 10 kilometres in length closes the angle between a river confluence: it is punctuated every 100 metres by a wide gateway through which cattle could be driven from the surrounding pastures. The pottery found on the site includes a roughly painted variety of the typical later Iron Age rouletted ware, which reoccurs at only five other earthwork sites running north from Bigo to Lake Albert. The distribution of these related sites suggests that the size of the Kitara kingdom might have been 150 kilometres from north to south and some 75 from east to west. In grassland country this might have comprised some tens of thousands of people and some hundreds of thousands of cattle. In general, the states formed as a result of the early Paranilotic influx were much smaller.

THE WESTERN NILOTES AND THEIR IMPACT

In East Africa in the fifteenth century Kitara was probably unique. By the early sixteenth century, however, Kitara had disappeared, and in its place there had arisen a new political configuration, based not on the central grasslands but upon the more mixed agricultural country to the north, the north-east and the south. The impetus for these changes was given by the infusion of a new wave of Nilotic migration, coming this time from the Western Nilotes of the Sudd region to the east and west of the White Nile. Presumably the causes of the Western Nilotic disturbances were linked in some way with those of their Paranilotic neighbours. It is noteworthy that only one of the three main sub-groupings of Western Nilotes was affected. These were the Lwo, whose original homeland was probably to the south of the Dinka and Nuer, and therefore bordered on that of the Paranilotes. At all events, the first effect of the Lwo dispersion was to redistribute the Lwo tribes into a rough circle around the Dinka–Nuer nucleus. The ancestors of the Bor Lwo settled to the west of the nucleus, around the lower Bahr al-Ghazal. The ancestors of the Shilluk settled to the north of the nucleus, on the White Nile around Fashoda, driving out an earlier set of riverain people, the Ap-Funy or Funj, who probably moved north to conquer the Gezira triangle between the Blue and White Niles, and to found the kingdom of Sennar on the ruins of the kingdom of 'Alwa (see Chapter 3). From Shillukland the ancestors of the Anuak moved up the Sobat and settled to the east of the nucleus around the modern Ethiopian frontier with the Sudan.

Whatever touched them off, all these movements seem to have developed through a temporary militarisation of Lwo people into the role of riverain pirates – a kind of African Vikings – who lived for the space of two or three generations mainly by plundering their neighbours. Their boats were of the flimsiest, but they provided the mobility which enabled small bands of warriors to make daring raids upon the cattle, crops and persons of less warlike communities. Like other martial hordes – for example, the Galla of Ethiopia (see pp. 55–9) or the Mane of Sierra Leone and Liberia (see pp. 88–9) – the Lwo were adept at incorporating captives, especially young males, into their societies, so that their numbers increased at a staggering rate. Numbers added to military strength, but also to the mouths that had to be fed, and this in turn quickened the pace of territorial expansion. At length, for reasons almost as obscure as those of the original disturbance, there would come the decision to abandon military life and to settle as a ruling group in the midst of a subject population. Here again, the Lwo were very flexible. They incorporated their subjects into their own clans, drawing only a distinction between the *jo-kal*, the people of the chief's enclosure, and the *lwak*, or herd of conquered clients. It was through their women that the *lwak* moved gradually into the *kal*, with polygamous chiefs begetting enormous numbers of children by conquerors and conquered alike.

The same pattern was followed by what was probably the main body of Lwo emigrants, which moved southwards and right out of the former Nilotic sphere in the southern Sudan, into Central Sudanic-speaking territory in northern Uganda and into Bantu territory further south. Here, the initial line of penetration ascended the White Nile towards Lake Albert. A great military encampment was established beside the river at Pubungu, some 20 kilometres below the river's exit from the lake. This was in the heartland of the Madi people, who occupied both banks of the White Nile from Lake Albert to the Dufile rapids astride the Sudan–Uganda frontier. From Pubungu expeditions radiated in all directions, bringing in booty and captives from the Madi and other Central Sudanic peoples such as the Lugbara and the Lendu. The captives were incorporated into the Lwo formations, and this swelled the appetite for further adventure and

128

20 The upper Nile basin and the East African plateau (4): Nilotes and later Paranilotes (Plains), 17th–18th centuries

conquest. In this way there began a long process of assimilation which in the course of two centuries was to transform all but a tiny remnant of the Madi people, and other peoples living to the north of Lakes Albert and Kyoga, into Lwo-speaking Acholi, Alur, Lango and Kumam.

Unfortunately, no Iron Age archaeological research has yet been undertaken in northern Uganda, and we can therefore only guess at the reasons why the peoples of this region were able to be absorbed linguistically and culturally by the Western Nilotic immigrants. We do not, for example, know for certain that the Madi and their neighbours were iron-using at the time of the Lwo invasions, though we must presume that they were. It may have been just that this region was the closest to the Western Nilotic homeland and therefore received the largest proportion of Lwo immigrants. Or it may have been that the social and political organisation which grew from the Lwo war-camps, in which the chief acted as a major redistributor, first of booty and later of tribute, was positively attractive to peoples

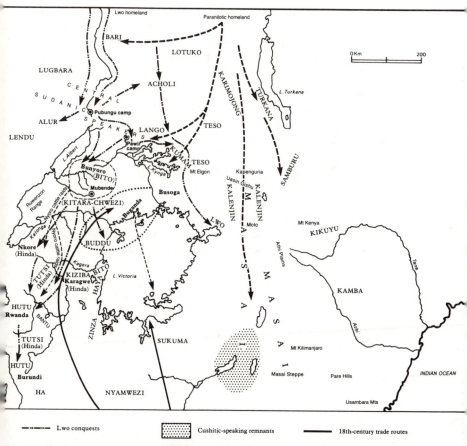

who had hitherto lived in much smaller and more dispersed communities. At all events, there was a fundamental difference between the political and cultural impact of the Lwo in northern and in southern Uganda, between their impact on the Central Sudanic peoples and their impact on the Bantu. For, in general, when the Lwo came into contact with the Bantu, even as outright military conquerors, it was the Bantu language that prevailed and Bantu social organisation towards which Lwo rulers made large compromises. It was only among the Bantu of western Kenya, living around the Kavirondo Gulf of Lake Victoria, that Lwo migrants were able to establish distinct communities of Lwo-speaking people.

The most significant of the Lwo conquests into Bantu territory was that which destroyed the Chwezi kingdom of Kitara. It can be roughly dated from genealogical, and probably also from astronomical, evidence to the closing years of the fifteenth century or the opening years of the sixteenth. In Lwo history it probably followed soon after the establishment of the war-camp at Pubungu. It was probably carried out by a war leader called Olum Labongo, remembered in Bantu traditions as Rukidi, 'the northerner', the founder of the Bito dynasty of Bunyoro and the founding ancestor of a whole circle of lesser Bito dynasties which gradually came to rule over much of southern Uganda. Tradition tells that the Chwezi ruler and his followers fled from Bigo at the approach of the Lwo armies and that Rukidi occupied for a time the capital of the Chwezi kings. The archaeological excavation of Bigo has, in fact, demonstrated that the centre of the site was radically reconstructed in a way that might well indicate the advent of Lwo rulers. Nevertheless, traditions equally make it clear that in the long term a capital in the grasslands proved unsuitable for a Lwo dynasty, which soon retreated to the region around and north of Mubende, where agriculture as well as pastoralism could be practised, and it was here, in the northern half of the old Kitara kingdom, that the new Lwo-ruled kingdom of Bunyoro developed. It is said that the bodies of the first three Bito kings were carried north to the neighbourhood of Pubungu for burial. This may be some indication of the period for which the Bito and their henchmen remained Lwo-speaking foreigners in a Bantu world. Thereafter, we may suppose, the Bito spoke the Nyoro language of their Bantu subjects, and intermarriage between Lwo and Bantu had gone so far that there was no longer any sense of racial difference.

Meantime, as was only to be expected, there had taken place in the southern half of the old Kitara kingdom a regroupment of the more distinctively pastoral population which had fled southwards with their cattle at the time of the Lwo invasions. Here, leadership came from the Hinda clan, which claimed a relationship with the Chwezi, and which succeeded in establishing a loose-knit hegemony on either side of the Kagera river, in Karagwe to the south of it and in Nkore to the north. The Hinda dynasty was in its way as significant as the Bito one. Its scions spread out in all directions, and soon there were a dozen or more Hinda-ruled states, reaching from south-western Uganda through north-western Tanzania to the southern confines of Burundi. The Nyiginya dynasty, which in the early seventeenth century began the building of a centralised state in Rwanda, probably derived from the same source. It would appear that in all these states the impetus of political growth was connected with the management of cattle in relation to the needs of cultivators. Whereas the early pastoralists of the region had settled only in the grasslands and had lived a life almost entirely separate from that of the cultivators to the east and west of them, the next phase was one in which some pastoralists interpenetrated the surrounding farmlands, lending out their cattle in twos and threes to cultivators, who valued them for their milk, but above all for their manure, and were prepared to pay for their loan with gifts of food and drink and other services of a feudal kind. Naturally, as it spread, this system invited the intervention of political entrepreneurs, men of power who were able to enforce the observance of the contract. This seems to have been the reason for the spread of Hinda dynasties in the farmlands of the Haya and Zinza peoples living between the Karagwe grasslands and Lake Victoria. In Rwanda and Burundi a similar process occurred with the westward penetration of Tutsi pastoralists from the eastern grasslands into the rich mountain valleys of the Nile–Congo watershed, with their dense populations of Hutu cultivators. At first the penetration was peaceful, but later the payment of tribute was enforced by military means, and chiefdoms grew in size. The emergence of large, centralised conquest states was only the last stage in the process, gathering noticeable momentum during the early seventeenth century in Rwanda and during the late seventeenth century in Burundi.

For more than two centuries after their foundation, the northern Hinda states had to endure the constant attrition of an aggressive and expanding Bunyoro. Whenever Bunyoro needed cattle, it raided Nkore, and sometimes also Karagwe and eastern Rwanda. Though the direct rule of the Bito kings never extended far to the south of Mubende, tributary states, some with Bito sub-dynasties, stretched to the shores of Lake Victoria between the Katonga and Kagera rivers, including what later became the Ganda province of Buddu and the 131

Haya state of Kiziba south of the lower Kagera. According to the traditional history of Bunyoro, even central Buganda was ruled by a Bito dynasty descending from the twin brother of the Lwo conqueror, Rukidi. Even if this claim now looks dubious, there can be no doubt that during most of the sixteenth century Buganda suffered successive defeats at the hands of Bunyoro armies and that it was forced to retreat within very restricted frontiers. Only in the seventeenth century, and even then only slowly, did Buganda recover its poise. When it did so, however, it was to the accompaniment of a new political principle of resounding significance. It was that conquered territory must be fully integrated, not by setting up an hereditary sub-dynasty to rule it, but by a system of appointed governors and by the deliberate absorption of the conquered people into the Ganda clans. Thus, when Buganda expanded its territory, the result was a real access of power, which made the next step easier than the previous one. By the late seventeenth century Buganda had recovered all the territory lost to Bunyoro. By the mid-eighteenth century it controlled the shores of Lake Victoria from the Kagera to the Nile. It was still a smaller country than Bunyoro and its dependencies, but politically and militarily it was far more coherent. All important appointments were held at the king's pleasure. A network of well-kept roads linked the capital with the provinces. Royal commands flowed outwards and tribute and services flowed in. Moreover, by the late eighteenth century Buganda was already indirectly involved in trade with the coast and the outside world. The king's ivory-hunters ranged widely around the peripheries of the state. His caravans travelled regularly to the south of the lake, and were soon to be augmented by a fleet of long-distance canoes. Imported cotton textiles were already in use at the royal court, along with cups and saucers, plates and cutlery, which would before long be followed by fire-arms and world religions. Thus, although the direct impact of Western Nilotic infiltration was felt most directly in northern Uganda and, within the Bantu world, in Bunyoro, the indirect results were much more widely spread. The Hinda states were one kind of response. The transformation of Buganda into a centralised, expansive and outward-looking polity was another response to the same challenge.

THE LATER PARANILOTES AND THEIR IMPACT

It was no accident that in the eighteenth century the long-distance trade routes connecting Buganda with the Indian Ocean coast had to make a wide detour through central Tanzania instead of passing directly through the Kenya highlands. The reason was the presence, right across the central highland region of Kenya and northern Tanzania, of specialised pastoralists pursuing a highly mobile and warlike existence which would have posed an impossible threat to the passage of trading caravans. These peoples were Paranilotes, but of a later dispersion than the Kalenjin. Sometimes called the Plains Nilotes in order to distinguish them from the Highland Nilotes of the earlier dispersion, they included such peoples as the Bari and the Lotuko of the Sudan–Uganda frontier region, the Karimojong and the Teso of north-eastern Uganda, the Turkana and the Samburu of north-western Kenya; but the most important and widespread ethnic sub-grouping was the Masai, whose arena eventually extended from the north-western highlands of Kenya to the plains of central Tanzania.

Of the origins of these peoples it is only possible to say that they must have been relatively close to the ancestors of the Kalenjin and relatively distant from those of the Western Nilotes. Probably they emerged from the same south-eastern Sudan–south-western Ethiopian borderlands as the Kalenjin, but some three or four centuries later. Perhaps the Paranilotic homeland was particularly liable to extreme climatic fluctuations, so that in times of extended drought migration was the only alternative to disaster. At all events, the second Paranilotic dispersion seems to have begun about a century later than that of the Western Nilotic Lwo. The westward movement of the Bari across the southern borderlands of the Sudan is placed by tradition later than the first southward thrust of the Lwo, but before the final stages of Western Nilotic migration into northern Uganda. Again, it is clear that Lwo-speakers were at one time spread right along the northern shores of Lake Kyoga, but that many of them were later absorbed by Paranilotic Teso moving in from the north-east, while even a group like the Lango, which kept its Lwo speech, was much penetrated by Paranilotic influences. All this suggests that the seventeenth century was the period of greatest movement, and probably it was at this time also that the ancestors of the Samburu and the Masai, followed by those of the Karimojong, began to encircle the Lake Turkana basin to the west and the south.

Like all other migrants who set out to seize country already occupied by others, the later Paranilotes could succeed only by force of arms. In so far as they were specialised pastoralists, however, interested in cattle and in the monopolisation of scarce grasslands, they were more than simple conquerors; they were destroyers, or at the least extruders. The Masai, especially, were conquerors of this destructive kind. They believed that cattle had been put in the world 133 for their own exclusive use. Their social organisation was essentially military and based on an age-set system which made it the duty of boys to herd cattle and of young men to plunder and defend cattle, so that the middle-aged and elderly might enjoy the possession of cattle and plan the strategy for obtaining more and more. The impact of the Masai can be seen most clearly in relation to the western highlands of Kenya, where the distribution of abandoned 'Sirkwa holes' shows that the Kalenjin were once in possession of the whole plateau. The Masai intrusion left them clinging to the outside edges of their former territory. The Uasin Gishu Masai occupied the central grasslands from Kapenguria to Molo, with half of the Kalenjin survivors to the west of them and the other half to the east. Probably it was the same story in the Rift Valley, the Athi Plains and the Masai Steppe. The Masai could enjoy excellent relations with some kinds of neighbours, particularly those practising a different economic way of life in a different ecological setting, such as the Kikuyu in the forested foot-hills of Mount Kenya or the Pare in the hills to the east of the Masai Steppe, with both of whom the Masai regularly exchanged their hides and their surplus women for iron tools and weapons. But to inhabit the same kind of territory as the Masai was to invite attack, and the main significance of this later Paranilotic occupation of the eastern grasslands was that it erected an almost impenetrable screen across the natural and direct routes between the rich region to the west of Lake Victoria and the Indian Ocean coast.

Hence the growing importance towards the close of our period of the region to the south of Lake Victoria, inhabited by a series of fairly closely related peoples of whom the Nyamwezi formed the central group. This was not on the whole a rich land capable of supporting a dense population. Most of it was rather dry country covered with thorny bush, in which agricultural communities had constantly to divide and sub-divide, sending out colonies to considerable distances to find suitable land on which to settle. Chieftainship, though fairly ritualised, remained small in scale: there was no basis for the elaborate court life or the hierarchies of officials found in Buganda, Bunyoro and the larger interlacustrine states. Among small communities separated from each other by fairly large tracts of uninhabited bush, hunting remained an important part of the economy, and it may be that the availability of rare skins and particularly of ivory was what turned the minds of the Nyamwezi and their neighbours to the possibilities of long-distance trade. So far as we know at present, it was only during the eighteenth century that migrants from Usagara and other districts near the coast began to settle among the Nyamwezi, bringing with them such curiosities as conus-shell discs and ivory 'spirit-horns', which sometimes caused them to be recognised as chiefs. Thus the connection between coast and interior was established, and the response of the Nyamwezi seems to have been spectacular. Within two or three generations of the breakthrough, they had created a near-monopoly of the long-distance carrying trade to the deep interior. Within their societies prestige came to be associated with distant travel, and in the mid-nineteenth century the explorer Burton was to report how, among the children, every boy carried about in his daily round a tusk of ivory proportionate to his strength, so that, when older, he would be prepared for a man's most serious employment as a caravan porter. By this time, Nyamwezi caravans linked the coast with the interlacustrine region, the whole vast region around Lake Tanganyika and the Copperbelt of southern Zaïre and northern Zambia, and some of them had even penetrated as far west as Angola. By the end of the eighteenth century, however, the system was probably still confined to the region south of Lake Victoria and east of Lake Tanganyika. Even on that scale, its existence made possible, in some of the great interlacustrine kingdoms, the outward-looking attitudes which were to be so indispensable for their nineteenth-century development.

On the East African plateau, as we have seen, the essential feature of the 'later Iron Age' was the advent of northern influences from the basin of the upper Nile, associated in pottery manufacture with roulette-decorated wares, the widespread distrubution of which betokened a much more complete occupation of the land by food-producers than had occurred in Early Iron Age times. Specifically, it meant a diffusion of both specialised pastoralism and of mixed cattle- and cereal-farming among populations which had previously been much more exclusively agricultural. In southern Central Africa the 'later Iron Age' means something very different. The key region here is the Shaba (Katanga) province of south-eastern Zaïre, where the later Iron Age material culture seems to have resulted from a period of accelerated development within the region itself. Primarily this was an improvement in metallurgical techniques which occurred in and around the northern Copperbelt, and which resulted in a general enrichment of the whole material culture. From Shaba it spread southwards into Zambia and Malawi, and westwards into the Kasai province and Angola. The transitional phase between the Early and later Iron Age culture in Shaba province probably began towards the end of the first millennium A.D., but successive stages of its develop-ment continued to ripple outwards until about the seventeenth cen-tury. In social and political organisation, the crucial developments probably occurred fairly late on, making some use of systems and ideas which spread southwards from the later Iron Age states of the East African plateau, especially those situated in Rwanda, Burundi and the Kivu province of Zaïre. Not many parts of southern Central Africa were suited either to specialised pastoralism or to the kind of economic and political interaction between pastoralists and cul-tivators characteristic of the later Iron Age cultures of the East African plateau. Nevertheless in both north-eastern and south-western Zam-bia there were some societies in which pastoral aristocracies played an important role, and the same was certainly true of later Iron Age societies in Zimbabwe.

THE LUBA AND THE LUNDA

The central population of the Shaba region was the Luba. They lived between the Lualaba and the Bushimai, in a land drained by a hundred rivers and tributary streams running northwards in long, straight parallel valleys towards the forested centre of the Congo basin. Though Lubaland is often described as savanna, in fact its valleys are mostly filled with forest galleries, and even the intervening ridges are quite heavily wooded. It is essentially a land of fishermen and riverside planters, who use the ridges mainly for hunting, and who are prevented by the prevalence of the tsetse-fly from keeping many cattle. Archaeologically, Lubaland is best known at its eastern extremity, where the Lualaba flows through a series of lakes filling the lowest parts of the Upemba depression. Here, at the end of the first millennium lakeside fishermen, almost certainly Luba, were moving into a phase of of later Iron Age culture known as Early Kisalian. This was succeeded from about the eleventh till about the thirteenth century by a phase called Classical Kisalian, which may have overlapped from about the twelfth century onwards with another, intrusive culture called the Kabambian. Kisalian pottery, though distinctive, is clearly reminiscent of Early Iron Age wares, and its metal artifacts,

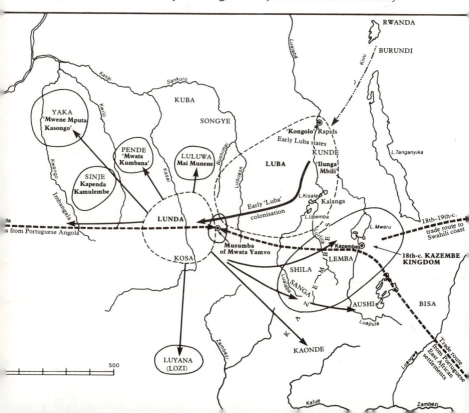

both jewellery and weapons, are mostly of iron. Kabambian pottery, by contrast, is almost undecorated, though finished with a shiny red slip, and its characteristic metal goods are of copper, including very elaborate articles of jewellery and large quantities of small copper croisettes, which must have been used for currency and must indicate the existence of a considerable network of local trade.

All these developments in material culture appear to have preceded the political reorganisation of Lubaland which forms the starting-point of Luba traditional history, and which perhaps refers to a period around the fourteenth and fifteenth centuries. The traditions describe a double process of infiltration and conquest which established ruling lineages known as Balopwe, whose members came to hold all but the most local kind of chiefly offices in a series of four main kingdoms embracing most of northern and central Lubaland. The southern part of Lubaland was unaffected. As with the Kintu traditions of southern Uganda, the Luba traditions have personalised and telescoped a process which must have operated over a wide geographical area and through a considerable period of time. The first such personification is that called Kongolo, which is also the name of an ancient settlement area at the head of the Lualaba rapids to the north of eastern Luba-land. The second figure is that of Ilunga Mbili, who is associated with the region to the east of the Lualaba, then occupied by peoples called Kunde and Kalanga. As traditionally presented, Ilunga reached Lubaland during the lifetime of Kongolo, and married his daughter, whose son Kalala eventually overthrew and succeeded his maternal grandfather. But this is a common traditional formula for concealing and legitimising a change of dynasty. The reality was probably that one set of outside influences was followed, perhaps much later, by a second. At all events, from these episodes northern Lubaland acquired some political coherence, which was reinforced by many of the common rituals of centralised kingship systems in use from Dar-fur to Zimbabwe. Like so many others, Luba kings ate and drank in secret and concealed other natural functions. They practised royal incest with their queen-sisters, shared ritual authority with their queen-mothers, and used spirit mediums to communicate with their royal ancestors. Human sacrifices were a part of the elaborate rituals surrounding their death and burial. As their principal symbol of authority they used royal fire, kindled at their accession and kept burning until their death, from which the fires of all subordinate chiefs had annually to be rekindled.

The developments referred to in the traditions of Kongolo and Ilunga Mbili used to be described as the first and second Luba 'empires'. This was certainly to convey a wholly misleading conception of the nature of political change in this and other parts of Africa during our period. No more than in the Uganda of the Kintu traditions were large kingdoms created by invading armies at one fell swoop. The earliest Luba states were certainly very small and probably very numerous. The more successful among them grew slowly at the expense of the others. Defeated dynasties often migrated to try their luck elsewhere. Above all, military forces were minute. Often they consisted of little groups of hunters, who naturally tended to be more mobile and better armed than the settled communities of farmers and fishermen.

The same considerations apply when we turn from the early history of the Luba to that of their western neighbours, the Lunda, who lived astride the Kasai and its tributaries. The key figure connecting the history of the two regions is that of Chibinda Ilunga, presented in oral tradition as a Luba hunter who moved into eastern Lunda and married Lueji, the 'granddaughter' of a small-scale Lunda chief called Yala Mwaku, eventually succeeding him as ruler. Lueji's 'brothers', Kinguri and Chinyama, refusing to recognise Chibinda's authority, migrated westwards and southwards and founded dynasties among the Imbangala of central Angola (see Chapter 11, p. 159) and the Luyana (Lozi) of north-western Zambia. In this case, it is today accepted that the names in the story are not those of individuals but rather of hereditary titles. Similarly, the relationships attributed to them are those of 'perpetual kinship', indicating seniority or juniority in the foundation of the title by the use of kinship terms such as 'father', 'son' or 'brother', while conquests and amalgamations are referred to as 'marriages', with the senior or victorious partner described as the husband and the subordinate one as the wife. The Chibinda Ilunga of the tradition is likewise not to be understood as a personal name but as the leadership title of a Luba hunting expedition despatched westwards into Lunda country by the ruler of one of the Luba states to the east. Throughout the region described in this chapter, it was in fact the custom for large-scale military or hunting expeditions to be commissioned by the ruler, who conferred his own title upon the leader as his personal representative. The subordinate chiefs would contribute their own contingents to the expedition, the officers in charge of which would bear the titles of the chiefs whom they represented. In this way, an expedition was organised as a scale-model of the parent kingdom. All that was necessary to complete the act of political reproduction was for the expedition to settle permanently in its hunting-grounds, imposing its authority over the people of the area concerned. A new state would have come into being with a superstructure similar to its parent's, and the acquiescence of the parent state would be secured by the payment of tribute, at least for a time.

The essential message of the tradition of Chibinda and Lueji is therefore that a long process of centralising conquest and amalgamation of small Lunda chiefdoms was set in motion by an adventuring band of Luba origin, causing some of the older Lunda authorities to submit to them, while others moved away in an attempt to maintain their independence by imposing themselves on other Lunda living further to the west and the south. It was a process, not an event. It consisted of often-repeated episodes, widely spread over time and space. In the words of Joseph Miller, who has contributed much to the modern understanding of the problem, 'Early Lunda history should be . . . visualized as a gradual movement through several stages of political development characterized by progressively more centralized state structures.'[1] What began as the conquest of a tiny corner of Lundaland by a handful of Luba adventurers developed into an indigenous movement among the Lunda themselves. Probably it took some two or three centuries to reach the stage where most Lunda-speaking people had been welded into a single main centralised state ruled by a dynasty stable enough for its historical traditions to present a sequence of individual reigns, each associated with a set of important events. This stage was reached only around the middle of the seventeenth century, when a ruler (*mwant*, or *mwata*) called Ya Nawej (or Yamvo Naweji) achieved a position of such prestige that all his descendants took his name for their title, so that the main Lunda kingdom was known as that of the Mwant Yavs or Mwata Yamvos.

Lunda kingship seems to have developed as a much more effective instrument of political centralisation than its Luba progenitor. Very largely, this was because the pre-existing Lunda system of small matrilineal chieftainships over village communities (*tubungu* or *mwantangand*), each completely independent of its neighbours but yet arranged in groups observing ties of perpetual kinship, was one which could be peculiarly easily integrated under a central superstructure providing defence and security in exchange for taxation and tribute. The classic pattern of accommodation between Lunda *tubungu* and Luba kingship (*bulopwe*) was worked out in a group of fifteen village settlements occupying a section of the valley of the upper Bushimai where all the later capitals (*musumba*) of the growing kingdom were to

[1] *Kings and Kinsmen: Early Mbundu States in Angola* (London, 1976), p. 115.

be built. The *tubungu* were recognised as 'chiefs of the land', rulers of the traditional communities, and the priestly intermediaries with the unseen world of ancestral spirits. In token of this, the *tubungu* of the fifteen original settlements held positions of the highest honour at the royal court, and exercised a central role in the selection, initiation and investiture of successive kings. As the kingdom expanded beyond the original nucleus, fresh groups of related *tubungu* made their submission to the kingship and were confirmed in their traditional functions. The only royal official operating at the local level was the *chilolo*, who established a village of his own at some central point among a group of related village settlements. Unlike that of the *tubungu*, the authority of the *chilolo* was purely secular and mainly fiscal. He collected the tribute from his district and forwarded it to his permanent representative at the royal court. In districts close to the capital the tribute was paid mainly in beer and foodstuffs. More distant districts paid in salt or copper, or else in manufactured goods such as tools and weapons, palm and raphia textiles, pots and basketry. The peripheral districts in a constantly expanding circle were those in which organised expeditions were still operating, and these returned the products of warfare and hunting, especially ivory and slaves.

The initial direction in which the Lunda state expanded was westwards, across the Kasai to the Kwilu. All this country was already Lunda-speaking. Moreover, even before the arrival of the Mwant Yav's expeditions, this had been the direction taken by the eastern Lunda refugees, the followers of the Kinguri and the Chinyama title-holders in their flight from the Chibinda Ilunga. These had prepared the way for the later state-builders. Already during the reign of Mwant Yav Nawej, these western Lunda provinces were visited by long-distance trading caravans from the Portuguese colony in Angola, bringing guns and cloth, spirits and tobacco, which were exchanged for the slaves and ivory captured by the Mwant Yav's frontier forces. Henceforward the tribute requirements of the state were increasingly geared to the needs of the long-distance trade. Expeditions were undertaken among non-Lunda peoples to the north and south of Lundaland, and in time this led to conquest and permanent occupation. The first non-Lunda to be absorbed were the Kosa living to the south of eastern Lundaland, and the significance of this extension of the kingdom was that it opened the door to a whole new line of eastward expansion to the south of the Luba kingdoms, among the still stateless peoples of the Congo–Zambezi watershed plateau, such as the Kaonde and the Sanga, the Lembwe and the Shila, the Lemba and the Aushi. Here, in the late seventeenth and early eighteenth centuries a series of expeditionary leaders bearing the title of Kazembe established tributary kingdoms too distant to be effectively controlled by the parent state, but where the supposed Lunda ancestry of the ruling groups was sufficient to maintain loose bonds of community and mutual respect. In the later eighteenth century the easternmost of these Kazembes, operating from a capital in the fertile and densely populated Luapula valley south of Lake Mweru, built up an empire considerably larger than that of the Mwant Yavs, which stretched from the sources of the Lualaba to the south-western shores of Lake Tanganyika. Meanwhile, at the opposite end of the Lunda dominions, similar colonies were being formed beyond the effective borders of the parent state, of which the largest was that founded among the Yaka people of the Kwango valley by a Lunda conqueror who took the title of Mwene Mputa Kasongo. Others were the kingdom of Kapenda Kamulemba among the Shinje, that of Mwata Kumbana among the Pende and that of Mai Munene among the Luluwa.

Thus, by the later eighteenth century a wide swathe of Central Africa from the Kwango to Lake Tanganyika was under the rule of Lunda kingship, directly or indirectly tributary to the Mwant Yav residing in his capital town of Musumba, which was rebuilt in every reign but always in the narrow plain between the Bushimai and Lulua rivers. To the westward this great political complex traded with the Portuguese of Luanda through the Imbangala, who were themselves in a sense an offshoot of the Lunda expansion. To the eastward it traded through the Bisa and other intermediaries with the Portuguese on the Zambezi, and would soon do so directly with the Swahili Arabs of the Zanzibar coast. In its geographical extent the Lunda empire of the eighteenth century was by far the largest political hegemony to emerge anywhere in Bantu Africa. In sheer size it rivalled the largest states of the Sudanic belt. Yet this Lunda hegemony was in reality only the very lightest kind of superstructure. Except for tribute payments, every village community in the empire was self-governing, and at least in the more distant districts the amount of tribute was mainly determined by the local willingness to pay. In these circumstances the longer-distance tribute payments became almost indistinguishable from trade, because substantial gifts were made in return for them. If it is true that tribute was the life-blood of the empire, it was not only, or even mainly, for fiscal reasons, but because tribute helped to stimulate the arteries of commerce. The military forces of the Mwant Yav were never large. Expeditions of three or four hundred men, with only a handful of guns and mainly armed with swords and spears, were sent to capture slaves and to hunt elephants for their ivory in the Luba-ruled territories to the north and east of the capital. Otherwise little compulsion was used. But the flow of tribute ensured that all roads led to the Musumba, which thus remained the principal centre of redistribution in Central Africa until, in the mid-nineteenth century, outside trading caravans became well enough armed to carve their own direct routes to the resources they wished to exploit.

THE SOUTH-EASTWARD SPREAD OF LUBA SYSTEMS – MARAVI, BISA AND BEMBA

During the same period that Luba systems of centralised kingship were spreading out westwards into Lunda territory and beyond, a similar movement was in progress to the east of the Lualaba, in the region between Lake Mweru and the lower Zambezi, and in all probability reaching to the Zimbabwean plateau as well. But whereas the westward movement produced results which were still clearly visible during the nineteenth century, the traces of the south-eastward movement had been nearly obliterated, on the one hand by the expansion of the Lunda Kazembes across the area of its origin, and on the other hand by the invasion and settlement of the Ngoni peoples of Zulu origin right up the highlands of the Malawi–Zambia frontier. These developments of the late eighteenth and early nineteenth centuries have caused the suppression of much traditional evidence concerning earlier periods, and it has only been through the very careful scrutiny of what little survives, in the light of early Portuguese documentation of the region, that it has been possible to reconstruct the outlines of its earlier history.

It is clear that the most significant group involved in this whole process was that which called itself Maravi or Malawi (meaning 'flames') in order to distinguish the immigrants regarded as being of Luba origin from the Nyanja, Chewa and Manganja populations among whom they had settled. The leading element among the Maravi was the Phiri clan, which provided the royal dynasties for a number of loosely organised kingdoms existing in the region to the west and south of Lake Malawi at least from the fifteenth century and perhaps somewhat earlier. The senior Maravi kingdom, which apparently sired the others, had its capital towns among the Nyanja people around the southern shores of the lake. It was ruled by Phiri kings who bore the title of Kalonga, and whose queens, bearing the title of Mwali, had to be drawn from the Banda clan. To the south of the Kalonga's kingdom, among the Manganja of the lower Shire was 143

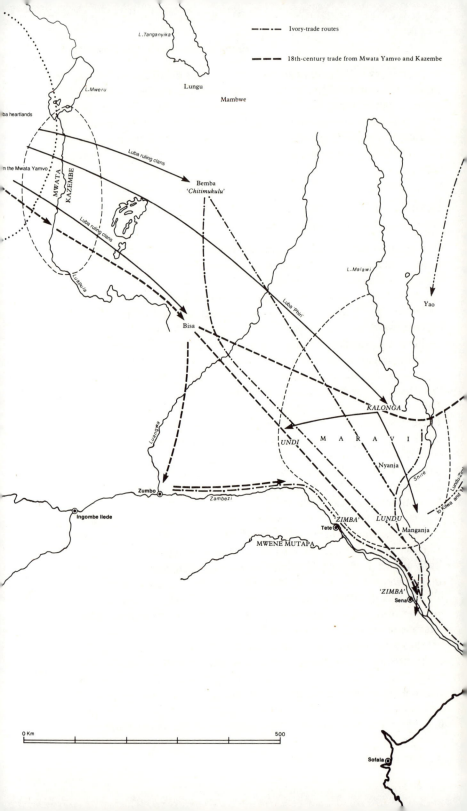

L.Tanganyika

Lungu

Mambwe

L.Mweru

ba heartlands

m the Mwata Yamvo

MWATA KAZEMBE

Luba ruling clans

Luba ruling clans

Luapula

Bemba
'Chitimukulu'

L.Malawi

Luba Phiri

Yao

Bisa

Luangwa

KALONGA

UNDI

M A R A V I

Nyanja

Zumbo

Zambezi

Ingombe Ilede

Snire

to Kilwa and M

Lundu-Zimba

'ZIMBA'
Tete

LUNDU

Manganja

MWENE MUTAPA

'ZIMBA'
Sena

0 Km   500

Sofala

another Phiri kingdom, that of the Lundu. A third Phiri kingdom, of which the ruler's title was Undi, was founded during the sixteenth century among the Chewa living to the west of the Kalonga's kingdom, in the area where the modern Zambia–Malawi frontier meets that of western Mozambique.

The Maravi kingdoms have sometimes been described as confederations, in that they were all composed of smaller kingdoms ruled by hereditary dynasties, of which the rulers lived, like the paramount kings, in capital towns called *zimbabwe* and were addressed by the same honorific title of *mambo*. As in the Lunda kingdoms, a very wide autonomy existed even at the level of village communities, which were ruled by chiefs of the land (*mwene mudzi*) each supposedly descended from the founding settler. In the Maravi states kingship was essentially concerned with tribute, and tribute involved a two-way process of acceptance and redistribution which came very close to trade. Kings stored the grain collected as tribute and used it to relieve famine. They redistributed cattle and salt. Above all, they conducted long-distance trade with outside regions in iron goods and ivory. The Maravi were renowned as miners, smelters and smiths, and their tools and weapons were in demand all over the lowland country north and south of the lower Zambezi, where iron was very scarce. The Maravi were likewise deeply involved in the ivory-trade. Their country abounded in elephants, which they trapped in pits, and it was the immemorial custom that the tusk which fell nearest to the ground was the tribute payable to the *mambo*. The inception of the ivory-trade on the lower Zambezi can be dated from the rich trading site of Ingombe Ilede, just above the Luangwa confluence, to a period around the late fourteenth or early fifteenth century, and it is likely that the valley of the Shire tributary, running down to the Zambezi from Lake Malawi, would have begun to contribute to the trade at least by this date. If the Maravi conquerors were not already established in the lands of their settlement, it is likely that their advent soon after would have given a new dimension to the trade through an enlargement of the political framework within which it could operate.

Certainly, in the sixteenth century, when the Portuguese replaced the Swahili Arabs on the lower Zambezi (see Chapter 12, pp. 177–9), and when their captains began to place monopolistic restrictions on the trade of the river, the reactions of the Maravi were swift and formidable. First the Lundu, and later the Kalonga, sent fearsome military expeditions eastwards through the country of the Lomwe and Makua to open alternative trade routes with the Indian Ocean coast from Angoche Island in the south to Kilwa in the north. The forces of

145

the Lundu, remembered variously as the Marundu and the Wazimba, practised terror tactics of the most extreme kind by killing and eating their war captives in a manner reminiscent of the Imbangala (themselves an offshoot of the Luba military system) in the hinterland of the Portuguese colony of Angola (see Chapter 11). In 1588 or 1589 a Zimba band sacked Kilwa and Mombasa, and were only narrowly defeated outside Malindi. In 1592 other bands destroyed Portuguese forces sent against them from Tete and Sena. The situation was only restored in 1622, when the Kalonga with Portuguese help defeated the Lundu, and extended his own trading network to the Indian Ocean coast. This hegemony continued until the end of the seventeenth century, when it was gradually replaced by that of the Yao, who ran their ivory caravans down the Lujenda and Rovuma valleys to Ibo and Kilwa.

To the north of the Maravi kingdoms, and linking them geographically with those of the Luba and Lunda, were the multiple small states of the Bisa and the Bemba. Here the population as a whole was culturally akin to that of eastern Lubaland, though it included some elements drawn from the patrilineal and partly cattle-keeping peoples, such as the Lungu, Mambwe and Ila, who lived in the high watershed country to the south of Lake Tanganyika. The ruling groups were certainly of Luba origin. The royals were known as *balopwe* and the capitals as *musumba*. Some time in the seventeenth century a fresh group of Luba royals of the Bena Ngandu or Crocodile clan established themselves in a part of Bembaland under a chief with the title of Chitimukulu. During the eighteenth century the Chitimukulus gradually built up a ritual pre-eminence among a circle of some twenty neighbouring Bemba states, which in the nineteenth century was misinterpreted by early European observers as a political paramountcy. In reality however, the Chitimukulus never exercised political or economic control over their client dynasties. In all secular matters these dynasties, like those of the Bisa, acted independently, their power deriving largely, as Andrew Roberts has expressed it, 'from their command of material wealth and their ability to circulate it among their subjects'[2] – through the interconnected systems of tribute and trade. All this was a region rich in ivory, but very deficient in iron-ore. Tools and weapons had therefore to be imported, either from the Mambwe and Lungu to the north-east or else from the Maravi to the south. In the eighteenth century, with the establishment of the Kazembe's kingdom on the Luapula, the Bisa became the

[2] *A History of the Bemba* (London, 1974), p. 182.

commercial intermediaries between the eastern Lunda on the one hand and the Maravi and the Portuguese on the other. Like the Nyamwezi of central Tanzania and the Yao of northern Mozambique, the Bisa became specialists in the organisation of long-distance caravans. A Portuguese officer who travelled through their country in 1831 described a society in which the villages were inhabited mainly by old men, women and children, because most of the adult men were away on caravan service. Above all, the Bisa carried the ivory and copper of the Mwata Yamvo's kingdom and all its southern offshoots and sold them, first to the Portuguese at Tete and Zumbo, and later increasingly to the Yao on the south-eastern shores of Lake Malawi, whose own caravans carried them on to the Swahili coast, where prices were higher than on the Zambezi.

In 1806 the Portuguese governor of Angola sent two literate African trading agents (*pombeiros*) on a mission to explore the overland route from Luanda to Tete. So far as is known, this was the first caravan to cover the whole distance from one Portuguese colony to the other. The mission took five years to accomplish, but only because the Mwata Kazembe of the Luapula, jealous for his own monopoly over the central part of the route, delayed the travellers at his capital for four years. The actual travelling time for the double journey was less than one year, and at no stage was it necessary for the caravan to diverge from well-beaten tracks with river ferries and recognised halting-places, nor from a framework of authority sufficient for goods to be carried in reasonable security. At the time of the pombeiros' journey, these routes had all been in existence for nearly a century. The economic watershed between east and west, which was also the last link to be forged in the chain of communications, lay on the borders of the Mwata Yamvo's home territory and that of the Luapula Kazembe. This marked the main divergence between an export trade in slaves which flowed mainly to the west and a trade in ivory which flowed mainly to the east. Copper moved in both these directions, but also in others; it was much less exclusively an article of intercontinental commerce. Imports from the Atlantic coast consisted of European textiles, arms and ammunition, glass beads and other hardware, and of Brazilian rum and tobacco. An incidental introduction, perhaps more significant than any of these things, was the Brazilian root-crop called manioc or cassava, which spread into the heart of the continent along the trade routes. It was capable of much more intensive cultivation and of much longer storage than the millet and bananas which it increasingly replaced. It was thus particularly significant as a staple food for towns and trade routes, and all the greater chiefs developed plantations, cultivated by slaves, from which to exercise the hospitality expected of them. The main imports from the Indian Ocean coast were Indian textiles and other manufactured goods. 'King Cazembe', the pombeiros noted, 'has tea-pots, cups, silver spoons and forks . . . and gold money. He has a Christian courtesy: he doffs his hat and gives good day.'[3]

Throughout this region the connection between political organisation and long-distance trade is so obvious that it would be peculiarly satisfying if the whole process of state-formation could be linked with the development of trade routes. In such a scheme the ivory-trade would assume the key position. Already attested in the region around the lower Zambezi by the tenth century A.D., it would have by this theory have spread its tentacles up the Zambezi tributaries – the Shire and the Luangwa – to the copper-rich watershed between the Zambezi and the Congo, and thence, using the hunting organisations of the Luba and the Lunda, extended itself westwards to the Kwango before meeting the rival system spreading inland from the Atlantic. There are unfortunately at least two flaws in this otherwise attractive theory. The first is the ubiquitous tradition that political systems spread mainly from north to south – from Songye to Luba, and thence to Lunda on the one hand and Maravi on the other. The second is the chronological evidence, which seems to indicate that only in the late seventeenth or early eighteenth century did the Zambezi trading system make contact with that of the Congo basin. The momentum for change thus appears to have been political rather than economic, and its direction seems to have been down the centre of the sub-continent from north to south. In this region, no less than in the interlacustrine region to the north of it, political developments seem to have had precedence over economic ones, unless indeed the economic factors were of a much more local kind. Here, Andrew Roberts has delineated more clearly than any other author the significance of a rich and populous stretch of river valley as the focus of political integration, both in the case of the Kazembe's kingdom on the Luapula and in that of the Luyana (Lozi) kingdom on the upper Zambezi. In the Luapula valley the economic basis for a dense population consisted in the combination of fishing with flood-plain agriculture, using manioc, introduced by the Lunda conquerors, as an easily storable and relatively trouble-free starchy root-crop. On the upper Zambezi the Luyana pastured great herds of cattle on the wide

---

[3] *Lacerda's Journey to Cazembe in 1798; also the Journey of the Pombeiros*, tr. R. F. Burton (London, 1873), p. 230.

flood-plain of the river and practised intensive agriculture at the edges of the valley. In both areas density of population and fixity of settlement favoured the imposition of a structured system of territorial chieftainship, and the development of military forces capable of conquering and laying under tribute the scattered and shifting societies of the less favoured countryside all round. Roberts has described the Kazembe's capital as 'a clearing-house where the products of the river were exchanged for those of the surrounding woodland',[4] and the same was certainly true of the much more centralised system evolved by the powerful Luyana kings during the course of the late seventeenth and eighteenth centuries. Here, as elsewhere in Africa, we have the salutary reminder that human societies evolve not only in accordance with their received inheritance but in response to the promptings of diverse environments.

[4] *A History of Zambia* (London, 1976), p. 95.

As we have seen, the area of direct Lunda rule was bounded on the west by the Kwango, the westernmost of the great rivers flowing northwards into the Kasai and the Congo. Between the Kwango and the Atlantic coast the three main ethnic and linguistic groupings at the beginning of our period were the Mbundu in the south from the Kwanza to the Loje, the Kongo in the north on both sides of the Congo river below Lake Malebo (Stanley Pool), and the Teke in the north-east, straddling the narrows of the river above the lake. The ancestors of all these peoples had no doubt been long settled in this general region – probably, in fact, since the penetration of the great forest by the first western Bantu cultivators during the closing centuries of the first millennium B.C. Nevertheless, it would appear that until the eve of our period the homeland of the Kongo people had been mainly to the north of the lower Congo, and that most of the country to the south of the river had been occupied by the northern Mbundu. Although the earliest large state to develop in the region may well have been that of the Teke, it seems likely that the main impulse to state-formation elsewhere came from the expansion of Kongo people from an area remembered in tradition as Bungu, situated between the upper Niari and the middle section of the lower Congo. This expansion had a military as well as a migrational character, which may have been based on the possession of superior weaponry deriving from a sudden spurt of technological innovation around the rich copper and iron deposits of Mindouli on the borders of Kongo and Teke country. At all events, conquering Kongo bands moved westwards to the Atlantic coast north of the Congo estuary, where they established the three kingdoms of Loango, Kakongo and Ngoyo, while other bands crossed the river to the south and created the nucleus of what was to become the great kingdom of Kongo.

In so far as the legends of origin can be interpreted, they suggest an initial cluster of Kongo settlements in the province of Mpemba, immediately to the south of the Congo river from Bungu. The newcomers occupied sites on the northern edge of the Angolan plateau, where iron-ore was plentiful, and it was here that their leader (the Na Kongo or Manikongo) established what was to be the permanent

150

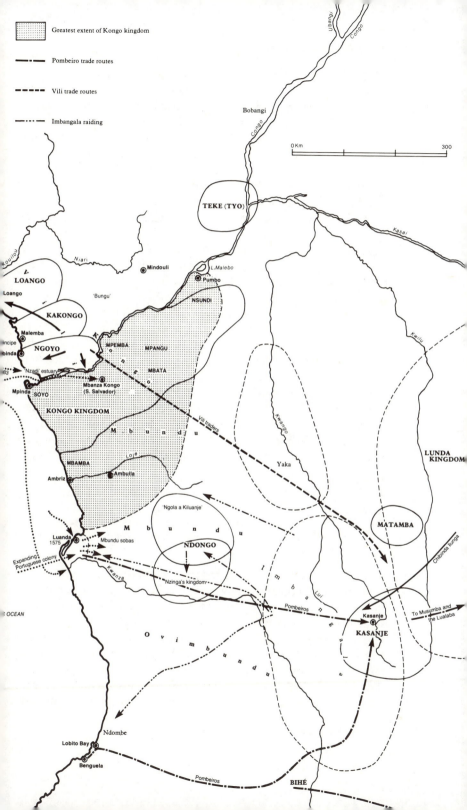

Greatest extent of Kongo kingdom

Pombeiro trade routes

Vili trade routes

Imbangala raiding

Bobangi

Ubangi

Congo

Kasai

TEKE (TYO)

0 Km 300

Niari

Mindouli

L.Malebo

Pumbo

LOANGO

Loango

'Bungu'

NSUNDI

Kwilu

KAKONGO

Malemba

NGOYO

MPEMBA

MPANGU

'Nzadi' estuary

MBATA

Kwango

Mbanza Kongo
(S. Salvador)

Mpinda

SOYO

KONGO KINGDOM

M b u n d u

Vili traders

Yaka

LUNDA
KINGDOM

MBAMBA

Loje

Ambriz

Ambulla

'Ngola a Kiluanje'

MATAMBA

Luanda
1575

M b u n d u

Mbundu sobas

NDONGO

Expanding
Portuguese colony

Nzinga's kingdom

I m b a n g a l a

Chibinda Ilunga

To Musumba and
the Lualaba

Kasanje

Kwanza

Pombeiros

Lui

OCEAN

KASANJE

O v i m b u n d u

Ndombe

Lobito Bay

Benguela

Pombeiros

BIHÉ

capital of the kingdom at Mbanza Kongo (São Salvador). The Kongo settlers are said to have married the daughters of the local Mbundu population and to have recognised the priestly authority of their chiefs (*kitome*). However, the Kongo asserted their own political predominance, and no doubt the centres of their excellent ironworking industry became the natural markets to which the Mbundu farmers of the surrounding areas brought their produce and their manufactures for trade and tribute. Their numbers and their cultural impact were together strong enough to secure the prevalence of the Kongo language, in which the word 'Mbundu' came to denote only the unassimilated people of the remoter areas who could lawfully be taken into slavery. Meantime the concentration of population around Mbanza Kongo soon produced a shortage of cultivatable land. Famines occurred and organised bands of colonists were sent out under Kongo chiefs to establish new settlements in the surrounding regions. Some of the expeditions went north-east to Nsundi and Mpangu, the provinces between Mpemba and Lake Malebo. Others went eastwards to Mbata. Others again went westwards to Soyo and Mbamba, the provinces between Mpemba and the Atlantic coast. Each expedition was led by a chief selected by the Na Kongo, who was accompanied by representatives from each of the main Kongo clans, consisting of an elder with his wives and children and subjects. From the boasting-songs handed on from father to son in these clan segments, the Belgian missionary Van Wing was able, some five hundred years later, to reconstruct a vivid picture of the dispersal.

On our departure from Kongo [goes one account] there were nine caravans under nine chiefs with their staffs of office. We brought with us the basket containing the relics of our ancestors which are used in the installation of chiefs. We brought the grass rings for the chiefs' roof-tops. The paths we travelled were safe. The villages we built were peaceful . . . We kept all together. We were careful not to separate . . .[1]

Although some accounts suggest the opening up of new agricultural land, previously occupied only by pygmy hunter–gatherers, much of the expansion must have repeated the circumstances of the original settlement, with Kongo people and their assimilated adherents forcing their authority upon older Mbundu populations. Above all, it was a structured expansion, in which the migrants maintained their links with the central monarchy. Tribute flowed into the capital, and the principal chiefs were appointed by the king, each of them taking as the main symbol of his allegiance a brand from the royal fire and

[1] J. Van Wing, *Etudes Bakongo* (Brussels, 1921), pp. 78–80.

passing it down the line of authority from his own provincial capital. When the Portuguese reached the region in the 1480s, the western provinces of Soyo and Mbamba had already been extended to the seacoast, and the royal armies were fighting the Teke on the frontiers of Nsundi in the north-east. From the genealogical evidence about the central dynasty recorded somewhat later, it would appear that the king who was ruling at the time of the Portuguese contact was either the fourth or the fifth of his line. It is therefore reasonable to date the conquest of Mpemba to the late fourteenth or the early fifteenth century.

By the beginning of our period, therefore, the Kongo kingdom was the largest state in western Central Africa. It was not, however, the only state to have developed to the stage of having a hierarchy of chiefdoms paying tribute to a central dynasty. In the north-east the Teke had probably evolved something similar at an even earlier date, which may have been the prototype for the early Kongo development in Bungu. The three coastal states to the north of the Congo estuary were likewise hierarchical structures, owing allegiance to blacksmith kings, which were the result of a process of Kongo settlement and conquest parallel to that which occurred to the south of the river. Finally, all down the eastern side of the main Kongo kingdom, and curving round it to the ocean on the south, lay a region which was pervaded by mobile groups practising the blacksmith's art which showed a propensity to develop into hierarchical state systems wherever conditions were favourable. In his study of the history of the southern Mbundu called *Kings and Kinsmen* Joseph Miller has shown that the earliest layer of political authority in central Angola was one based on ruling clans each supposed to be descended from the first agricultural settlers of a particular small locality. For regalia the ruling clan-heads employed cult objects carved in wood called *lunga*, which were essentially immobile, each being connected with a particular unexpandable piece of territory. However, the next layer of political authority was one introduced by immigrant groups of blacksmiths, arriving from the north, who used regalia made of iron, called *ngola*, which symbolised a type of authority that was essentially mobile, expansive and hierarchical. *Ngola* emblems could be carried about from place to place. They could be used to wean people away from their local *lunga*-based loyalties into new and wider groupings. As itinerant craftsmen, smiths were necessarily traders, interested in the security of the paths connecting one small state with another. They were also armourers, making weapons for hunting and warfare. They were ideally placed to organise warrior bands and to become the military patrons of small communities of settled farmers. Miller postulates a period of central Angolan history when rival organisations of *ngola*-bearing warrior–smiths were competing for political authority over groups of *lunga*-owning territorial chiefdoms among the southern Mbundu. At about the same time as the Kongo kingdom was expanding its authority over the country of the northern Mbundu, one of the several *ngola*-bearing chieftainships was emerging supreme in the contest for control of the southern Mbundu. Its ruler assumed the title of *ngola a kiluanje* (the conquering *ngola*), and it was from this title that the early Portuguese navigators applied the name Angola to all the country south of Kongo. By the early sixteenth century the Ngola's kingdom had become the centralised state of Ndongo, with a hierarchy of chiefs at several levels, and an army that was capable of blocking any further southward expansion by the Kongo.

THE PORTUGUESE AND THE OPENING OF THE ATLANTIC

Such in outline was the situation in western Central Africa when in 1483 a Portuguese caravel captained by the famous navigator Diogo Cão, sailing southward on a voyage of exploration from Elmina, encountered muddy water several miles offshore and turned eastwards to investigate. Thus Cão reached the Congo estuary, called by the local people Nzadi (whence Zaïre), and made contact with the subjects of the Manikongo, Nzinga a Nkuwu. In the course of a later voyage in 1485–6 Cão visited the capital, twenty-three days' march inland, and then sailed home with a party of Kongo emissaries, who on their arrival in Lisbon were baptised into the Christian faith and placed in a monastery for initiation into western ways. They were returned to Kongo in 1491 with a fleet of three caravels, carrying Portuguese priests, masons, carpenters and soldiers, a selection of domestic animals including horses and cattle, samples of European cloth and other manufactures, even a printing-press complete with two German printers. The ships anchored at Mpinda in the Congo estuary, and after a brief halt to baptise the provincial governor of Soyo, who was an uncle of the Manikongo, the expedition proceeded to the capital, where Nzinga a Nkuwu and five of his leading chiefs were baptised on 3 May 1491. A thousand of the Manikongo's subjects were detailed to assist the Portuguese masons in the building of a church. Meanwhile the Portuguese soldiery accompanied the armies of the king in a campaign to defend the north-eastern province of Nsundi from Teke raiders, in which European fire-arms contributed to a decisive victory and to the capture of many prisoners-of-war.

Most of the Portuguese now departed, carrying away a valuable cargo of ivory and slaves. The priests and craftsmen remained in Kongo, where the king's profession of their faith proved short-lived. However, that of his son Nzinga Mbemba, the governor of Nsundi, baptised as Afonso in 1491, developed into a lifelong commitment to Christianity and the Portuguese alliance. On the death of Nzinga a Nkuwu around 1506, Afonso won a disputed succession and reigned until about 1543. These years marked the zenith of Portuguese influence on Kongo.

From the very beginning of his reign Afonso made serious efforts to transform his loose-knit African empire towards what he understood of the pattern of a Christian state of the Renaissance period in Europe. He sent for more missionaries and technicians, of whom the first contingent arrived in 1512. He stepped up the flow of Kongo students to Lisbon. He himself studied the laws of Portugal, which were sent to him in five great volumes, and informed himself in detail about the etiquette of the Portuguese court and the ranking system of European society. Soon his provincial governors were known as dukes, and his military leaders and court officials as counts and marquises, while the sartorial fineries sent from Lisbon were distributed in the inner circles of the Kongo aristocracy. It should not be assumed that such changes were merely superficial. Probably they symbolised a general hardening of the social structure in Kongo, whereby members of the conquering clans which had spread out from Mpemba into the surrounding provinces now became increasingly consolidated into a ruling class. Likewise, the early spread of Christianity probably helped the process of social differentiation. It was a classic case of 'conversion from the top'. In 1513 Afonso took an oath of obedience to the pope, and three years later a Franciscan missionary wrote ecstatically of the king's Christian qualities.

It seems to me from the way he speaks as though he is not a man but rather an angel, sent by the Lord into this kingdom to convert it; for I assure you that it is *he* who instructs *us*, and that he knows better than we do the Prophets and the Gospel of our Lord Jesus Christ and the lives of the saints and all the things concerning our Holy Mother the Church . . . For he devotes himself entirely to study, so that it often happens that he falls asleep over his books, and often he forgets to eat and drink in talking of the things of Our Lord.[2]

However, within Kongo society, the spread of the faith seems to have followed aristocratic channels, affecting the court at São Salvador and

---

[2] Letter from Rui d'Aguiar to King Manuel of Portugal of 25 May 1516, in A. Brasio (ed.), *Monumenta Missionaria Africana*, vol. I (Lisbon, 1953), p. 361.

diffusing from there to the provincial capitals by a transformation of the traditional system of educating the sons of chiefs in the households of the great. Seen from the Kongo end, Christianity was the route to royal favour, the badge of the successful faction within a ruling group. Its connections with the universal Church were very slender, depending upon a dozen white missionaries, a few uncertainly motivated European craftsmen and a handful of Bakongo students returned from Portugal, among them a son of Afonso who had been priested in Lisbon and consecrated to the episcopate in Rome. Like the *ngola* hierarchies among the Mbundu, the new religion was perhaps seen by the populace at large in the light of a powerful secret society introduced from abroad.

Of course, despite his Christian piety, Afonso was throughout his reign deeply involved in the capture and sale of slaves to the Portuguese. It was the inevitable price which he had to pay for his European advisers and for the material luxuries with which he rewarded his chief subjects. Without doubt, his slaving wars gave a military impetus to his kingdom and consolidated his authority in the border regions to the east and the south. The condition of success in these adventures was, however, that the trade should remain a royal monopoly. Hence his growing disquiet with the Portuguese sea-captains who tried to trade directly with his subjects and even with his enemies. The official trading expeditions were soon supplemented by those of Portuguese colonists, many of them transported convicts, who had been settled since the 1490s on the islands of São Tomé and Principe, whose sugar estates required large numbers of agricultural slaves. These men felt no obligation to support the alliance between Portugal and Kongo. They sailed up and down the coast, trading with the subordinate chiefs of the Manikongo and with others beyond his sway. They discovered the Kwanza river and sailed up its slow-flowing waters to make contact with the Ngola a Kiluanje. Indeed, it is likely that the final emergence of the Ngola as the supreme power among the southern Mbundu was due to wars of conquest stimulated by the demand for slaves of the São Tomé settlers. At all events, the unofficial Portuguese were now in touch with the Manikongo's most powerful rival, and a series of official missions, beginning in 1520, all failed to bring the situation under control. So long as Afonso lived there was no direct confrontation, but thirteen years after his death, in 1556, there was war on the frontier between the armies of the Manikongo and those of the Ngola in which the Kongo forces suffered a severe defeat. It was not the end of the Portuguese alliance with Kongo, but

certainly it marked the moment when the civilising mission of Portugal was overtaken by the economic interest of the Atlantic slave-trade now centred on the growing plantations of Brazil. The situation between the kingdom of Benin and the principalities of the Niger Delta had been reproduced in western Central Africa.

THE YAKA, THE PORTUGUESE AND THE IMBANGALA

It was in connection with the war of 1556 between Kongo and Ndongo (the kingdom of the Ngola) that the Portuguese first heard of people whom they called 'Jaga', who lived in the far interior and who sent warrior bands of extreme ferocity to fight alongside the Mbundu of Ndongo. Though the Portuguese later applied the term to other peoples using similar methods of warfare, there can be little doubt that at this stage it referred to the Yaka people who inhabited the middle reaches of the Kwango valley and who were the eastern neighbours of the Mbundu and the Kongo. Along with the Teke, who lived to the north of them, the Yaka had probably been among the main victims of the slave-raids conducted by the Kongo since the opening of the Atlantic trade. With the weakening of the Kongo kingdom following the death of Afonso, the raided became the raiders, joining forces with the Mbundu not only for the defence of Ndongo but in subsequent invasions of Kongo territory. These began during the reign of Afonso's grandson, Diogo (1545–61). His successor, Bernardo (1561–7), was killed while fighting the Yaka on the eastern frontier. The next king, Henrique (1567–8), died in a war against the Teke. His successor, Alvaro (1568–87), had barely acceded when the whole eastern side of the Kongo kingdom was laid waste by a great invasion of Yaka war-bands, which swept through the provinces of Mbata and Mpemba, capturing and sacking São Salvador itself in 1569. Alvaro fled with his courtiers to an island in the lower Congo and sent desperate appeals for help to his Portuguese allies. Meanwhile, the Yaka made profitable contact with the São Tomé traders at the ports on the Congo estuary, to whom they sold thousands of their Kongo captives including members of the royal family and other notables.

So far as the Portuguese were concerned, it seemed at first that once again São Tomé had triumphed over the metropolis. However, when news of the disasters in Kongo at last reached Lisbon in February 1571, it provoked a revolution in Portuguese policy towards western Central Africa as a whole. On the one hand, an expeditionary force of some six hundred Portuguese soldiers was quickly despatched to help Alvaro of Kongo to regain his throne. On the other hand, the decision was taken to abandon further attempts to negotiate a peaceful relationship with Ndongo, and instead to grant a royal charter to Paulo Dias, the grandson of the great explorer Bartholomew Dias, permitting him to conquer the territory between the southern frontier of Kongo and a line thirty-five leagues to the south of the Kwanza, of part of which he would be the hereditary Lord Proprietor, and of the rest governor for life on behalf of the Portuguese Crown. The unspoken premiss of the charter was that there would be perpetual warfare between the colony and the Ngola of Ndongo, at whose expense all conquests behind the coastal belt would have to be made. The preamble to the charter stated that conquest would promote the spread of the Christian faith, and it clearly envisaged that this would be mainly achieved by the conversion of war captives prior to their despatch as slaves to the New World. In Kongo the Portuguese expeditionary force was successful in restoring Alvaro in 1574. The Yaka, unnerved by their first experience of fire-arms, were soon driven back to their bases on the eastern frontier. The Kongo kingdom entered upon a second long period of stability, lasting till the mid-seventeenth century, during which the slave-trade centred upon the markets on the Teke frontier, above all that of Pumbo near the southern shore of Lake Malebo. The traders who organised caravan traffic to this market became known in Portuguese as *pombeiros*, and so dominant was their role that the term was later applied to all traders operating in the far interior of western Central Africa. Meanwhile, in 1575 Paulo Dias carried out the occupation of Luanda Island. In the following year a bridgehead was established on the mainland, in the neighbourhood of the modern town.

For nearly two hundred years the colony of Angola developed essentially as a gigantic slave-trading enterprise. The garrison seldom numbered more than one thousand European troops, armed with matchlocks and scattered in half a dozen small forts in or near the Kwanza valley. To these there were gradually added some thousands of slave soldiers, who fought with bows and spears. The strategy was to conquer first one and then another of the small Mbundu chieftainships, forcing the local rulers (called *sobas*) into a state of allegiance in which they paid tribute in slaves, whom they obtained by attacking their independent neighbours farther inland. Those most inclined to resist migrated inland and placed themselves under the protection of the Ngola of Ndongo, who soon began to mount major campaigns against the advancing frontiers of the colony. The territorial expansion of the Portuguese was thus slowed, but the slave-trade was fed by the casualties of this frontier warfare. Already by the last quarter of the sixteenth century the export of slaves from Luanda to Brazil averaged between five and ten thousand persons a year. Alongside the purely military activity there grew up a commercial enterprise based largely on the local coastal trade of the Portuguese up and down the coast of western Central Africa. The pombeiros who traded into the interior of Kongo with the salt and sea-shells of Luanda returned not only with slaves but with tens of thousands of the fine raphia cloths of the forest margins, which were in high demand with the Mbundu. Other pombeiros accompanied the military expeditions of the colonial garrisons and traded in the intervals of warfare.

Besides the direct trading and warfare between the Portuguese and the Mbundu, the Angolan slave-trade was augmented by a third and more gruesome factor. This was the activity of nomadic bands of people who had entirely abandoned the food-producing way of life and who lived by raiding others, consuming their crops and their cattle and felling their oil-palms for palm-wine, before moving on to repeat the process elsewhere. Because of the similarity of their operations to those of the Yaka bands which raided the Kongo kingdom in the 1550s and 60s, the Portuguese described these people indiscriminately as 'Jaga'. In point of fact there may have been no connection at all between the Yaka, who spoke a language closely akin to Kongo, and the more southerly bands who operated among the Mbundu and their neighbours to the south, who came to be known as Imbangala. These represented in some sense the extreme fringe of the westerly migrations of older Lunda lineages and political titles away from the reorganisation of Lunda society by the dynasty descending from the Chibinda Ilunga (Chapter 10, p. 139). But although many of these groups maintained the tradition of their Lunda origins and of their long march to the west, only a small fraction of them can in reality have had Lunda blood in their veins, because the migrants had incorporated fresh elements at every stage in their journey. Indeed, taken at their face value, Imbangala traditions appear to relate that, after crossing the Kasai, the main body had adopted the singular custom of destroying their own children at birth and of keeping up their numbers by adopting adolescents from the peoples whom they conquered on their travels. In reality, as Joseph Miller has shown, the so-called destruction of children referred to a system of military initiation known as the *kilombo*, in which lineage ties were utterly renounced, and children, whether born in the group or adopted, were brought up communally in quasi-military formations.[3] At all events,

[3] *Kings and Kinsmen* (London, 1976), p. 234.

this elimination of family life was the ultimate adaptation to an economy of militaristic parasitism. Even more effectively than the Nguni migrants of the nineteenth century, the Imbangala 'cultivated with the spear'.

The first written description of an Imbangala band was made by an English sailor, Andrew Battell, a war captive of the Portuguese, who employed him as the captain of a coastal trading vessel operating out of Luanda. Around 1600 Battell sailed southwards to Lobito Bay to buy foodstuffs for the colony. He found that the local community of Ndombe people had been destroyed by a band of some 16,000 Imbangala, who were living in a stockaded war-camp, eating and drinking the fruits of their conquest. At least on certain ritual occasions, human flesh was consumed with relish. Battell painted an intimidating picture of the leader of the band, Kalandula.

He weareth a palm-cloth about his middle, as fine as silk. His body is carved and cut with sundry works, and every day is anointed with the fat of men. He weareth a piece of copper cross his nose, two inches long, and in his ears also. His body is always painted red and white. He hath twenty or thirty wives, which follow him when he goeth abroad; and one of them carrieth his bows and arrows; and four of them carry his cups of drink after him. And when he drinketh, they all kneel down, and clap their hands and sing.[4]

As befitted a desperado of his period, Battel ferried a detachment of Kalandula's followers across the Kuvu river to attack another Ndombe settlement living on the site of Old Benguela, and sailed back to Luanda with the first of many cargoes of very cheap slaves. When, five months later, the band moved away into the interior in search of fresh victims, Battell and fifty other Portuguese merchants followed in their train. It was the beginning of a long partnership between Portuguese slave-traders and Imbangala bands, which were soon operating around all the frontiers of the colony and of Ndongo.

KONGO, NDONGO, MATAMBA, KASANJE, LOANGO

Thanks to the military and commercial activity of the Portuguese and to the operations of the Imbangala bands in the interior, the mainspring of historical change during the seventeenth and eighteenth centuries lay in the southern half of the region. The first crucial issue concerned the survival of Ndongo, and it centred on the astonishing career of a female ruler, Nzinga Mbande, who inherited the Ngola-

[4] E. Ravenstein (ed.), *The Strange Adventures of Andrew Battell* (London, 1901), pp. 31–2.

ship in 1624. Nzinga appreciated that the best hope for her kingdom, beset by the Portuguese on the west and by the Imbangala on the north and south, lay in establishing the position of an intermediary in the slave-trade, whereby Ndongo would become an ally of the Portuguese and the main source of slaves would be transferred from her own dominions to those of her eastern neighbours. Already before her accession Nzinga travelled as an envoy to Luanda, where the outlines of such an arrangement were agreed and were sealed by her own solemn baptism as Dona Ana Nzinga, the Portuguese governor standing godfather. The honeymoon proved, however, of short duration. During the second year of her reign Dona Ana appealed for Portuguese help against the Imbangala invaders of her kingdom. Forces were sent, but soon turned to slave-raiding on their own account. Western Ndongo was overrun and refugees converged upon Dona Ana's headquarters in the east. From there she led them north-eastwards to conquer and settle the region of Matamba between Ndongo and the middle Kwango. Abandoning all her Christian connections, and adopting much of the military organisation of the Imbangala, she succeeded in building up a powerful slave-raiding and middleman state, which remained of importance till the second half of the eighteenth century. After flirting briefly with the Dutch, who captured and ruled Luanda from 1641 till 1648, Dona Ana renewed the treaty relations with the Portuguese in 1656, and died, once more in the arms of the Church, in 1663 at the age of eighty-one.

Meanwhile, to the south of Matamba, the Imbangala bands were at last beginning to settle down. In some sense, the process may be traced back to the second decade of the seventeenth century, when several Imbangala bands closed in on both sides of the Kwanza valley in order to be in regular touch with the Portuguese frontier and the main Luanda trade route. In these circumstances the bands started to treat some sections of the local Mbundu less as temporary victims and more as long-term subjects. On the one hand Mbundu youths were initiated into the *kilombo* formations, and on the other hand the Imbangala masters became progressively Mbunduised, taking Mbundu wives and adopting Mbundu lineages. As the Portuguese pushed their advanced posts further into central Ndongo, the Imbangala followed the example of Dona Ana and retreated further into the interior in order to maintain their independence. Some time around 1630 one large group reached and conquered the region lying in the angle of the Lui and the Kwango rivers, henceforward known, after the leadership title of the conquering commander, as Kasanje. The original settlers were soon joined by others, and there emerged a new and powerful state, and one which enjoyed an even more strategic situation than that of Matamba to the north of it, for across the Kwango from Kasanje lay the western frontier lands of the great kingdom of Lunda with its well-policed trade routes running east to Musumba and the Lualaba (see Chapter 10, pp. 141–2). Until around the 1680s the slave-trade of Kasanje was supplied mainly by the captives from its own wars of conquest. Thereafter an increasing proportion came from the frontier wars of the Lunda. Kasanje became the great broker state of the region, trading with the Lunda on the Kwango frontier and with the Portuguese pombeiros at market-places on its western borders. In the words of David Birmingham, 'The Portuguese now needed to play a much less active military role in Angola; they organized the final purchase and shipment of slaves, but most of the actual capturing of slaves passed out of their hands.'[5]

The rise of Angola, Matamba and Kasanje was accompanied during the late seventeenth and eighteenth centuries by the disintegration of the kingdom of Kongo. During the fifty years which followed the restoration of the monarchy after the Yaka invasions as many as a thousand Portuguese traders settled in the main towns of the kingdom, marrying local wives and founding a Luso-African bourgeoisie, whose descendants formed the core of a mercantile and nominally Christian community. The Church was still served by missionaries from Europe, but there were also some native clergy, and in the capital a small literate class of secretaries and bureaucrats helped the kings to collect their revenues and to conduct their relations with Luanda and São Tomé, Lisbon and Rome. Nevertheless, the expansion of the Portuguese colony and of the Imbangala bands operating around its fringes proved an increasing threat to the security of the southern provinces. In 1622 frontier disputes suddenly flamed into war and the Kongo armies were soundly defeated by a combination of Portuguese and Imbangala forces. On the death of the king during the same year, faction fighting broke out within Kongo itself and six rulers held the throne for brief periods during the next nineteen years. Stability was briefly restored under a king named Garcia II, who reigned from 1641 to 1661, largely thanks to the interval of Dutch rule at Luanda. With the return of the Portuguese, hostilities were resumed, culminating in 1665 in a great battle at Ambuila, when a Kongo army said to number 70,000 was virtually wiped out.

After the battle of Ambuila the Kongo kingdom broke up. The Manikongo, Antonio, had perished on the field, and none of the

[5] *Trade and Conflict in Angola* (Oxford, 1966), p. 132.

contenders for the succession was able to establish his authority over more than a limited area. The coastal province of Soyo had already been independent for some years. The southern province of Mbamba was overrun by slave-raiding bands. In the north two rival dynasties competed indecisively until 1709, when one of them succeeded in reoccupying the capital, though with a greatly reduced territory. In these circumstances the old trade routes fell into disuse. The trade of the regions to the east of Kongo was tapped from Matamba to the south and, increasingly, from the rising commercial states of the Vili people to the north of the Congo estuary. Among these, Loango (see p. 150) had at first the predominance. Itself a producer of raphia cloths and salt, which were in wide demand throughout the region, Loango became the broker for the copper of Mindouli and the ivory of the far interior, brought by river to Lake Malebo. From there the Vili traders began in the eighteenth century to ascend the southern tributaries of the Congo, selling fire-arms to Matamba and Kasanje and bringing out the ivory of western Lunda. An important strength of the Vili was that their European trade connections were with the Dutch, and later with the French and English, rather than with the Portuguese. They were thus able to obtain more favourable terms of trade and also access to the all-important long-distance trading commodity of fire-arms. From the late seventeenth century onwards the accent in the export trade to the Dutch, French and British shifted increasingly towards the slave-trade, and here again the Vili distinguished themselves as suppliers. Their main raiding grounds were in the northern part of the former Kongo kingdom, and so the southern Vili states – Kakongo with its port at Malemba, and Ngoyo with its port at Cabinda – began to overtake Loango.

To the south of the main Luanda trade route up the Kwanza valley to Kasanje in Imbangala country lay the Benguela highlands, which were inhabited by Ovimbundu and related peoples. At least as early as the seventeenth century the Ovimbundu had begun to form little states, similar in structure to the Kongo kingdom, but with some Lunda features, passed on, no doubt, by the Imbangala. By the middle of the eighteenth century the Ovimbundu states were deeply involved in the Atlantic slave-trade, feeding, initially, into the Ndongo–Luanda system, but increasingly trading direct with Benguela. Benguela had been founded early in the seventeenth century as a colony of settlement for Portuguese fishermen and farmers rather than, as in the case of Luanda, for traders. Some of these Benguela farmers moved inland and settled all over the highlands, married local women, and became *sertanejos*, backwoodsmen. By the middle of the

163

eighteenth century, however, Benguela began to overtake Luanda as the main Portuguese slaving port. The impact of this upon the Ovimbundu states was dramatic. At least seven of these – including Mbailundu and Bihé – grew into large kingdoms. The Ovimbundu kingdoms raided far into southern and western Angola for slaves, cattle and ivory. Long-distance trade was organised by the Ovimbundu themselves, or very frequently by *sertanejos*, the pombeiros of the south. By the end of our period, the Ovimbundu kingdoms dominated a huge area south and west of the Kwanza and north of the Cunene, and raided or traded even further afield: they were the most south-westerly frontiers of the political and social influences of the great Kongo and Lunda traditions.

The people who lived in the very south of modern Angola and all over northern Namibia were related linguistically and culturally to the Ovimbundu. Most sections of these South-Western Bantu were cattlekeepers – their cattle coming originally from the Bantu of the middle Zambezi via a narrow corridor along the Okavango river. The Ovambo and Nkhumbi built up dense populations in the fertile flood plains of the Cuvelai and Cunene rivers; to their west, the Nyaneka people inhabited the fairly productive Huila highlands, the escarpment of which falls directly to the Namib desert of coastal southern Angola and Namibia – one of the most arid areas of Africa. The Herero, the most southerly of the South-Western Bantu, had abandoned agriculture and become wholly cattle nomads (the only Bantu group to make the complete transition). The Nyaneka and the Herero were in contact with the Korana and Bergdama Khoi-speaking Negro hunters, and the Herero with the Nama Khoi pastoralists of central Namibia. By the end of the eighteenth century the Nyaneka, Nkhumbi and Ovambo had become caught up in the slave- and ivory-trading activities of the Ovimbundu, *sertanejos* and Portuguese from Benguela. Their response was to coalesce into a number of chiefdoms, but these never became as powerful as the Ovimbundu kingdoms. It was not until the middle of the nineteenth century that Cape traders from Walvis Bay and Portuguese from Moçamedes penetrated northern Namibia and southern Angola, and traded firearms to the chiefdoms, which led, fairly rapidly, to their breakdown.

THE INDIAN OCEAN BACKGROUND

We saw in Chapter 9 that until almost the end of our period the later Iron Age societies which were emerging on the great interior plateau of East Africa had practically no connection with the Indian Ocean coast. From Mogadishu in the north to Mozambique Island in the south, the Zanzibar coast was a world of its own, based on the coastal plain and the offshore islands, oriented towards the sea and exploiting only tenuously even the immediate hinterland as a source of ivory and slaves. The population of the coast was almost entirely Negro and Bantu-speaking, and much of it was still organised on purely African and ethnic lines. The Pokomo of the lower Tana valley, the Giriama and the Digo north and south of Mombasa, the Bondei around the mouth of the Pangani, the Zaramo between Dar es Salaam and the Rufiji, the Makonde and the Makua between the Rovuma and Mozambique Island were all basically coastal peoples, who lived by a combination of fishing, hunting and farming and who governed themselves in small clan and family units with very little reference to the strangers who lived in their midst. Even on some of the islands, such as Pemba and Zanzibar, there were some wholly African communities which existed independently of any system of alien rule. Nevertheless, the dynamic societies of the Zanzibar coast were those which had grown up around the seaside villages and small towns originally founded by traders and settlers who had arrived by sea from Somalia, southern Arabia and the Persian Gulf. Even these communities were largely African in their ethnic composition, for the immigrants, though reinforced in every generation, generally inter-married with the locals and built up large households of dependants and slaves. In all of them Bantu languages were spoken, and even the upper classes used a Bantu lingua franca, called Kiswahili, which was most closely related to the languages of the Kenya coast around Mombasa, though laced with words of Arabic origin. Language apart, these communities were linked by the facts that the ruling groups professed Islam, that their economic activities were largely bound up with the maritime trade, and that their social and material culture was   165

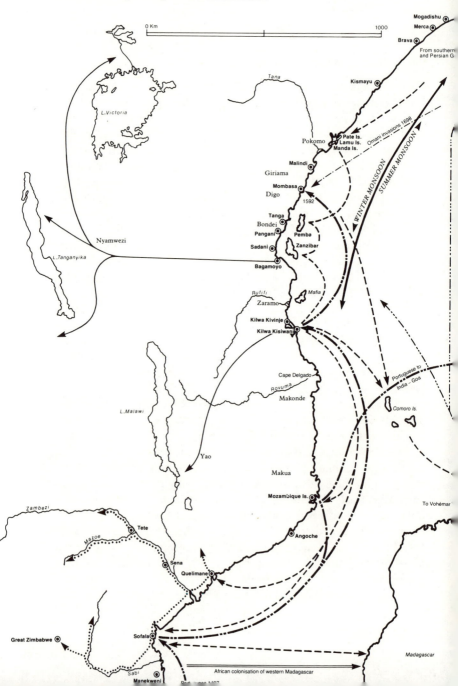

0 Km   1000

Mogadishu
Merca
Brava
From southern
and Persian G.

Kismayu

Tana

L.Victoria

Pate Is.
Pokomo   Lamu Is.
Manda Is.
Omani invasions 1698

Malindi

Giriama

Mombasa
Digo
1592

Nyamwezi

Tanga
Bondei
Pangani
Pemba
Sadani
Zanzibar
Bagamoyo

L.Tanganyika

WINTER MONSOON

SUMMER MONSOON

Rufiji
Mafia

Zaramo

Kilwa Kivinje
Kilwa Kisiwani

Cape Delgado
Rovuma
Makonde

Portuguese to
India – Goa

Comoro Is.

L.Malawi

Yao

Makua

Mozambique Is.

To Vohémar

Zambezi

Tete

Mazoe

Angoche

Sena
Quelimane

Great Zimbabwe

Sofala

Madagascar

Sabi

African colonisation of western Madagascar

Manekweni

largely influenced by their overseas contacts. An important difference from the Islamic societies of sub-Saharan West Africa was that the rulers, even if mainly African, thought of themselves as foreigners. *Ustaarabu*, 'to be like an Arab', was the touchstone of civilisation.

At the beginning of the fifteenth century the pattern of Islamic trade and settlement on the East African coast was already well established. It had started on the offshore islands as early as the eighth century with the partial conquest and settlement of Zanzibar Island. By the ninth and tenth centuries the islands of Manda and Pemba were both regular ports of call on a long-distance route that extended as far south as 'Sofala' – a stretch of low-lying coast which probably included the site of the later port of that name, well to the south of the Zambezi delta. Arabs were not the only foreign visitors to this southerly region, for the first Indonesian settlement of the previously uninhabited island of Madagascar must have occurred by this period, and large fleets of Indonesian sailing canoes had been sighted by Arab seamen in the waters off Aden. The goal of all these voyages, according to the tenth-century Arab geographer al-Masudi, who had himself sailed the route, was a great kingdom of the blacks where ivory of the best quality was to be had in profusion, and gold. These commodities were transshipped at Shiraz on the Persian Gulf and used for the trade with India and China. Thenceforward Arab and Persian settlement along the coasts of Somalia, Kenya, Tanzania and Mozambique had developed steadily. Mogadishu, Merca, Brava, Malindi and Mombasa were settled by the twelfth century, and Kilwa at the beginning of the thirteenth. The coast of East Africa, being lined with coral reefs, afforded an unlimited supply of soft, easily cut stone, which hardened with exposure to the air, and the main settlements were soon equipped with stone-built ramps and sea-walls, mosques and pillar-tombs, palaces for the rulers and urban housing for the well-to-do who lived within the city walls. By the fifteenth century many other towns had grown up at places like Pate and Lamu, Gedi and Kilifi, while in between them smaller settlements were to be found at intervals of a few kilometres all down the coast.

Economically, these Swahili Arab settlements were self-supporting in the essentials. Their inhabitants lived on fish and goatsmeat, bananas and coconuts, millet and rice. In the northern cities at least, they wove their own camel-hair cloth. Further south cotton was planted, spun and woven, so that Muslims might be clothed with the required attention to decency and dignity. The settlements had masons and boat-builders, blacksmiths and leatherworkers. The climate was humid, but otherwise pleasant. Life, as James S. Kirkman   167

24 The approaches to Zimbabwe (1): Arabs and Portuguese on the East
    African coast

has written, was 'colonial and comfortable'.[1] So far as luxuries were concerned, however, the Swahili cities formed part of a vast network of exchange covering the whole of the Indian Ocean and the China Sea. The dhows came southwards in their hundreds with every winter monsoon, filled with luxury textiles of silk and cotton, carpets, hardware, glazed pottery from Persia and porcelain eating-bowls from Canton. They sailed northwards again every summer, loaded with the hard mangrove poles vital for house-building in the treeless lands of the Gulf, with rice from Madagascar to feed the hungry cities of the north, with the large, soft ivory used especially for women's bangles in all the Hindu countries, and with the copper and gold of Zimbabwe which helped to fertilise the trade of the whole system. Curiously enough, slaves are little mentioned as objects of export. Presumably, they were more easily obtained in the countries of north-eastern Africa, where larger states with better-organised armies were constantly warring with their neighbours. That it was gold which really sustained all the other branches of the East African coastal trade can be demonstrated both from the history of Kilwa and from that of

[1] *Men and Monuments of the East African Coast* (London, 1964), p. 110.

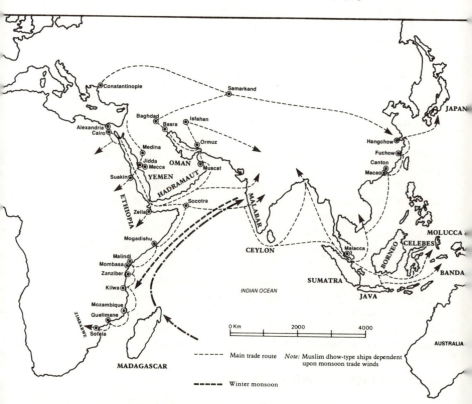

- - - - - Main trade route   *Note: Muslim dhow-type ships dependent upon monsoon trade winds*

━━━━ Winter monsoon

━━·━ Summer monsoon

Zimbabwe, which was the only sector of the vast interior which was deeply penetrated by long-distance trade with the coast.

The strategic significance of Kilwa was that it marked approximately the limit of a single season's sailing for dhows based in southern Arabia and the Persian Gulf. South of Cape Delgado the monsoon winds diminished and ships sailing beyond this point risked a whole year's delay in making their return. Kilwa was thus the natural port of transshipment for the Sofala coast and also for Madagascar. With its magnificent, sheltered roadstead between the island and the mainland, it was the natural headquarters for vessels plying over the southern sector of the route. Extensive archaeological investigation carried out over seven seasons by Neville Chittick has established the importance of the settlement and the chronological stages of its development. Founded about 1200 by a dynasty claiming to have originated in Shiraz on the Persian Gulf, but which had probably been settled for some time on the Somali coast before moving further south, Kilwa grew steadily through the thirteenth century. It reached its peak of prosperity during the fourteenth century under a new dynasty, that of the Mahdali, whose origins and main connections were with Aden rather than the Gulf. During this period much of the town was rebuilt in stone, the Great Mosque was enlarged and adorned with vaults and cupolas, and a splendid new palace, the Husuni Kubwa, was erected on a low cliff overlooking the roadstead at the northern tip of the island. This was equipped with a reception hall of great magnificence, with an elegant octagonal bathing pool on the edge of the cliff and with a large warehouse compound for the storage of trade goods. The numerous finds of Chinese porcelain associated with the buildings of this period show the growing wealth of the Mahdali sultans. For small transactions a minted copper coinage was in widespread use. Three-legged steatite eating-vessels made in northern Madagascar prove that there was regular trade with the great island, the bulk of which was probably in foodstuffs, especially rice. A contemporary site at Vohémar in north-eastern Madagascar shows the existence there of at least one Muslim settlement which was importing the same trade goods as Kilwa. However, the indigenous chronicles of Kilwa, compiled in the sixteenth century, leave no doubt that the main commercial interests of the town lay along the Sofala coast. By the fourteenth century, if not before, Sofala had come to denote a specific settlement in the neighbourhood of the modern Beira, which was ruled by governors sent from Kilwa. The fourth of the Mahdali sultans, Daud, had held this post during his father's reign, and both he and his successor were said to have grown rich on 169

25 The approaches to Zimbabwe (2): Muslim trading activities in the Indian Ocean

the Sofala trade. Though Kilwa seems to have suffered a brief period of decline at the end of the fourteenth century, the fifteenth century saw a marked revival, and when the Portuguese first landed at Sofala in 1497 they found it still ruled by a Kilwa governor. It can be concluded that during most of the fourteenth and fifteenth centuries Kilwa controlled the lines of maritime communication leading southwards to Madagascar and the Mozambique mainland. As we shall see, this period corresponds with the great period of Shona political development on the Zimbabwean plateau and the lowlands of central Mozambique. It was also the period when western Madagascar was extensively colonised by African peoples from Mozambique. These migrants are likely to have been attracted by the seafarers' tales of fishing waters and pastureland as yet unoccupied by the Malagasy, who were still concentrated around the northern and eastern coasts of the island. Some of the colonists may even have been transported in Arab shipping. Others may have been emboldened to follow by canoe in the wake of the larger ships.

THE STATES OF ZIMBABWE

The historiography of Zimbabwe has hitherto painted a picture far too concentrated upon the highland plateau south of the middle Zambezi, to the virtual exclusion of the lowlands between the plateau and the coast. The impression has been created that states emerged in the interior without any reference to events at the coast, and that a great gold-mining industry developed without any stimulus from a world market. Ritual citations have been made from the tenth-century writings of al-Masudi, but little attempt has been made to explain them. Only with the emergence of the Mutapa empire in the fifteenth century has Shona rule in the coastal lowlands generally been discussed in any detail. However, the recent discovery at Manekweni, only 50 kilometres from the coast at Vilanculos, of a stone-built capital site with a series of radiocarbon dates running from about A.D. 1150 to about 1600 has shown that right through the period of stone building at the plateau site of Great Zimbabwe the same culture was present in the lowlands of central Mozambique.[2] Moreover, Garlake's excavations have shown that at Manekweni, as at most of the comparable sites on the plateau, cattle ownership was the main preoccupation of the ruling class and prime beef the diet of those who inhabited the main stone-built enclosure.[3] It thus becomes quite reasonable to

[2] P. S. Garlake, 'An investigation of Manekweni, Mozambique', *Azania*, 11 (1976), 25–48.
[3] Garlake, 'Pastoralism and Zimbabwe', *Journal of African History*, 19 (1978), 479–93.

26   The approaches to Zimbabwe (3): Zimbabwe/Mutapa/Butwa

suppose that al-Masudi's 'great kingdom of the blacks', rich in cattle
and with access to plenteous supplies of ivory, was a kingdom situated
in the lowlands of the Sofala coast. Very likely it was the ancestor of
the kingdom known to the sixteenth-century Portuguese as Kiteve,
then a somewhat unwilling tributary of the Mwene Mutapa, but in
earlier times an important broker state linking the maritime enterprise of the Arabs with the sources of gold and ivory in the interior.
While the political systems of Kiteve, and of other neighbouring
Shona states, were undoubtedly of African origin, it is thus per-
fectly conceivable that the stimulus to large-scale gold-mining and
ivory-hunting should have resulted from the contacts with the

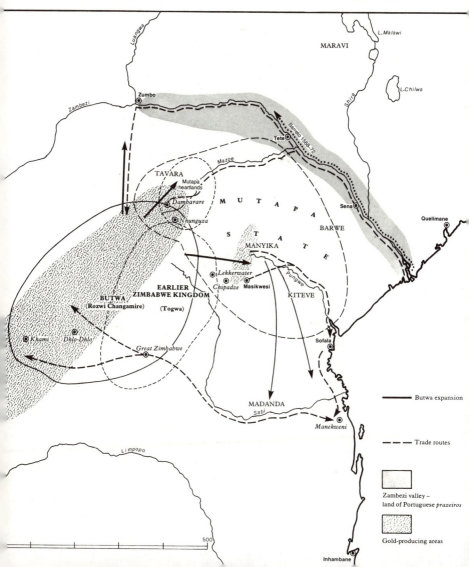

maritime traders of the Indian Ocean coast. As in so many other regions of Africa, it was easiest for the largest concentrations of political and economic power to develop in the interior, away from direct contact with the outsiders who would tend to play off one coastal state against another. Nevertheless, the external trade could be a powerful influence even in the politics of interior regions.

There is no doubt that at the beginning of our period the dominant state of the interior plateau was that centred since the end of the eleventh century at Great Zimbabwe. The capital was not itself in gold-producing country, which stretched around it in a wide arc from the west to the north-east. Rather, the place seems to have been chosen for its temperate climate and varied agricultural potential, midway between the dry grazing-land of the west and the misty mountains and damp valleys adjoining the eastern scarp. Here, in a landscape of little ridges topped with granite boulders and valleys dropping gently to the Sabi river, a royal township, supplied with beer and vegetable food by the local cultivators and with milk and meat from royal herds kept moving round the country in a regular pattern of transhumance, could be comfortably supported for more than four centuries. At its western extremity an unusually steep, granite-covered hill rising sheer from the valley floor was the ritual centre and, traditionally at least, the royal burial site of the kingdom. In the valley below its southern cliffs the royal enclosure had its main gateway facing towards the hilltop shrine. The town stretched away to the east along the valley floor. For the first two centuries of its existence Great Zimbabwe was a fairly modest settlement. The royal enclosure was roughly walled with uneven slabs of granite. The holy hill had huts of pounded ant-hill standing upon roughly piled stone platforms. The local pottery was plain and undecorated. Only towards the end of the thirteenth century was there a sudden enrichment of the whole site, with improved styles of stone building, with burnished and richly decorated pottery, with jewellery of gold and ingots of copper, and with imported Chinese porcelain and Persian glazed wares. A copper coin has been found which was minted at Kilwa in the early fourteenth century. Later on in this century, the whole of the royal enclosure was surrounded by a new girdle wall, ten metres in height, and built in courses so even and uniform as to give the appearance of cut stone. Again, during these centuries there appeared a few other stone-built sites constructed in the same style, though on a smaller scale, and yielding a selection of the same local artifacts and luxury imports. These sites – at Chipadze, Lekkerwater, Nhunguza and Ruanga – were spread around the north-eastern edges of the plateau. These again were primarily pastoral sites, although they might also have commanded some of the more important areas of gold-production in relation to trade routes descending towards the Zambezi valley. It looks very much as though they were the provincial outposts of a Great Zimbabwe kingdom that was expanding its territory northwards during this period.

Essentially, the evidence for the political character of the kingdom based on Great Zimbabwe rests upon the archaeological evidence that a single widespread 'court culture' co-existed with a number of local 'plebeian cultures'. As Peter Garlake has expressed it, 'While most of the later Iron Age ceramic traditions of Zimbabwe can be equated with particular Shona dialect clusters, this does not apply to the Great Zimbabwe tradition. This represents a social or political entity spread over the whole interior plateau and, as Manekweni demonstrates, far beyond. It existed at the same time and in the same areas as other traditions and presumably interacted with them.'[4] The implication of all this would seem to be that the rulers of Great Zimbabwe were a minority, not necessarily of foreign origin, but at the very least a tightly organised, aristocratic group which established its authority over most of the area by conquest and succeeded for an unusually long time in maintaining a superstructure of political, economic and military power, heavily fortified by religious magic. Such was certainly the impression gained by the Portuguese when they began to penetrate the region in the early sixteenth century. By that time, however, the geographical centre of power had changed. Great Zimbabwe had been deserted, or at least had ceased to be a place of any importance. The paramount dynasty of the region had its headquarters on the northern edge of the plateau above the Zambezi valley. The great question about how far it is legitimate to project backwards from the situation covered by the Portuguese turns upon how much continuity there was between the new system and its predecessor. On the whole the evidence suggests that the element of continuity was large.

The abandonment of Great Zimbabwe as a major capital site is documented in archaeology by the fact that its luxury imports were all of the fifteenth century or earlier. The rise of the new political centre in the north is roughly datable from the tradition that the founder, Nyatsimba Mutota, preceded by either four or five generations the Mwene Mutapa with whom the Portuguese entered into direct relations in the 1560s. This would place the origins of the Mutapa dynasty around the middle of the fifteenth century, when (following a widespread cliché of African traditions of conquest) Mutota was sent by his

[4] Garlake, 'Investigation', p. 43.

father, a king reigning in a stone-built capital far to the south, to seek for fresh sources of salt. These were found in the land of the Tavara at the northern edge of the plateau, with easy access, moreover, to great herds of elephant living in the broad valley of the middle Zambezi. The Tavara were conquered, and Mutota's successor Matope went on to extend this kingdom into a great empire comprising most of the lands between Tavara and the Indian Ocean coast formerly subject to the Togwa dynasty of Great Zimbabwe. The story has some loose ends, notably about the precise relationship of the new paramount dynasty to the old one. What is sure from the archaeology of the northernmost sites built in the Great Zimbabwe tradition at Nhunguza and Ruanga is that, by the time of the emergence of the Mutapa state, the influence of the southern capital was already well established over most of the northern plateau. The conquest of Tavara could therefore have originated in a relatively modest expansion, perhaps carried out by the frontier regiments, into the country west of the Mazoe valley. Mutota, the commander of the expedition, was very likely a Togwa prince, who asserted his independence only slowly, after the fashion of the many Kazembes who separated themselves from the Mwata Yamvos (pp. 141–2). The significance of the episode may have become apparent only when the second ruler, having become rich by exploiting the copper of Chidzurgwe and the ivory of the middle Zambezi valley, sent his armies eastwards to open a route to the coast. The Togwa government at Great Zimbabwe may have continued to function normally throughout this phase of the northern secession. Only when Matope's armies overran Manyika, and the coastal states of Kiteve and Madanda, may the old capital have become untenable through the northward diversion of the main long-distance trade routes.

At all events, by the time the Portuguese reached the coast of Mozambique, the centre of Shona power had already shifted from south to north. De Barros, the great historian of Portuguese enterprise in the Indian Ocean, writing about 1550, reported information collected at Sofala about a capital of the ancient gold-mines called Zimbabwe, which was 'built of stones of marvellous size, and there appears to be no mortar joining them'. It was still 'guarded by a nobleman' and there were always some of the Mwene Mutapa's wives quartered there. The sixteenth-century capital, however, was approached up the Zambezi, where the Swahili Arabs of the east coast had already established trading settlements at Quelimane, Sena and Tete. From Tete it was a mere five days' march up the Mazoe valley to the fairs on the edge of the metropolitan district where the foreign merchants were required to trade. The capital town itself, lying beyond the region of granite outcrops, was built, like most other African towns, of clay, wood and thatch and surrounded by a wooden stockade, which could be circumambulated in about one hour. It contained a public enclosure where the king did his business; another for his wives and their attendants, who were said to number three thousand; and a third for the pages and bodyguards, who were young, unmarried men recruited from all parts of the kingdom and destined for later service as soldiers and administrators. The annual distribution of brands from the royal fire was here, as in so many other African kingdoms, the main symbol for the conferment of authority. The royal shrines, and the cult of the royal ancestors involving the ritual consultation of the spirits through living mediums, were served by priests called *mhondoros*, whose descendants have continued to live around the site of the capital until the present day. It has been from them that the best traditions of the dynasty have been recorded.

THE PORTUGUESE AND THEIR IMPACT

The Portuguese who entered the Indian Ocean in 1497 in the three ships commanded by Vasco da Gama were already consciously bound for India. Their expedition was the culmination of ten years of research by explorers despatched through the Middle East, who had travelled the Red Sea and the Persian Gulf as far as Cananor in the pepper country of south-western India. The Portuguese knew that their prime objective was to begin the capture of the spice-trade from the Arabs who had hitherto monopolised it. What they had still to learn by experience was that trade goods brought from Lisbon were of little interest to the Hindu merchants of Calicut, Goa and Cananor. What the Indians wanted were gold and ivory. What the Portuguese had to do, therefore, was to oust the Arabs from the trade of Sofala. This could be achieved only by force. The new plan was put into operation in 1505, when Francisco de Almeida was appointed the first governor of Portuguese India. His headquarters were at Goa, but his command included both shores of the Indian Ocean. On his way out, he subjected and built forts at Sofala and Kilwa and imposed a Portuguese monopoly on their external trade. Within eight years, the trade of Kilwa was so nearly defunct that the fort there was demolished and the garrison withdrawn. There could be no firmer proof of the economic dependence of Kilwa on the Sofala trade. By about 1515 the Portuguese had established virtually complete naval superiority over Arab shipping in the Indian Ocean, operating from a chain of fortified bases on Mozambique Island, at Ormuz and Muscat in the Persian Gulf, at Diu, Goa and Cochin in western India, and at Malacca in the strait between the Malay peninsula and Sumatra. Henceforward, the luxury trade of the Sofala coast followed almost its ancient pattern, but with the elimination of the Arabian link. Indian silks, cottons, glass beads and hardware were brought to Mozambique in Portuguese ships, transshipped into coastal and river vessels and used to buy gold and ivory from the various states of the Mutapa empire at the fairs still visited by the Swahili Arab merchants of Sofala and Inhambane, Quelimane, Sena or Tete. The gold and ivory reaching Mozambique from the interior was forwarded to Goa and there used to fertilise the trade in spices. But between south-eastern Africa and South Asia the Portuguese were now the carriers.

Once they had firmly established this position, the Portuguese did not greatly concern themselves with the rest of eastern Africa or with the trade which continued in small vessels plying up and down the coast from southern Arabia. They maintained friendly relations with Zanzibar and Malindi, but to the other Swahili settlements north of Cape Delgado they behaved mainly as pirates, making brief naval expeditions to loot their accumulated wealth. Generally speaking,

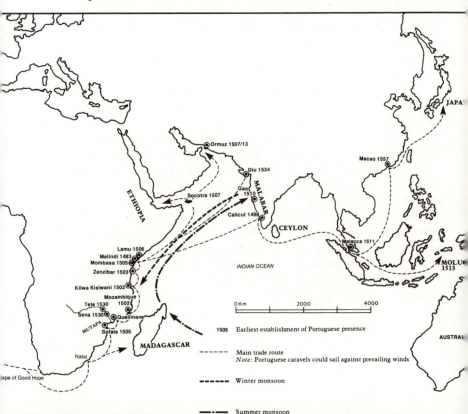

there were no garrisons north of Mozambique until, in 1592, the Portuguese decided to occupy Mombasa. Even this was a defensive measure, undertaken to block the southward penetration of the only Muslim fleet which they had not succeeded in destroying – that serving the Ottoman provinces in the Red Sea. Their installation at Fort Jesus in Mombasa was accompanied by a closer control of the offshore islands from Lamu to Kilwa, but it did not involve them in any relations with the peoples of the mainland. Like that of the Swahili Arabs before them, Portuguese interest in the African interior was limited to the lands immediately above and below the Zambezi. Even here, their objectives were few and simple. They needed to ensure that the production of gold and ivory continued, and if possible that it increased. And they needed to see that as much as possible of what was produced would pass out of Africa through their own hands and not leak away into the small-boat traffic of the Swahili Arab system. To achieve the first aim, they needed good relations with the Shona kings, who controlled the production of their subjects. To achieve the second, they needed to extend their own system of communications up the Zambezi and install themselves alongside the settlements of the Swahili merchants.

During the first sixty years of the sixteenth century relations between the Portuguese and the Shona developed amicably enough. Besides the official garrisons, a number of private adventurers and deported criminals, many of them drawn from the Portuguese settlements in Asia, were landed at Sofala. They quickly made their way into the hinterland as backwoodsmen (*sertanejos*), living alongside the Swahili merchants at the inland fairs, and even taking service with the Shona kings as interpreters and political advisers. One of them, Antonio Fernandes, succeeded between 1512 and 1516 in travelling through virtually all the important Shona states from Kiteve and Manyika in the east, through the Mwene Mutapa's metropolitan district and on to the kingdom of Butwa in the far south-west, modern Matabeleland. With the help of such rough-and-ready ambassadors, the Captains of Sofala were able to work out a system of commercial relations with the Mwene Mutapa and his tributary kings. The first serious breakdown occurred in 1561, when a Jesuit missionary, Gonçalo de Silveira, penetrated to the Mwene Mutapa's court, persuaded his host to accept Christian baptism, and a few days later was himself murdered at the instigation of the Muslim traders at the capital. After lengthy preparations, the Portuguese in 1568 mounted an expedition of a thousand men under Francisco Barreto, conceived partly as an anti-Muslim crusade and partly in the hope of bringing the gold-

27 The approaches to Zimbabwe (4): Portuguese trading activities in the Indian Ocean

producing areas under Portuguese control. In most respects it was a disastrous failure. Though penetrating far up the Zambezi, the greater part of the force succumbed to tropical diseases, and by 1572 the survivors had retreated to their base. Nevertheless, the expedition had some important results. The Swahili Arab traders of the Zambezi were massacred with revolting cruelty and their places taken by Portuguese traders, whose descendants and successors, taking African wives and assimilating progressively to African customs, gradually developed into the largely self-governing 'estate-holders' (*prazeiros*) of the lower Zambezi valley. Sena and Tete retained tiny garrisons, supported henceforward by increasing numbers of African mercenaries and dependants, which became an important factor in the politics of the Shona states to the south of the river valley and of the Maravi states to the north.

The relationship of the Portuguese with the eastern Shona states after the Barreto expedition has been aptly described by J. R. Gray as one of 'subordinate symbiosis'.[5] Throughout the remainder of the sixteenth and the whole of the seventeenth century the Mutapa kingdom, like those of Manyika, Kiteve and Madanda, retained basic control of its territory and of the economic production of its subjects. In particular, fierce penalties were exacted from any individual or group attempting to mine gold without the ruler's licence. Equally, every Portuguese Captain on taking up his office at Mozambique paid a subsidy (*curva*) to the Shona rulers for permission to trade at the established fairs, where a duty of 50 per cent was further levied on all trade goods imported. It was only during comparatively rare moments of internal disorder, during succession struggles, rebellions and inter-state warfare, that Shona kings sometimes appealed to the Portuguese for military help. It was during such crises that successive Mwene Mutapas ceded peripheral land in the Zambezi valley for Portuguese *prazos*, and occasionally, as in 1607 and 1629, signed treaties (which were never put into effect) giving the Portuguese possession of the gold-mines or declaring themselves the vassals of the Portuguese Crown.

More realistically, what did happen during the seventeenth century was that the Mwene Mutapas gradually lost their paramountcy over other Shona states. Kiteve, Madanda and Manyika all ceased to pay tribute. This would probably have happened in any case, but it may have happened rather sooner as a result of the Portuguese contacts with these states. Again, a new state, that of Barwe, emerged in the southern part of the Zambezi valley. The most serious threat to the Mutapa kingdom, however, seems to have come from the south and the south-west, that is to say, from the central lands of the old Togwa kingdom of Great Zimbabwe. The course of events in this part of the region is more obscure than elsewhere, but already in the early sixteenth century there were reports of a ruler with the title of Changamire who invaded the Mutapa kingdom from a base in the southern part of the plateau. By the seventeenth century this title was definitely associated with the Rozwi dynasty of the rising state of Butwa. The main towns of Butwa were stone-built in the general style of Great Zimbabwe, and they included such sites as Dhlo-Dhlo, Naletale, Khami and Matendere – all in the area between Bulawayo and Fort Victoria. Though lacking any pre-sixteenth-century deposit, all these sites are rich in material of the seventeenth and eighteenth centuries. They testify to the existence of a state with sophisticated local industries, which was in addition wealthy enough to import all the luxury goods of the Portuguese Indian Ocean trade. At first this long-distance trade probably passed through Kiteve and Madanda. Latterly, the entrepôt market was at the Portuguese trading station at Zumbo, at the confluence of the Zambezi and the Luangwa.

By the late seventeenth century Butwa, under the leadership of a Changamire called Dombo, was actively challenging the hegemony of the Mutapa kingdom in the region as a whole. In 1684 Dombo's forces encountered and decisively defeated those of the Mwene Mutapa Mukombwe on the southern borders of the metropolitan district. In 1693 Mukombwe died, and there ensued a succession struggle in which the Portuguese backed one contestant and Dombo another. Dombo thereupon razed the fair-town of Dambarare, situated at the very approaches to the Mutapa capital, and wiped out the Portuguese traders and their entire following. In 1695 Dombo overran the rich, gold-producing state of Manyika, and even descended to the lowlands on the eastern edge of the country to destroy the Portuguese fair at Masikwesi. Dombo now controlled the whole arc of gold-producing territory from Butwa in the south-west to Manyika in the north-east. Unlike the Mwene Mutapas, who had always permitted subordinate rulers to bring their own tribute to the capital at the time of the annual ceremonies, the Changamires installed their own tax-collectors to reside in the conquered provinces. The control of mining could thus be effectively enforced. Although the fair at Masikwesi was eventually reopened, it remained a firm principle of the Butwa hegemony that henceforward no Portuguese should set foot upon the plateau. Trade with Butwa itself was carried out through Zumbo, whence only the

African agents (*mussambazes*) of the Portuguese traders were permitted to organise caravans to the main towns of the country. The main consequence of Butwa's dominance over the Zimbabwe plateau, which lasted throughout the eighteenth century, was that the Portuguese in the Zambezi valley shifted their interests increasingly from the south bank to the north. Here Portuguese backwoodsmen and prospectors who had been expelled from the Shona states made numerous, mostly small, gold strikes in the lands of the Maravi, Chewa and Nsenga peoples, whose earlier political unity was fast crumbling at this period. In these circumstances most of the gold was mined under various arrangements with local chiefs by the *prazeiros* and *sertanejos* who set up temporary mining camps (*bares*), which were worked by their retainers and slaves. Meanwhile, the ivory-trade of the Luangwa basin and the Kazembe's kingdom on the Luapula was being carried through the Maravi country by the Bisa, and it was the hope of attracting this trade to the Zambezi settlements rather than to the Zanzibar coast that inspired the exploration of a coast-to-coast route described in Chapter 10 (pp. 146–7).

THE RETURN OF THE ARABS

On the East African coast to the north of Cape Delgado the zenith of Portuguese power was reached during the forty years from 1592 till 1631. Under the watchful eyes of the Fort Jesus garrison, the former ruling house of Malindi, transplanted now to Mombasa, reigned over Malindi, Mombasa and Pemba. North of Malindi the island settlements of the Lamu archipelago were all careful to pay tribute. There were Portuguese *sertanejos* settled on Zanzibar, Pemba and Pate, and Augustinian missionaries at Mombasa, Zanzibar and Faza. The situation was not, however, completely peaceful. In 1595 or 1596 the Swahili governor of Pemba was poisoned on becoming a Christian. Even the friendly Sultan Ahmad was always complaining of the insulting treatment he received from the Portuguese Captains of Fort Jesus. His son and successor, Hassan, quarrelled openly with the Portuguese and in 1614 ran away to the mainland. He was replaced, first by a brother who was deposed four years later, and then by a nephew, Yusuf Chinguliya, who was taken away to Goa and educated for twelve years in an Augustinian priory before being allowed to assume office. How little the Portuguese were really tolerated is best shown by the sequel. In the year after his return to Mombasa Yusuf abjured Christianity for his native Islam and incited a revolt of the townspeople in which the entire Portuguese garrison was massacred.

The neighbouring towns joined in the rebellion and the first punitive expedition of eight hundred Portuguese sent from Goa in 1632 was beaten off. Yusuf thereupon demolished the fort and decamped to Arabia, whence he continued the struggle in a series of naval raids.

Though the Portuguese reoccupied Mombasa and rebuilt Fort Jesus in 1635, they never recovered their former control of the northern coast. It was a period when the Portuguese empire all round the world was suffering disasters at the hands of the Dutch, who between 1631 and 1641 conquered Pernambuco, Elmina, Luanda, Ceylon and Malacca. The Portuguese had already in 1622 been ejected by the Persians from Ormuz, and in 1650 the Omanis drove them from Muscat on the opposite shore of the Persian Gulf. There were Omani merchants settled in all the towns along the East African coast, whose trade was taxed and hampered by the Portuguese, and it was inevitable that the Omanis of the Gulf should follow up their own liberation by fomenting trouble in East Africa. Already in 1652 their fleets raided Pate and Zanzibar, wiping out the Portuguese settlers. In 1660 they attacked the town of Mombasa under the noses of the Portuguese in the fort. In 1669 they raided as far south as Mozambique Island. The Mombasa garrison, increasingly isolated, at last succumbed in 1698 to an Omani siege lasting two and a half years. The place was briefly recaptured by the Portuguese in 1728–30, but in general it was Arab sea-power that dominated East African waters north of Cape Delgado throughout the eighteenth century. Once more the big sailing dhows of the Persian Gulf replaced the small coasting vessels of the Portuguese period. The Swahili communities of the coast, now increasingly supplied with fire-arms, began to develop the slave- and ivory-trade of the far interior. Symbolic of this new commercial interest was the emergence of a new Kilwa, situated on the mainland 20 kilometres to the north of the medieval island site. Unlike its predecessor, the new Kilwa faced inland. It was the coastal base of new caravan routes leading far to the west. In the early 1770s Kilwa was visited by a French trader, Morice, who was interested in building up a regular supply of slaves for the sugar plantations of Mauritius and Réunion. He was told of the existence of a great inland sea, which must have been Lake Malawi, and beyond it of an immense country, which had been traversed in two months by native caravans to another ocean with ships manned by Europeans.

The case of Kilwa was not, however, unique. On the Kenya coast, the old towns of Mombasa and Malindi, Pate and Lamu did not perhaps change their characters very greatly. They had survived the Portuguese period, and they were to survive into modern times, 181 mainly as the centres of slave-worked plantation agriculture, more or less self-contained within the coastal belt. But other towns grew up in the later eighteenth century, especially along the Tanzanian coast – Tanga and Pangani, Saadani and Bagamoyo – which like Kilwa Kivinje were oriented inland, and were to develop as the coastal termini of trade routes leading westwards to Lake Tanganyika and the Congo basin, to Uganda, to Kilimanjaro and north into Kikuyu and Kavirondo. As we saw in Chapter 9 (pp. 132–5), it was around the third quarter of the eighteenth century that the kingdoms of the interlacustrine region began to receive some luxury imports from the outside world, while by the end of the century even bulky goods like cotton textiles were appearing in some quantity. Here, as on the more southerly routes to Lake Malawi and beyond, it was at this stage the peoples of the interior who did most of the actual travelling. It was not until the nineteenth century that the coastmen themselves started to go inland in any numbers. But already in the eighteenth century the trade of the interior was becoming one of their main preoccupations.

13   The peoples of the south

THE KHOISAN AND THE SOUTH-EASTERN BANTU

After the Sahara desert, the great spaces of southern Africa include more land that is too dry for cultivation than any other region of Africa. In most of southern Angola, in virtually all of Namibia and Botswana, in much of the western Cape Province of South Africa, rainfall is less than fifty centimetres a year. River valleys apart, all this is at best ranching country. It is only the eastern third of the sub-continent, comprising the Transvaal, southern Mozambique, Swaziland, Natal, the Orange Free State, Lesotho, the Transkei and the eastern Cape Province, that offers the possibility of dense agricultural settlement. Such is the geographical logic underlying the distribution of language families – to the west the old Khoisan languages of the surviving hunter-gatherers and specialised pastoralists, to the east the Bantu languages of the Iron Age cultivators. Of the two language families Bantu was of course the intruder, but the intrusion had begun to occur early in the first millennium A.D. By the beginning of our period the linguistic frontier was not significantly different from that obtaining in 1800, although in 1400 there would certainly have been large enclaves of Khoisan speech within the Bantu sphere. These enclaves would essentially have been those of San-speakers, the sur-vivors from the old hunting and gathering population of southern South Africa who in the eighteenth century still formed identifiable communities inhabiting all the mountainous country of the Drakens-berg, Lesotho and the eastern Cape Province, much of the Orange Free State plateau and the valleys of the Orange and the Vaal. Khoi-speakers occupied much wider territories, stretching from southern Angola around both sides of the Kalahari desert to the Cape Province, where they formed the main population all the way from the Orange to the Kei.

Unlike the San, most of the Khoi were pastoralists rather than hunter–gatherers, living in communities of five hundred to one thousand persons, and keeping herds of longhorn cattle and flocks of fat-tailed sheep. Their practice of shepherding may have begun in Stone Age times, for sheep-bones have been found in association with stone tools and pottery in cave sites near the Cape of Good Hope, which have been dated to around the beginning of the Christian era. Cattle must have come significantly later, and must have reached the northern Khoi through Bantu country in Angola or Zambia during the Iron Age, probably even later Iron Age, times. Certainly, however, by the beginning of our period the Khoi were the supreme cattle-keepers of southern Africa. Their staple diet was the milk of cows and of ewes. Their clothing was of leather and sheepskin. They gelded their bulls and used them for riding and baggage. Though not skilled as smiths, they knew the use of metals, wearing a profusion of copper ornaments and wielding some iron weapons in addition to wooden bows and staves. Certainly, the Khoi interacted continuously with the Bantu farmers to the east of them. The clicking sounds of the Khoi languages were transmitted to their Bantu neighbours, both Sotho and Nguni, and the South-Eastern Bantu words for 'cattle',

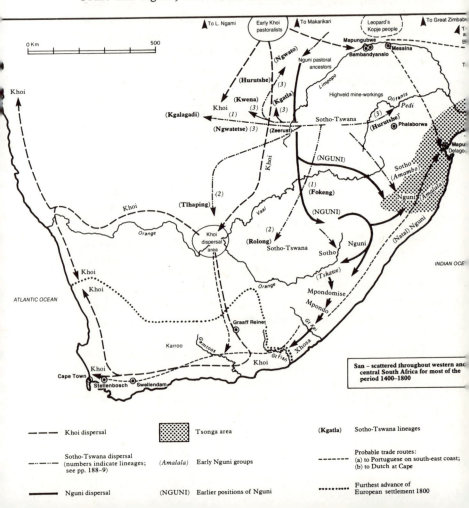

– – – – Khoi dispersal	Tsonga area	**(Kgatla)** Sotho-Tswana lineages
Sotho-Tswana dispersal (numbers indicate lineages; see pp. 188–9)	*(Amalala)* Early Nguni groups	Probable trade routes: – – – – – (a) to Portuguese on south-east coast; (b) to Dutch at Cape
—— Nguni dispersal	(NGUNI) Earlier positions of Nguni	••••••••• Furthest advance of European settlement 1800

San – scattered throughout western and central South Africa for most of the period 1400–1800 'sheep' and 'milk' are all of Khoi origin. The Khoi were no race of downtrodden clients. Intermarriage with them conferred prestige even upon the ruling houses of the Bantu. Most of the land of southern Africa was theirs. Because of the inadequate rainfall upon that land, however, it was inevitable that most of it should be sparsely occupied and difficult to defend – not against cultivators, for whom it held no attraction, but against fellow pastoralists equipped with fire-arms and wheeled vehicles who pressed in upon them during the last century of our period.

Anthropologists and linguists are agreed that the South-Eastern Bantu comprise three main sub-divisions – the Tsonga, the Sotho-Tswana and the Nguni. The Tsonga are the people of southern Mozambique, who at one time also populated most of Swaziland and Natal. These were cultivators and fishermen of the coastal plain, keeping few cattle, and paying even marriage dowries in hoes and other metal goods. They were the oldest of the Bantu inhabitants of southern Africa, with their roots in the Early Iron Age and their main affiliations with the coastal Bantu of central and northern Mozambique and the eastern parts of Tanzania and Kenya. Next there were the Sotho-Tswana, basically the Iron Age population of the Transvaal highveld, which later spread across the Orange Free State towards Lesotho and Botswana. The Sotho practised a mixed economy of agriculture and cattle-keeping, with a tendency to live in large, almost urban, settlements, which were often protected by stone walling. The northern Sotho had a particularly well-developed interest in mining and metallurgy, in copper and gold as well as iron, with dates for mining sites going back into the first millennium at Phalaborwa and other sites on the north-eastern side of the plateau. Finally, there were the Nguni, who during the past six or seven hundred years have occupied the lowlands between the Indian Ocean coast and the escarpment of the great interior plateau, in Natal and the Transkei. The Nguni were more strongly pastoral than the Sotho, living in beehive huts around their cattle kraals, which were dispersed more or less evenly across the landscape. Though everywhere within easy reach of the sea, the Nguni, like many other pastoralists in Africa, maintained a rigid taboo against eating fish. All this suggests that the pastoral element among them came from the interior, and probably only in later Iron Age times, since the major dispersion of cattle in southern Africa seems to have occurred within this period. Logic would suggest that the Nguni ancestors must have entered South Africa across the upper Limpopo from eastern Botswana or western Zimbabwe, where the beginnings of the later Iron Age were associated

185

28 The peoples of the south

with a strong emphasis on pastoralism. At this rate their initial area of settlement would have been to the west and south of the Sotho, perhaps on the plateau between the Vaal and the Orange, whence the later expansion of the Sotho-Tswana would have caused them to migrate through the Drakensberg passes towards the coast.

Naturally enough, at the beginning of our period the most developed part of the region, both economically and politically, was the north-east. The Tsonga, after all, were the local population of Inhambane and Delagoa Bay (Maputo). They had been in touch with the maritime trade of the Indian Ocean for almost as long as the Shona of Kiteve and Madanda. The Zimbabwe-like site at Manekweni dating from about A.D. 1100 (see pp. 170–1) stood in Tsonga territory and perhaps represented the extension of a Shona political system over a northern Tsonga population. Further south the Tsonga were organised in their own small kingdoms, which controlled the approaches to the Limpopo valley with its riches in copper and ivory; to its southern tributary, the Olifants, with its gold, copper, tin and iron exploited since the end of the first millennium and to similar sources of wealth in Swaziland and the eastern Transvaal. In its heyday Manekweni may have controlled an overland route from the Bazaruto Islands to the northern loop of the Limpopo, where just upstream from Messina and its copper-mines there stood a southerly counterpart of Great Zimbabwe in the cliff-top and valley sites of Mapungubwe and Bambandyanalo. Later Iron Age occupation began in an unspectacular way around the eleventh century with a settlement based around a large cattle kraal but also practising agriculture with very simple material equipment. By the fourteenth and fifteenth centuries, however, Mapungubwe had become a rich centre, with complex daga houses built on stone platforms, containing abundant iron tools, black burnished pottery, spindle-whorls, beads and ornaments of gold and copper, and at the centre of the site some extremely rich burials, accompanied by gold and copper jewellery and gold-plated figurines of animals, the grave-goods from eleven burials containing some thirty-two kilograms of gold. Mapungubwe thus has every appearance of having been a capital site and ritual centre, contemporary with the richest period of Great Zimbabwe and probably influenced by it, yet showing signs of a distinct cultural tradition, which originated in the Leopard's Kopje sites of western Zimbabwe and which may have been the work of people more like the Sotho-Tswana than the Shona.

That mining and pastoralism do not normally go hand in hand was recognised by the Sotho themselves in the popular saying that 'where the hammer is heard, the lowing of cattle is not there'.[1] It is not only that pastoralists make a significantly smaller use of metal tools than cultivators. It is also that mining, especially for gold and copper, was essentially a communal activity undertaken with agricultural tools and at seasons of the year when large numbers of people were free from work in the fields. Nevertheless, there can be no doubt that both activities were highly significant in the history of the Sotho expansion. The whole of the Transvaal plateau from the Zoutpansberg in the north to the Witwatersrand in the south is pitted with ancient workings and with the remains of countless smelting furnaces. Much of the evidence comes from terrain that must have been quite unsuited to cattle-keeping, either because of tsetse-fly or because it was covered with a dense thorn forest which had to be slowly and painfully cleared before the land could be used for agriculture or grazing. The miners and metalworkers of the central plateau, consuming much wood in their smelting and forging, performed an important function in clearance as well as by their manufactures. At the same time, in the more open lands to the west and south of the highveld plateau, mixed farming with a strong pastoral element was bringing about a rapid increase of Sotho-Tswana population, which led in turn to further territorial expansion. The density of later Iron Age settlement throughout a wide arc from Zeerust in the south-western Transvaal to Lydenburg in the south-east is shown by the thousands of stone ruins spread across this area. Most of them probably date to the last three centuries of our period, but a few may go back to the thirteenth century or earlier.

The ruined towns [wrote the missionary Robert Moffat, who travelled through the region a few years after it had been laid waste by the Ndebele migrants of the early nineteenth century] exhibited signs of immense labour and perseverance, every fence being composed of stones, averaging five or six feet high, raised apparently without either mortar, line or hammer. Everything is circular, from the inner fences which surround each house, to the walls which sometimes encompass each town. The remains of some of the houses . . . were large . . . the walls of clay with a small mixture of cow-dung, and so well polished that they had the appearance of being varnished. The walls and doorways were neatly ornamented with architraves and cornices. The pillars supporting the roof, in the form of pilasters projecting from the wall, and fluted, showed much taste.[2]

According to traditions gathered from all the different areas of the Sotho-Tswana dispersion, it was from this region that clan sections

[1] Cited in *The Cambridge History of Africa*, vol. III (Cambridge, 1977), p. 604.
[2] Cited in Cecil Northcott, *Robert Moffat, Pioneer in Africa* (London, 1961), p. 138.

hived off to colonise much of the Orange Free State, Lesotho and Botswana. No doubt, the expansion was due at least as much to the increase of the cattle as to that of the human population. However, it should not be seen as the first occupation of a virgin land. Possibly, as we have seen, it involved the extrusion of an earlier Bantu population which moved away south-eastwards to become the Nguni. Certainly, at some stage it involved the infiltration and eventual absorption of earlier populations of Khoi and San. Of these, the Khoi were already herders, and to them the advent of the Sotho meant the competition of fellow pastoralists equipped with later Iron Age tools and weapons, practising some agriculture alongside their herding activities and consequently living in larger and denser communities. In these circumstances the language and culture of the newcomers would have prevailed over those of the more scattered herders. It was the same with the San, except that there was probably more scope for the co-existence of hunters with herder–farmers in separate communities than for the co-existence of old-style and new-style herders.

On the whole, it was the size and density of Sotho-Tswana settlements that distinguished them most sharply not only from the Khoi and San but also from the Nguni people of Natal and the Transkei. Although the earliest numerical estimates come from just after the end of our period, they are not inconsistent with the scale of the ruin sites, most of which are considerably earlier. There is also the consideration that when Sotho-Tswana settlements reached something like an 'optimum size', colonists tended to hive off and found new settlements elsewhere. Seen in this light, the figure of 15,000 persons, which recurs frequently in early-nineteenth-century estimates for various different settlements from the Transvaal to southern Botswana, can perhaps be taken as a rough indication of the optimum size. Such a settlement would be surrounded by a single enclosing wall or fence, within which there might be as many as fifty subdivisions, each comprising a group of kinsfolk numbering between two hundred and five hundred. Cultivated lands would stretch for several miles beyond the walls and beyond these again there would be a much wider circle of grazing-land, dotted with peripatetic cattle-camps. Each settlement with its agricultural and pasture lands would in reality constitute an autonomous state, although its ruling lineage would recognise ties of perpetual kinship with the settlement from which its founders had hived off. The chronology of the Sotho-Tswana expansion may one day be established through radiocarbon datings. Meanwhile, the genealogical evidence concerning the ruling lineages and their relationships to one another suggests that the earliest Sotho pioneers, associated with the Fokeng and Kgalagadi lineages, had spread throughout the area well before the beginning of our period. The next wave of migrants, associated with the Rolong and the Tlhaping, have genealogies going back to the fourteenth century. A third wave, associated with the Hurutshe lineage and comprising the ruling dynasties of the Kwena, Ngwato, Ngwaketse, Kgatla and Pedi, appear to have spread outwards from the southern Transvaal during the late fifteenth or early sixteenth century.

The history of Nguni settlement in the lowlands of Natal, Swaziland and the Transkei presents more fundamental problems than that of the Sotho-Tswana on the interior plateau. There is an important problem of definition which arises from the obviously diverse origins of the Nguni people, even within the Bantu context. In this book we apply the term 'Nguni' to the pastorally oriented element which gave the later Iron Age population of the lowlands its economic and social character. It is important to remember that, before the arrival of the pastoralists, the northern coastlands at least were occupied by Tsonga-speaking people (in Nguni terms, Amalala), and the immediate hinterland by people of eastern Sotho origin (in Nguni terms, Amambo). It is possible that the linguistic unity of the Nguni peoples derives from a fusion of these earlier strata. It is even conceivable (although we think unlikely) that the pastoral element which became so dominant in Nguni society was not of Bantu but rather of Khoi origin. It seems to us more probable that the Nguni pastoralists were already Bantu-speaking on their arrival in the lowlands, and that they came from some very early, pre-Sotho colonisation of the southern Transvaal. At all events, the crucial development of the early part of the present millennium was the slow clearance of the forests which had previously covered most of the lowland area, and the opening up of the land to a system of farming in which, although millet and vegetables were regularly planted, pride of place was given to cattle-keeping. The pattern of settlement was based upon the cattle kraal, the care of cattle was the essential business of the male population, and the social values of wealth and status depended primarily upon the resources in cattle of the patrilineal kinship group.

As a result of the great upheavals which affected the northern half of Nguniland with the rise of the Zulu nation just after the end of our period, it happens that historical traditions for the period from the fifteenth till the eighteenth century have survived better in the south than in the north. From these it would appear that the royal clans of the Xhosa, Mpondo and Mpondomise peoples all descend from the same Tshawe lineage, which had its earliest remembered centre 189 somewhere among the sources of the Mzimvubu River. This was at the end of the sixteenth century. During the seventeenth century the dynasty moved down the Mzimvubu to the coast, and from there divided, as its followers spread out across southern Natal and the Transkei. By the mid-seventeenth century the Xhosa capital was established on the Kei. In 1702 there occurred the first skirmish between the Xhosa frontiersmen and the Dutch cattle-traders from Cape Town in the valley of the Fish River. For northern Nguniland the genealogical evidence is much more fragmentary, and it is safer to rely on the scattered references in Portuguese writings of the sixteenth and seventeenth centuries. These show that, at least by the middle of the sixteenth century, all the country from the Transkei to northern Natal was thickly settled by people whose main wealth lay in their herds of sleek, well-fed cattle. They also show that throughout this region chiefs were known by the Nguni word *nkosi*, which differentiated these Africans from the Khoi to the west of the Kei and from the Tsonga living to the north of Santa Lucia Bay in the far north of Natal. A journal kept by one of the survivors from a Portuguese ship wrecked on the coast of Transkei in 1593 describes an overland march of four months from the Bashee river to Delagoa Bay, through the whole length of the Nguni country.

These Kaffirs [wrote the anonymous author] are herdsmen and husbandmen . . . Their husbandry is millet . . . From this millet, ground between two stones or in wooden mortars, they make flour, and of this they make cakes, which they bake under the embers. Of the same grain they make wine, mixing it with a lot of water, which after being fermented in a clay jar, cooled off and turned sour, they drink with great gusto. Their cattle are numerous, fat, tender, tasty and large, the pastures being very fertile. Most of them are polled cows, in whose number and abundance their wealth consists. They also subsist on their milk and on the butter which they make from it. They live together in small villages, in huts made of reed mats, which do not keep out the rain . . . The dress of these Kaffirs is a mantle of calf-skins, with the hair on the outside, which they rub with grease to make it soft. They are shod with two or three soles of raw hide fastened together in a round shape, secured to the foot with thongs and with this they run with great speed. They carry in their hand a thin stick to which is fastened the tail of an ape or of a fox, with which they clean themselves [i.e. whisk away flies] and shade their eyes when observing.[3]

There can be no doubt that 'these Kaffirs' were Nguni or that

---

[3] C. R. Boxer (ed.), *The Tragic History of the Sea, 1589–1622* (Cambridge, 1959), pp. 121–2.

they had already settled in a density which presupposed that forest clearance was already far advanced.

THE TAVERN OF TWO OCEANS

The Portuguese and the Dutch influenced southern Africa from opposite ends. To the Portuguese the Cape of Good Hope was, despite its name, a cape of storms, which was best given a wide berth by their ships sailing to and from the East. As their main trading interest in south-east Africa was in the region of the Zambezi, so the main revictualling point for their Indian convoys was established at Mozambique Island. This, as we saw in Chapter 12, became the centre of a coasting trade which during the sixteenth and seventeenth centuries stretched from the Lamu archipelago in the north to Delagoa Bay in the south. It was towards Delagoa Bay that the trade of the Sotho-Tswana and the Nguni was mainly oriented, and the Tsonga were the middlemen. By far the richest trade was, of course, that of the northern Sotho, who sold their copper and gold for Indian textiles and hardware. In comparison, the Nguni, despite their prosperous herds, had nothing that could be sold abroad but skins and ivory. Nevertheless, the shipwrecked mariners of 1593 noticed that, even as far south as Pondoland, the Nguni were wearing in their ears red beads made in India, which had been carried by the Portuguese to Mozambique and thence to Delagoa Bay, where they had been bartered for ivory. It would appear that at least some of this ivory had been carried overland for more than 1,000 kilometres to the port of shipment. If such distances were being covered in the rather difficult terrain of the lowlands, it would seem likely that the network of trails connecting the Sotho settlements on the plateau could have been even more extensive, particularly since the Sotho had learned from the Khoi how to bridle oxen and use them as beasts of burden. While it is true that in their trading activities at Delagoa Bay and Inhambane the Portuguese were merely carrying on a tradition begun by the Swahili Arabs, there can be little doubt that the Portuguese system carried more goods into and out of southern Africa than the Arabs had done, and that by the end of the period, with the expansion of world demand for ivory and the higher prices paid for it, the economic influence of the Portuguese in the north-east of the region may still have been nearly as important a factor as that of the Dutch in the south. Furthermore, it is possible that the introduction of maize by the Portuguese, and the spread of its cultivation outwards from Delagoa Bay, may have had demographic consequences of the utmost importance, 191 causing population to increase faster in the north of the region than in the south, and so paving the way for the destructive warfare of the early nineteenth century.

Meanwhile, however, there was developing around the Cape of Good Hope a rival pole of outside influence which was destined, in the nineteenth century at least, to overtake by far that of the Portuguese in the north-east. With the discovery by the Dutch in the early seventeenth century of sailing routes to the Far East based upon the trade winds of the Atlantic and southern Indian Ocean, whereby voyages were made in wide sweeps across the two oceans, the Cape, with its anchorage uniquely sheltered from southerly gales at Table Bay, assumed a new significance as the best single landfall between Holland and Java. Though French and British ships had used it intermittently as a watering-point, where it was often possible to obtain cattle by barter from passing bands of Khoi, it was the Dutch who formally occupied the place in 1652, when Jan van Riebeeck sailed in with three ships and 125 paid servants of the Dutch East India company. The plans contained no hint of African colonisation. There was to be a fort, surrounded by a market-garden and a stock-farm, a place where crews and passengers could rest on their long journeys to and from the East, while their ships were restocked with fresh meat, fruit and vegetables for the second leg of the voyage.

It took the more enterprising of the pioneers just five years to exchange their Company employment for individual grants of land on the Cape peninsula and to obtain a supply of Javanese slaves to perform the manual labour of the settlement. Within ten years the Company's suppliers had discovered that meat was more cheaply and easily obtainable by sending agents to trade with the Khoi of the interior ('the Hottentots' Holland', as they called it) than by stock-farming within the settlement. The cattle-traders, ranging far and wide, with 'loyal' Khoi from the Cape peninsula for their servants and guides, were soon able to see how thinly populated and ill-developed was the land, how small and mutually hostile the communities of Khoi and San who grazed and hunted over it. Already by the 1670s there were little wars developing, arising from real or suspected thefts on either side, in which the settlers and their clients would seize the sheep and cattle of the Khoi bands nearest to the colonies, facing the owners with the choice of becoming either semi-servile dependants or fugitive hunters. The only Khoi who fared well in the new circumstances were those who acted as middlemen with the cattle-traders from the colony. These took the white man's trade goods, his horses, his arms and ammunition, and moved ever further inland towards the frontier between the Khoi and the Bantu, where they obtained cattle and ivory and skins and ostrich feathers which made up the long-distance trade of the Cape.

The colony itself grew slowly but steadily, the number of whites reaching 2,000 by the first decade of the eighteenth century, 5,000 by the mid-century and 16,000 by the end. The slave population grew in parallel, and in a slightly higher proportion, the original Indonesian element being augmented by Africans from Mozambique and Madagascar. There were also Khoisan who had accepted dependence and security within the colony. Among the whites males at first predominated. There was some intermarriage, much concubinage and, especially among the female slaves, much casual miscegenation with the crews of passing ships. Thus there emerged the part of the population later to be called Cape Coloured. Cape Town itself remained first and foremost a port. Its inhabitants let rooms to travellers, supplied stores for the ships and smuggled contraband. What was significant for the future, however, was the spread of white farmers into the countryside. In so far as this consisted of European-style mixed farming in the coastal region to the east of Cape Town, it was encouraged by the Company as a means of forestalling rival European settlements, and its progress can be roughly charted by the new administrative districts established at Stellenbosch in 1685, and at Swellendam in 1745. But there were also the frontiersmen, the *trekboers*, who moved right out of the narrow belt of Mediterranean climate on to the dry plateau, where extensive pastoralism combined with hunting was the only possible basis for existence. Here, where five acres were needed to support one cow, the six-thousand-acre holding became normal and many trekboers had two holdings. The area of land taken into European possession in this way during the course of three or four generations was staggering, and from all of it Khoisan populations were dispossessed. Many were killed, many were driven out, many were taken into servitude. And for the most part it was accomplished with no more organised effort than could be mounted by a group of trekboers using their own hunting fire-arms.

The dry *karroo* country behind the Cape, with its sparse and help-less Khoisan population, in fact proved the Achilles heel of Africa. Had the well-watered, wooded country of Natal and the Transkei extended westwards to the Cape, it would certainly have been occupied, long before 1652, by Bantu farmers with a later Iron Age material culture and a corresponding density of population and capa-bility of defence. In those circumstances a maritime staging-post in Table Bay might well have grown up as an African Gibraltar, or at least as a southern African Elmina or Mozambique. It was the *karroo*, with its insignificant bands of late Stone Age hunters and herders, which offered the conditions in which a handful of frontiersmen, acting on their own initiative and without the armed support of any government, could create a permanent bridgehead of white settlement in the interior with the confidence and momentum to continue its expansion in every generation. This is not to say that the Khoisan offered no resistance. There was a steady process of retreat and regroupment, often under the leadership of Khoi or mulattos who had earlier in their lives come closest to white culture as frontier trading agents or escaped slaves. By the last quarter of the eighteenth century the Khoi based in the mountain ranges to the north of the Great Karroo were reported to be moving in bands of up to one thousand persons, with at least a sprinkling of horses and guns. A temporary check was in fact imposed to the white advance, but only while a corresponding process of white regroupment prepared the way for the Great Trek.

How different was the relative strength of Dutch and Bantu from that of Dutch and Khoi was shown during the second half of the eighteenth century, when Dutch and Xhosa frontiersmen began to interact regularly in the region between the Gamtoos river and the Fish. Both sides were operating in country hitherto occupied by Khoi, and both were in search of Khoi cattle and grazing-land. While there were many sharp skirmishes which later went by the name of 'Kaffir Wars', the Dutch at least understood the strength of the Xhosa too well to attempt any deep penetration. Moreover, while the government in Cape Town was prepared to turn a blind eye to the activities of the trekboers on the northern frontier, in the east it sought to keep them under control. In 1770 the official frontier was advanced from the Great Brak river, flowing into Mossel Bay, to the Gamtoos, with the object of reasserting control over those who had settled beyond the old frontier. In 1785 a new administrative district was created at Graaff Reinet on the Sundays river, with the same object. The frontier was now advanced to the Fish, but mainly in order to bring a degree of supervision to affairs in no-man's-land. It was only in the 1830s, with the full strength of a British colonial garrison in support, that the frontier was finally pushed back 150 kilometres from the Fish to the Kei. And there it remained. The southern Nguni were not conquered, but encircled.

Epilogue

At the end of the eighteenth century Africa as a whole was still far from losing its pre-colonial independence. Indeed, the only large area of theoretically dependent territory was that comprised within the Ottoman empire – Egypt, Tripoli, Tunis and Algiers – and even here the central authority had declined so far that the system could almost be described as rule by locally based military elites of foreign origin. The pashas of Timbuktu had a similarly theoretical relationship to Morocco, as did the Mazruis of Mombasa and various other East African coastal dynasties to the Albusaid Imams of Oman. European dependencies were in comparison very small. There was Mozambique Island, with its cluster of trading outposts and its nearly Africanised *prazo*-holders in the lower Zambezi valley. There was Angola with its two slightly garrisoned trade routes running inland from Luanda and Benguela. There were the fortified warehouses and slave-pens of Dutch, Danes and British on the Gold Coast and the Gambia, and of the French on the Senegal. And, in a class by itself, the Dutch colony at the Cape, soon to be taken over by the British, where the trekboers had expanded by the end of the century about halfway to the Orange River. Such dependent areas were neither the most important nor the most dynamic of African polities. Except for the Cape, none of them was expanding, and some were obviously wearing away.

Looked at from another point of view, the eighteenth century was of course the peak period of the African slave-trade, when it has been calculated that some 6,500,000 persons were transported across the Atlantic to the New World. This figure takes no account of those exported across the Sahara or the Indian Ocean. In the view of some writers this in itself is enough to situate the eighteenth century (and indeed the seventeenth and the sixteenth also) within the colonial period of African history. This, however, is to miss a vital distinction between the colonial period in the New World and the colonial period in Africa. It was because the European nations were engaged in opening up colonies in the Americas that they looked to Africa for slaves to meet the labour needs of their plantations in Brazil and the Caribbean. But to colonise is to occupy and rule another country by main force, and of this Africa knew very little until the late nineteenth century. The African states and corporations which engaged in the slave-trade, whether westwards across the Atlantic or northwards across the Sahara, did so for the most part as free and willing agents. This is not to say that commercial profit was their only motive, although sometimes it was so. Often enough, however, the slave-trade was an almost incidental element in national aggrandisement. A ruler extended his country's frontiers, and sold war captives in exchange for horses or fire-arms with which to extend the frontiers still further. Alternatively, a ruler sold captives for imported textiles and other luxuries, in order to reward his military captains for the last campaign and to whet their appetite for the next one. Eventually, the ruler of a state might reach a stage when the frontiers were so distant that the game was no longer worth the candle. Or the expanded frontiers might reach those of another rising power which had been pursuing the same course. Then the supply of slaves from that particular region would dry up, and the foreign merchants would be forced to seek another source. Neither did the trade in slaves – nor in any other goods – make those Africans who engaged in it dependent upon European (or Islamic) mercantile capitalist interests. It is true that Europeans supplied fire-arms and other commodities which African rulers found useful or desirable. But these rulers were not in any quantifiable sense 'dependent' on the European providers of fire-arms: these were useful as an improvement of technology, but the functioning of African states did not depend upon them. Rather, the European mercantile capitalists were dependent on Africa for the supply of slaves, which were crucial for *their* colonies in the New World.

Thus, although the slave-trade was an important and almost ubi-quitous element in the relations between Africa and the outside world, and particularly during the last century of our period, it was not the main motive force of social and political change in Africa itself. This is rather to be sought in the necessity felt in nearly every part of Africa during this period to seek the enlargement of political groupings. This necessity was probably in the main a function of the growth of population experienced in all the more favourable environments of the continent following the spread of later Iron Age technology. It was at least as marked in interior regions, such as Rwanda and Lunda and Asante and Oyo, as it was in the coastal areas or those of the desert frontier. It seems likely that, even if there had been no external contacts and no external slave-trade, the enlargement of political scale would still have been the dominant theme of our period, and that slavery and deportation would have been among its by-products. The medieval states of the Sahel – Ghana, Mali, Songhay, Kano, Katsina, Bornu, 'Alwa, Ethiopia – had all practised the removal of war captives from neighbouring states to the metropolitan districts of their own kingdoms. Asante, Oyo and Benin had all followed this example. The Lunda states all employed slaves in agriculture, especially in the neighbourhood of their capital towns. It is thought that there was a slave class in Kongo before the Portuguese contact. It is to be presumed that the stone-built capitals of Great Zimbabwe and its successor states were built by some kind of impressed labour. All in all, it seems likely that, even at the height of the Atlantic slave-trade, there were many more African slaves within Africa than outside it. At this rate, there would be no reason to assign a dominant role in African history to the supply of the external trade. By and large, it would seem that European traders proposed, but that African rulers disposed. This situation would remain broadly unchanged until the era of the rifle and the machine-gun, and meantime the enlargement of political scale among the indigenous states of independent Africa would continue.

If the end of the eighteenth century marks the end of the African Middle Ages, therefore, it is not because of any dramatic development in the unfolding of the historical process, but rather because of a change in the nature of the historical evidence. The nineteenth century saw the widespread exploration of independent Africa by literate observers. It saw the first recording of much oral tradition, of which the latest parts were the most reliable and the least disguised under hidden, esoteric meanings. From this time forward it is possible to reconstruct the history of nearly all of Africa in some detail and with a considerable degree of confidence. This we have tried to do in our book called *Africa since 1800*, of which the third, revised edition appears side by side with the present volume.

Suggestions for further reading

GENERAL

Roland Oliver (ed.), *Cambridge History of Africa*, vol. 3, *c. 1050–c. 1600* (Cambridge, 1977). Cited below as *CHA 3*
Richard Gray (ed.), *Cambridge History of Africa*, vol. 4, *c 1600–c. 1870* (Cambridge, 1975). Cited below as *CHA 4*
Basil Davidson, *Africa: history of a continent* (London, 1966)
J. D. Fage, *A History of Africa* (London, 1978)
Philip Curtin, Steven Feierman, Leonard Thompson and Jan Vansina, *African History* (New York and London, 1978)

BY CHAPTER

Chapter 3. Egypt and the Nilotic Sudan
I. Hrbek, 'Egypt, Nubia and the eastern deserts', *CHA 3*, pp. 10–97
P. M. Holt, 'Egypt, the Funj and Darfur', *CHA 4*, pp. 14–57
P. M. Holt, *Egypt and the Fertile Crescent, 1516–1922* (London, 1966)
Y. F. Hasan, *The Arabs and the Sudan* (Khartoum, 1973)
J. Spencer Trimingham, *Islam in the Sudan* (London, 1949)
E. M. Sartain, *Jalāl al-din al-Suyūtī* (Cambridge, 1975) [Egypt during the Circassian Mamluk period]
S. J. Shaw, *The Financial and Administrative Organisation of Ottoman Egypt, 1517–1798* (Princeton, N.J., 1962)
William Y. Adams, *Nubia, Corridor to Africa* (London, 1977)
Jay Spaulding, 'The Funj: a reconsideration', *Journal of African History*, 12, 1 (1972), 39–53

Chapter 4. The north-eastern triangle
Tadesse Tamrat, 'Ethiopia, the Red Sea and the Horn', *CHA 3*, pp. 98–182
M. Abir, 'Ethiopia and the Horn of Africa', *CHA 4*, pp. 537–77
Tadesse Tamrat, *Church and State in Ethiopia, 1270–1527* (Oxford, 1972)
J. Spencer Trimingham, *Islam in Ethiopia* (London, 1952)
M. W. Aregay, *Southern Ethiopia and the Christian Kingdom, 1508–1708* (Addis Ababa, in press)

Chapter 5. The states of Barbary
H. J. Fisher, 'The eastern Maghrib and the central Sudan', *CHA 3*, pp. 232–330, and 'The central Sahara and Sudan', *CHA 4*, pp. 58–141
J. M. Abun-Nasr, *A History of the Maghrib* (Cambridge, 1971)

C.-André Julien, *Histoire de l'Afrique de Nord*, vol. 2 (Paris, 1952); trans. C. C. Stewart and ed. J. Petrie (London, 1970)

Stanley Lane-Poole, *The Barbary Corsairs* (London, 1890)

Fernand Braudel, *The Mediterranean and the Mediterranean World in the Age of Philip II*, trans. S. Reynolds (2 vols., London, 1972–3)

A. G. B. Fisher and H. J. Fisher, *Slavery and Muslim Society in Africa* (London, 1970) [For chapters 5 to 8]

R. Cohen, *The Kanuri of Bornu* (New York, 1967)

Chapter 6. Western West Africa

N. Levtzion, 'The western Maghrib and Sudan', *CHA 3*, pp. 331–462, and 'North-West Africa from the Maghrib to the fringes of the forest', *CHA 4*, pp. 142–222

J. F. A. Ajayi and Michael Crowder, *A History of West Africa*, vol. 1 (London, 1971)

Abdallah Laroui, *A History of the Maghrib* (Princeton, N.J., 1978)

Henri Terrasse, *Histoire du Maroc* (2 vols., Casablanca, 1949–50)

Joseph M. Cuoq (trans. and ed.), *Recueil des sources concernant l'Afrique occidentale du VIIIe au XVIe siècles (bilād al-Sūdān)* (Paris, 1975)

E. W. Bovill with Robin Hallett, *The Golden Trade of the Moors*, 2nd edn (London, 1968)

Walter Rodney, *A History of the Upper Guinea Coast, 1545–1800* (Oxford, 1970)

Philip D. Curtin, *Economic Change in Pre-Colonial Africa: Senegambia in the era of the slave trade* (2 vols., Madison, Wisc., 1975)

John W. Blake, *West Africa: quest for God and gold, 1454–1578* (London, 1977; rev. edn of *European Beginnings in West Africa*, 1937)

K. Y. Daaku, *Trade and Politics on the Gold Coast, 1600–1720* (Oxford, 1970)

Chapter 7. Eastern West Africa

J. F. A. Ajayi and Michael Crowder (eds.), *A History of West Africa*, vol. 1 (London, 1971)

Philip D. Curtin, *The Atlantic Slave Trade: a census* (Madison, Wisc., 1969)

Thomas Hodgkin, *Nigerian Perspectives*, 2nd edn (London, 1975)

I. A. Akinjogbin, *Dahomey and its Neighbours, 1708–1818* (Cambridge, 1967)

S. O. Biobaku (ed.), *Sources of Yoruba History* (Oxford, 1973)

R. C. C. Law, *The Oyo Empire, c. 1600–c. 1836* (London, 1978)

Robert S. Smith, *Kingdoms of the Yoruba*, new edn (London, 1977)

A. F. C. Ryder, *Benin and the Europeans, 1445–1897* (London, 1969)

G. I. Jones, *The Trading States of the Oil Rivers* (London, 1963)

Chapter 8. From the Niger to the Nile

G. Nachtigal, *Sahara and Sudan*, vol. 4, trans. A. G. B. Fisher and H. J. Fisher (London, 1971)

A. G. B. Fisher and H. J. Fisher, *Slavery and Muslim Society in Africa* (London, 1970)

'Umar al-Naqar, *The Pilgrimage Tradition in West Africa* (Khartoum, 1972)
H. Carbou, *La région du Tchad et du Ouadaï* (2 vols., Paris, 1912)
J. Chapelle, *Nomades noires du Sahara* (Paris, 1957)
A. M.-D. Lebeuf, J.-P. Lebeuf and A. M. Detourbet, *La civilisation du Tchad* (Paris, 1950)
A. J. Arkell, 'The history of Darfur, 1200–1700 A.D.', *Sudan Notes and Records*, 32 (1951), 37–70, 207–38; 33 (1952), 129–55, 244–75
E. de Dampierre, *Un ancien royaume Bandia du Haut-Oubangui* (Paris, 1967)
Pierre Kalck, *Histoire de la République Centrafricaine* (Paris, 1974)

Chapter 9. The upper Nile basin and the East African plateau
Roland Oliver, 'The East African interior', *CHA 3*, pp. 621–69
E. A. Alpers and C. Ehret, 'Eastern Africa', *CHA 4*, pp. 470–536
B. A. Ogot (ed.), *Zamani*, 2nd edn (Nairobi, 1973)
M. S. M. Kiwanuka, *A History of Buganda* (London, 1972)
B. A. Ogot, *History of the Southern Luo*, vol. 1 (Nairobi, 1967)
J. E. G. Sutton, *The Archaeology of the Western Highlands of Kenya* (Nairobi, 1973)
Jan Vansina, *L'évolution du royaume Rwanda des origines à 1900* (Brussels, 1962)
D. W. Cohen, *The Historical Tradition of Busoga: Mukama and Kintu* (Oxford, 1972)
Godfrey Muriuki, *A History of the Kikuyu, 1500–1900* (London, 1974)

Chapter 10. From the Lualaba to the Zambezi
David Birmingham, 'Central Africa from Cameroun to the Zambezi', *CHA 3*, pp. 519–68, and *CHA 4*, pp. 325–83
Jan Vansina, *Kingdoms of the Savanna* (Madison, Wisc., 1966) [For Chapters 10 and 11]
Richard Gray and David Birmingham (eds.), *Pre-Colonial African Trade* (London, 1976)
Andrew Roberts, *A History of Zambia* (London, 1976)
Mutumba Mainga, *Bulozi under the Luyana Kings* (London, 1973)
A. D. Roberts, *A History of the Bemba: political growth and change in north-eastern Zambia before 1900* (London, 1974)
Edward A. Alpers, *Ivory and Slaves in East Central Africa* (London, 1975)

Chapter 11. The land of the blacksmith kings
Joseph C. Miller, *Kings and Kinsmen: early Mbundu States in Angola* (London, 1976)
David Birmingham, *Trade and Conflict in Angola* (Oxford, 1966)
W. G. L. Randles, *L'ancien royaume du Congo des origines à la fin du XIXe siècle* (Paris, 1968)
P. M. Martin, *The External Trade of the Loango Coast, 1576–1870* (Oxford, 1972)
K. David Patterson, *The Northern Gabon Coast to 1875* (Oxford, 1975)

Chapter 12. The approaches to Zimbabwe

H. Neville Chittick, 'The East Coast, Madagascar and the Indian Ocean', *CHA 3*, pp. 183–231

Eric Axelson, *Portuguese in South-East Africa, 1488–1600* (Cape Town, 1973; repr.)

Justus Strandes, *The Portuguese Period in East Africa*, trans. J. F. Wallwork (Nairobi, 1961)

W. G. L. Randles, *L'empire du Monomotapa du XVe au XIXe siècle* (Paris, 1975)

M. D. D. Newitt, *Portuguese Settlement on the Zambezi* (London, 1973)

H. Deschamps, *Histoire de Madagascar* (Paris, 1960)

Chapter 13. The peoples of the south

D. B. Birmingham and S. Marks, 'South Africa', *CHA 4*, pp. 569–620

Monica Wilson and Leonard Thompson (eds.), *The Oxford History of South Africa*, vol. I (Oxford, 1969)

Leonard Thompson (ed.), *African Societies in Southern Africa* (London, 1969)

R. Mason, *Prehistory of the Transvaal: a record of human activity* (Witwatersrand, 1978)

Richard Elphick, *Kraal and Castle: Khoikhoi and the founding of white South Africa* (New Haven, Conn., 1977)

J. S. Marais, *The Cape Coloured People, 1652–1937* (repr. Witwatersrand, 1968)

Index

Index

Arabs, 6, 8, 10, 31, 32, 38–40, 55, 60, 65, 67, 85, 109–13, 167, 171, 175, 181, 191
Aragon, 61, 65
Arbaji, 38, 39, 41
Aregay, Merid, 58
Arguin, island, 75
Arkiko, 58
arma, 84, 85
armies, *see* soldiers
Arochuku, 97
Aruj, 66, 67
Asante, 3, 90, 91, 98, 196, 197
asantehene, 90, 91
Asemmour, 82
asiento, 88
Askiya Ishaq, 83
Askiyas, 80, 81, 84, 105
Aswan, 37, 43
Atbara river, 10, 38, 47, 113
Athi Plains, 134
Atlantic coast, ocean, 4, 8, 13, 17, 18, 22, 30, 65, 72, 75, 85, 88, 92, 96, 100, 102, 147, 148, 150, 152, 156, 163, 192, 195, 196
Atlas mountains, 5, 7, 64, 65, 69
Atrun, 110
atta, 102
Augustinians, 180
Aures mountains, 64
Aushi, 141
Avungara, 116, 117
Awash river, 12, 45, 47, 53, 57
Awjila, 72
Awlad Muhammad, 73
Axim, 90
'Aydhab, 7, 37
'Ayn Jalut, 34
Ayyubids, 32, 35, 37
Azande, 22, 119
Azores, islands, 75, 77
Azurara, 75

Badagri, 98
Bagamoyo, 182
Baghdad, 8, 34, 35
Bagirmi, 20, 72, 107, 110–16
bagnois, 19
Bahr al-Arab, 114
Bahr al-Ghazal, 110, 114, 127
Bahri Mamluks, 34
Baida Maryam, 49
Bali, 48, 53, 55, 57
balopwe, 138, 146
Bambandyanalo, 186
Bambara, 81, 89

Bambuk, 77
bananas, 25, 147, 167
Banda, 20, 116–18
Bani river, 19
Bantu languages, peoples, 16, 22, 25, 26, 29, 59, 116, 118, 120, 126, 128, 130, 132, 142, 150, 164, 165, 183, 184–5, 188, 193, 194
Banu Hillal, 65, 110
Banu'l Kanz, 37, 38
Baqqara, 10, 38, 113
Baraytuma Galla, 57
Barbary coast, 71, 72
Barcelona, 65
bares, 180
Bari, 25, 133
Bariba, 100
Barquq, 35, 109
Barreto, Francisco, 177
Barwe, 178
Bashee river, 190
Basra, 8
Battell, Andrew, 160
Baya, 20, 116
Baybars, 34, 35, 37
Bazaruto islands, 186
Bedderi, 111, 112
bedouin, 5, 10, 36, 37, 65, 109, 110
Begemder, 54
Begho, 19
Beira, 169
Beja, 12, 40, 55
Bemba, 146
Bena Ngandu, 146
Benguela, 160, 163, 164, 195
Benguela highlands, 163
Benin, 3, 17, 19, 23, 30, 77, 92, 96, 100–2, 157, 197
Bénin (Dahomey), 17, 20, 90
Benin, Bight of, 2
Benue river, 100
Berberistan (Nubia), 43
Berbers, 2, 5, 60, 64, 65, 67, 69, 110
Bergdama, 164
beylerbey, 67, 68, 70
Bernardo (of Kongo), 157
beys, 44, 69, 70
Bigo, 127, 130
Bihé, 164
Bilma, 8, 72, 73, 105, 107
Birmingham, David, 162
Bisa, 142, 146, 180
Bito, 130, 131
Bizerta, 67
Blanco, Cape, 75
Blue Nile, 10, 38, 39, 54, 128

Index

Index

Index

Index